Celebrating Multiple Intelligences:

Teaching for Success

A Practical Guide Created by
the Faculty of The New City School

Copyright © 1994 by The New City School, Inc.
St. Louis, Missouri

ALL RIGHTS RESERVED

Graphic Design: Hawthorne/Wolfe, Inc.

Printed in the United States of America

ISBN 0-9643514-0-4

Sixth Edition – July 1997

**Visit New City School at
http://info.csd.org/newcity.html**

A practical guide created by the faculty of The New City School ©1994

Dedication

This book is dedicated to the students of The New City School. We are thankful for yesterday's students, whose enthusiasm has inspired us; we are appreciative of our current students, with whom we learn; we look forward to growing with the students of tomorrow.

Acknowledgments

We acknowledge, with gratitude, those who have given us their confidence and support. In particular, we acknowledge the support of The New City School Board of Directors. The value they place on our teachers, and this effort, is gratifying indeed.

We acknowledge the vision of Tom Hoerr, the director of The New City School. His commitment to learning and his effort to ensure that all children and teachers grow were the foundation for this book. His dedication and inspiration moved the faculty forward in completing this project.

And we would be most remiss if we did not acknowledge Dr. Howard Gardner. Without his creativity and inspiration, there would be no theory of Multiple Intelligences. He has been a friend of The New City School. He has given us his counsel, his thoughts and his time.

Special Thanks

At The New City School, working hard is the norm. Going beyond the call of duty is expected, but creating, designing and producing *Celebrating Multiple Intelligences: Teaching for Success* has required even more time, energy and insight than could ever have been imagined.

Thanks to all of the members of the MI Book Committee: Sally Boggeman, Mary F. Daly, Bonnie L. Frank, Monette Gooch-Smith, Jean Blockhus Grover, Tom Hoerr, Nancy McIlvain, Carla Mash, Julie Stevens, and Christine Wallach. Thanks, too, to Renee Barry and Karen Lechner for their typing and flexibility.

Monette Gooch-Smith and Julie Stevens, in particular, gave great amounts of time and skill. Carla Mash's persistence led to the creation of the index. Nancy McIlvain's sharp eye and love of editing were invaluable. We are grateful to Craig Jones who generously volunteered her time and expertise. We are especially thankful to Tom Hoerr, our director. He worked long hours behind the scenes while letting the members of the committee make many decisions. He provided guidance and support. His proclivity with words resulted in numerous articles. The time he spent reading every article and lesson plan resulted in valuable feedback that helped shape this book. And special thanks to Christine Wallach and Sally Boggeman, chairs of the MI Book Committee. They gave more time, talent, energy and skill than could ever have been expected, and they did it day after day after day of their summer vacation! Without their determination and dedication, this book would only be a dream.

Table of Contents

Contributors: Sally Boggeman, Susie Chasnoff, Linda Churchwell, Mary F. Daly, Danielle Egeling, Jean Blockhus Grover, Carla Mash, Joan Moldafsky Siwak, Monette Gooch-Smith, Christine Wallach, Denise A. Willis

Chapter 3. The Bodily-Kinesthetic Intelligence   71

Bodily-Kinesthetic: Out of the Gym and Into the Classroom
by Sally Boggeman and Lauren M. McKenna   73

Contributors: Sally Boggeman, Carla Carroll, Linda Churchwell, Diane Davenport, Danielle Egeling, Joycelyn L. Gray, Susan Matthews, Lauren M. McKenna, Christine Wallach, Stephanie Cunningham Wiles

Contributors: Carol Beatty, Carla Carroll, Mary F. Daly, Bonnie L. Frank, Jean Blockhus Grover, Carla Mash, Julie Stevens, Susie Tenzer, Stephanie Young

Contributors: Bonnie L. Frank, Joycelyn L. Gray, Jean Blockhus Grover, Elizabeth King, Susan Matthews, Suzy Schweig, Christine Wallach, Stephanie Cunningham Wiles, Denise A. Willis

Contributors: Sally Boggeman, Joe Corbett, Mary F. Daly, Diane Davenport, Bonnie L. Frank, Monette Gooch-Smith, Christine Wallach, Denise A. Willis

Contributors: Carol Beatty, Susie Chasnoff, Linda Churchwell, Joe Corbett, Eileen Griffiths, Jennifer Hartz Pass, Suzy Schweig, Monette Gooch-Smith, Denise A.Willis

Introduction

*by Sally Boggeman,
Tom Hoerr and
Christine Wallach*

Welcome!

This book represents, literally, thousands of hours of effort by New City teachers and administrators. But, as you might suspect, creating it has been a labor of love. Our five years of work with the theory of Multiple Intelligences (MI) has taught us that MI is not only a theory of intelligence; MI can be a philosophy about how kids learn, how teachers teach, and how schools operate. We hope that our efforts will make a difference for others, just as MI has made a difference for us.

Why a book about MI?

We want to share our ideas and approaches so that children and teachers everywhere can benefit from the MI theory. Precisely because it is not a theory of education or curriculum design, MI can be adapted by each school's faculty to the school's personality in the way that they see fit. The work of The New City School with MI, for example, is different than that of the Key School's program in Indianapolis, Indiana, or the efforts of the San Jose School in Jacksonville, Florida; that's OK! In fact, in this era of increasing public criticism of education and educators, and broad-sweeping nostrums, one of the attractions of MI is that its various implementations respect the identity and integrity of the teachers and schools which use it.

We realize that school environments and teaching situations vary quite dramatically. Almost all of our faculty has worked in other public, private, and parochial schools before coming to New City. We know that not every teacher has the advantage of working in a school in which the entire faculty is committed to MI, that not every teacher has the luxury of having her students' parents support efforts with MI curriculum and instruction. And we understand that not every teacher has the autonomy to take risks, learn, and grow. But we believe that there are things that we have learned which can be useful to others, regardless of their setting. We believe that good teachers grow and develop, regardless of — sometimes in spite of — their circumstances. This book can facilitate and support that growth and development.

There are other good books published about MI. But we are unaware of any books that have been written collaboratively by an entire faculty. As you will see, New City's implementation includes many different directions and permutations, from redesigning curriculum, to using portfolios, to emphasizing the personal intelligences, to addressing genuine understanding. This school-wide approach, coupled with the myriad of perspectives that come from an entire faculty, make *Celebrating Multiple Intelligences* a unique and encompassing vision of MI.

The New City School MI Implementation

Sometimes when we talk about MI, people say, "But you're a private school. We can't do the kinds of things that you do!" We disagree. Although we are an independent school, our per-pupil expenditure is no higher than the Missouri State average. Although we are an independent school, our students must take competitive standardized tests in the sixth grade to enter into private secondary schools. And, most important, because we are an independent school, each year our students' parents have the option of whether or not they will elect to continue to send their child to our school and pay thousands of dollars in tuition. We must provide a quality education to our students. That's accountability!

Children are children, and their needs and areas of potential talent are similar regardless of their race, ethnic background, or economic circumstances, and regardless of the kind of school that they attend. Yes, there are differences between independent and public schools, just as there are differences among various independent and among various public schools. And certainly New City is a different environment than most schools, public or private. But many of the MI practices which we adopted can be used in any setting. Implementing MI requires motivation, thoughtfulness, educating of all a school's constituencies (not just the students, but also the administration, the students' parents, and other teachers), and effort. In this respect, it is no different than any other educational innovation.

Credit

Credit goes to all of the various authors of the books and journals we have read, to the presenters of all of the workshops that we have attended, and to all of the teachers with whom we have talked and worked over the years. Our school is committed to staff development and professional growth; we believe that everyone in the building must learn and grow. As a result, we are constantly pulling in information from here and there, adapting and sharing it with others. That is why although the articles in this book list the authors' names, the lesson plans do not. Our feeling is that any lesson plan is, necessarily, an amalgam of ideas from a variety of sources, most of which the teacher has forgotten. To assign specific authors' names to specific lesson plans would mean that someone was probably being overlooked. Instead, all of the New City teachers responsible for creating lesson plans have been listed in each chapter.

How to use this book

We have tried to make this book as user-friendly as possible. It is organized by intelligence and section (preprimary, primary and intermediate). Preprimary includes three year olds through kindergarteners. Our primary classes are grades one, two and three. Our intermediate classes are grades four, five and six.

A practical guide created by the faculty of The New City School ©1994

Graphics are used so that the reader can either peruse the pages by looking at all of the lessons for a particular age or grade of child, or can focus on lessons designed for specific intelligences, regardless of the age of the child. Each lesson contains MI extension ideas for all of the intelligences. Of course, just as the intelligences are not totally distinct from one another, so, too, despite their major focus, each of the lessons utilizes a variety of intelligences.

The icons below are used to provide quick reference to the intelligence being discussed:

Interpersonal

Intrapersonal

Bodily-Kinesthetic

Linguistic

Logical-Mathematical

Musical

Spatial

A graphic designation on each lesson plan will help you to quickly see how it fits into your curriculum. The example shown below signifies an interpersonal activity for the primary grades (1, 2, and 3) in the area of science.

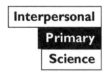

Each intelligence chapter begins with an article about that intelligence. We also include articles which go into some depth in explaining different aspects of our MI implementation; for example, we discuss our work with portfolios and our communication with parents.

What's next?
Creating this book is a first for us, and we would enjoy hearing your reactions to it. We would also be interested in learning about your work with MI. Please feel free to write us!

The New City School
5209 Waterman Avenue
St. Louis, MO 63108
Tel: 314/361-6411
Fax: 314/361-1499

And if you are ever going to be in St. Louis and would like to visit our school, please give us a call. We welcome visitors. Members of our faculty also present workshops on MI, so contact us if you would like to talk about our doing an MI workshop for your school.

Part 1.
The Multiple Intelligences

A practical guide created by the faculty of The New City School ©1994

Implementing MI Into the Classroom

By Tom Hoerr

Background

In creating his theory of Multiple Intelligences (MI), Howard Gardner was not designing a curriculum or preparing a model to be used in schools. Despite this, as Gardner notes with some surprise, educators have taken his theory and used it in many different ways. This is probably a response to the "King of the Hill" philosophy that seems to pervade education. The "educational establishment" seems to assume that (a) there's a hill; (b) the hill can be climbed best through succeeding on multiple-choice linguistic and logical-mathematical tasks; and (c) as educators, our job is to get our students up the hill, and create an academic hierarchy in doing so.

As James Fallows points out in *More Like Us,* there is no reason to assume that intellect (I.Q.) is distributed on the bell-shaped curve. While psychometricians have created standardized tests in which 68% of the population falls within one standard deviation of the norm, and schools have purchased the tests because they are cheap, easy to administer and acceptable to the public, we should not assume that this distribution of intelligence is necessarily the case. Standardized tests are very reliable; their validity, however, as measures of intelligence or academic understanding, leaves much to be desired.

There is no reason to assume that intellect (I.Q.) is distributed on the bell-shaped curve.

Indeed, in contrast, we look around us and see adults who are successful not because of their linguistic or logical-mathematical skills, but because of other qualities they possess. True, the adults who are successful typically can read, write and compute well; true, not being able to do these things is a disadvantage. But the world is full of successful people who did not excel on multiple-choice tests. And too many of us have seen talented and eager students have their desire for learning taken away because they didn't fit the profile for success that is sought in school. As a consequence, the label "learning disabled" is used with more and more frequency, slotting kids who learn differently and have different strengths.

Too many of us have seen talented and eager students have their desire for learning taken away because they didn't fit the profile for success that is sought in school.

With that background, it is not surprising that educators find merit in the MI model. And it makes sense that teachers who chose education because they wanted to help others would find MI a powerful tool for reaching their students.

The Theory

Gardner says that there are many different intelligences. He has identified seven (but also says that there may well be more). Intelligence is defined not as doing well on a test or memorizing the fifty state capitals, but as solving a problem or creating a product that is valued in a culture. "Solving a problem" encompasses computing two-digit multiplication, but it also includes forging a team, one capable of working collaboratively to accomplish a difficult task, from a group of individuals. "Creating a product" includes turning clay into a bust, but it also means developing a new dance. And "valued in a culture" means just what it implies: that others find merit in the work.

The criteria for an intelligence that Gardner sets forth are varied, ranging from "an evolutionary history and evolutionary plausibility" to "potential isolation by brain damage" to "susceptibility to becoming a symbol system." (For a far more detailed and richer explanation of the research and thinking behind MI, see *Frames of Mind* or *Multiple Intelligences: Theory Into Practice* by Howard Gardner; also see *In Their Own Way* by Thomas Armstrong).

Gardner's seven intelligences, and brief definitions, are listed below. (For background on how the intelligences have been manifested in some famous individuals, see *Creating Minds* by Howard Gardner.)

Children with strong B/K are highly coordinated, often tactile, and enjoy touching things.

Bodily-Kinesthetic (B/K) - using one's body, or part of it, to solve problems and communicate. Children with strong B/K are highly coordinated, often tactile, and enjoy touching things. They enjoy all sorts of athletics and would rather be a participant than a spectator.

Intrapersonal - being sensitive to one's inner feelings, knowing one's own strengths and weaknesses. These children often keep logs or journals and enjoy solitude. Sometimes their metacognition, their thinking about their thinking processes, is especially refined.

Interpersonal - being sensitive to and understanding others. A child with a strong Interpersonal Intelligence will work well with a group and often winds up playing a leadership role.

Linguistic - having the ability to use words and language in many different forms. Reading and writing come easily to these children and they typically do well in school.

Logical-Mathematical - having the ability to discern patterns and approach situations logically. Students who are strong here often calculate well and excel in scientific activities; they tend to be precise and methodical.

Musical - being sensitive to non-verbal sounds in the environment such as rhythms, pitch and tonal patterns. A child with a strong musical intelligence is likely to hum and easily turn sounds into rhythms. These children easily remember melodies.

Spatial - having the ability to form a mental model and to be able to maneuver and operate using that model. A strength in this area often means that the child does well at visualizing things and excels at representative drawings. These children think in images and pictures.

Our investigation and pursuit of a school in which learning is fun and kids come first has led us to MI. It has been an interesting and rich journey, and we look forward to sharing some of it with you.

Chapter 1:
The Interpersonal Intelligence

*Contributors: Sally Boggeman, Susie Burge, Susie Chasnoff,
Linda Churchwell, Danielle Egeling, Carla Mash, Joan Modafsky Siwak,
Monette Gooch-Smith, Susie Tenzer*

"But an important variable in leadership seems to be the ability to sense, to be aware of, what is going on in oneself as well as what is happening in the group or organization."

Joseph Luft

Web of the Interpersonal Intelligence

"I am Interpersonal because I like to talk, I like to go over to my friend's house and I like to have my friends over to my house."

"I'm Interpersonal because I get along with people. I have lots of friends. I can be a leader in a group and come up with ideas or I can be a follower and work with other people's ideas."

"I'm Interpersonal because I like to work in groups and hear someone else's point of view and what they are thinking."

- Enjoys cooperative games
- Understands the feelings of others
- Has lots of friends
- Prefers group problem-solving
- Can mediate conflicts
- Understands and recognizes stereotypes and prejudices
- Volunteers help when others need it

Jimmy Carter mediated meetings between Egyptian and Israeli representatives that resulted in a peace agreement.

Eleanor Roosevelt advocated for social reforms that helped the disadvantaged.

Lee Iacocca used his salesmanship and knowledge of power to get loans to keep Chrysler afloat.

Mother Teresa has devoted her life to communicating about the condition of the world's poor and seeking solutions to the problem through her personal efforts.

"The best way to cheer yourself up is to try to cheer somebody else up."

Mark Twain

A practical guide created by the faculty of The New City School ©1994

We're All In This Together

by Nancy J. McIlvain

Among the seven intelligences, it is the philosophy of The New City School that the two most important are the "Personal" Intelligences—Intrapersonal and Interpersonal. Through many opportunities for practice and feedback, one can develop the ability within the Interpersonal Intelligence to identify, assess and respond appropriately to the moods, temperaments, motivations and desires of others. While some seem to intuitively possess this strength, this is seldom the case. We, as educators, must address these skills thoughtfully and deliberately.

Schools Need to Address the Personal Intelligences

"Success" in life depends on successful relationships with other human beings—spouses, children, siblings, other family members, friends, peers, neighbors, colleagues, authority figures and subordinates. What better time could there be than during the formative years of one's life, in the safe environment within a nurturing community of learners and educators, to practice, interact and reflect on one's interpersonal skills? By the time we enter adolescence, and surely adulthood, the groundwork is set; our tolerance, empathy and understanding of the perspectives, desires and needs of others is in place. The probability of significant changes regarding flexibility, cooperation and socialization greatly decreases.

What better time could there be than during the formative years of one's life, in the safe environment within a nurturing community of learners and educators, to practice, interact and reflect on one's interpersonal skills?

Is there one among us who would say that interpersonal development is not important? Yet, how many schools make a concerted effort to teach and assess their students' interpersonal skills, such as the following?

- Understanding and appreciating the perspectives of others, including those of other races and cultures
- Showing concern and empathy
- Respecting others' individuality
- Making decisions based on appropriate information rather than stereotypes
- Cooperating with peers and adults
- Working at conflict resolution
- Behaving responsibly in a group situation
- Demonstrating the ability to compromise
- Expressing feelings
- Giving feedback constructively and appropriately

These attributes must be taught and assessed on a continual basis and, on the "front page" of our Progress Report, progress in these areas is reported to parents. They are not assumed to be included, as too often is the case, on the back page of the report card under "Works well with others" or "Respects the rights and opinions of others," phrases which are typically used to capture these areas.

At The New City School, what we value is what we measure and what we measure is what we teach.

At The New City School, what we value is what we measure and what we measure is what we teach. Teachers must become accountable for teaching our youngsters the skills they will need to be successful in life—at age four and age ten and age eighteen and age twenty-nine and age seventy-three and all ages in between. A sampling of activities compiled to support The New City School's teachers as they address and assess children in their Interpersonal Intelligence are:

- sorting children in a preprimary class and asking them how the people in one group or another are the same
- engaging primary-aged children in writing and discussion groups focusing on "If I were...(a person with a disability or Rosa Parks or a Taino Native American meeting Christopher Columbus)"
- having intermediate-grade students identify and discuss bias and stereotypes in literature, textbooks, advertisements and on television
- inviting guest speakers who use teamwork in their jobs
- providing opportunities for cooperative learning experiences and projects on a frequent basis

The Role of Reflection

The key is that this must be done frequently, so that children get in the habit of asking themselves these questions even when you don't.

An absolutely critical part of developing interpersonal skills is REFLECTION. On an ongoing, frequent basis, after completing cooperative learning experiences, students could be asked these kinds of questions:

- What role did you play in your group; were you a leader or a follower? Were you comfortable in that role?
- Were there times when you wanted to be the leader, but someone else in the group kept you from doing so?
- What did you do to move the group forward?
- How might you change your behavior next time?

There are times when you would ask the students to sit quietly and think about their answers to the above questions, without sharing aloud. Other times, you might have students share their reflections with a partner or the group. And yet, on other occasions, the students might be asked to enter their reflections in their journals. But, the key is that this must be done frequently, so that children get in the habit of asking themselves these questions even when you don't.

Of course, all students must learn to read and write and compute, but even more important is the ability to work and play and live successfully with others. Those who possess strong interpersonal skills might become teachers, counselors, salespeople, political leaders or religious leaders. However, teaching our students interpersonal skills does not mean that our goal is to guide them toward being bouncy and bubbly and extroverted, commonly thought of as the "cheerleader" type. As I stated in the beginning, we are helping children to develop the ability to identify, assess and respond appropriately to the moods, temperments, motivations and desires of others. We cannot assume that these critical skills will "just happen." They won't. WE must teach them.

We cannot assume that these critical skills will "just happen."

Conflict, Compromise, Cooperation

Interpersonal
Preprimary
Social Studies

MI Context: To build interpersonal skills through cooperative play and conflict resolution.

Learner Outcomes: Students compromise by using verbal skills.

Procedure:
1. Read the big book *The Land of Many Colors* by the Klamath County YMCA Family Preschool. Discuss the characters' feelings as the story is read.

2. Discuss how the characters resolved their problem peacefully.

3. Explain that the children will work together in groups of three or four to create a wall mural using only the supplies given them.

4. Distribute to each group one large and two small sheets of construction paper, one pencil, one glue stick, and one pair of scissors.

5. Stress the need to talk about what they want to make and who will draw, cut and assemble, as there are not enough supplies for everyone to have his own.

6. Facilitate discussion to help with compromise and cooperation.

7. Talk about the process: what was hard and easy.

Materials:
Each group will need: one large and two small sheets of colored construction paper, one pair of scissors, one pencil, one glue stick

Assessment / Reflection:
After hanging murals, discuss how a peaceful resolution was found.

MI Extensions:
Intrapersonal: Ask children how they felt when people in their group did not want to use their ideas. Videotape the groups working so the children can see their interaction and hear their discussion.

Bodily-Kinesthetic: Small groups act out for the class examples of how to work together in a group and how not to work in a group.

Linguistic: Brainstorm a list of words that express how they felt while working in their group.

Logical-Mathematical: Work in small groups to create a pattern with pattern blocks or unifix cubes. Children discuss the pattern they wish to make, come to agreement and work on it together.

Musical: Play Hap Palmer's song "Colors."

Teamwork

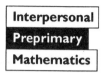

Interpersonal
Preprimary
Mathematics

MI Context: Children develop interpersonal skills by working together to complete a task.

Learner Outcomes: Three- and four-year-old children will make decisions and compromises as they share materials.

Procedure:
1. Divide the class into pairs. Keep in mind the personalities of the children. Put children together who might not choose one another. Place a child who can share easily with one who cannot. Put a verbal child with one less verbal.

2. Give each pair of children one puzzle to put together.

3. As children are working, talk to the pairs and to the whole class about how they are doing and if everyone is having a chance to work on the puzzle.

Materials:
Ten- to twelve-piece puzzles, one for each pair of children

Assessment / Reflection:
Observe how well the pairs are able to complete the task and if they cooperated and compromised. Ask the pairs to talk about how well they think they did.

MI Extensions:
Intrapersonal: Ask children to talk about what was easy and what was hard about working together to put together the puzzle.

Bodily-Kinesthetic: Give each pair one ball. They decide what they will play with it, i.e., throw, roll, bounce.

Linguistic: Read *Roxaboxen* by Alice McLerran. Discuss ways the children in the story might have cooperated as they played.

Logical-Mathematical: Give each pair one tray of several objects to sort.

Musical: Give each pair a container to use as a drum and two sticks. Ask them to make up a song on the "drum."

Spatial: Give each pair one piece of paper and two crayons to draw a picture of themselves.

Our Body Museum

MI Context: This lesson serves as a culminating project for the study of the human body. The gallery contains the projects the students have created during the unit. Ideas for exhibits can be found in the extensions to this lesson plan. With adaptation, this activity could be used at the end of any unit of study.

Interpersonal
Preprimary
Science

Learner Outcomes: The students will share information about their study of the systems of the body with parents and other students who visit the museum. Children serve as docents in the Body Museum.

Procedure:

1. Discuss museums with the class and ask the following questions:

   • What is a museum?
   • Who invented museums? Why?
   • How many people have ever been to a museum? What kind?
   • What types of museums are there?
   • Where are they located?
   • Who works in museums?
   • What exhibits might be found in a body museum?
   • Are there other people associated with museums?

2. Read the story *Katie's Picture Show* by James Mayhew, a story about a young girl visiting a museum. Discuss or role-play the book. What is the responsibility of a docent or guide in a museum?

3. Make a list of ideas as you challenge the students to brainstorm ways to turn the classroom into a body museum. Children could work in groups to decide who will be responsible for doing which jobs. The following jobs might be included:

   • notes home to parents telling them about the museum
   • letters to the student body
   • hanging up all of the bodies around the room
   • ads and reminders around the building
   • decorating the room

4. In small groups, role-play the part of a docent in a museum. In order to understand the perspective of both students and parents visiting the museum, give the children the opportunity to role-play things each might say, like to know or want to see. How would parent visitors be different from children visitors?

Materials:
Katie's Picture Show by James Mayhew, chart paper, museum projects

Assessment / Reflection:
Talk or draw in journals about the parts of this project that were easy, difficult, enjoyable or unpleasant. Can the students in the role of docent share information as they talk about their displays and those of other students? Have the class generate items which could be included on an assessment to be completed by visitors to the museum. Use the student list to develop the assessment sheet.

MI Extensions:
Interpersonal: Write or dictate a letter or story from a visitor's perspective after visiting the museum.

Bodily-Kinesthetic: Develop moves for a muscle circle game. Each child selects a muscle movement, i.e. kicking a soccer ball, moving on a balance beam, braiding hair. The first person makes a move. Then the second person makes the first child's move and then her own move. The game continues around the circle.

Linguistic: Share displays with the total class so that children are familiar with all of them. Make an audio tape of each child talking about herself to be played while people go through the museum.

Logical-Mathematical: Devise a way to organize the data from the assessment sheets that visitors filled out after their visit to the museum.

Musical: Make an audio tape of each child playing a musical instrument for about three minutes each. This musical-collage tape becomes the background to be played while people visit the museum.

Spatial:

Make a Me Body

1. In small groups, children look at themselves and at each other, paying attention to detail, color, shape and form. If mirrors are available, use them.

2. Outline each child on butcher paper. Children can do this in pairs, or ask a parent or older student to help. Children cut out their forms or send them home so parents can help.

3. Take a Polaroid picture of each child or a group picture so they will remember what they were wearing that day.

4. Use people-color crayons, markers, paint or pastels to decorate the Me Bodies and the clothes. Glue on yarn for hair and cut out material for clothing.

Masai Jewelry

MI Context: This lesson is part of a unit on Africa with a focus on understanding the Masai Culture. Any culture or tribe can be substituted.

Learner Outcomes: Children will develop the ability to create aesthetic works with limited resources while learning how to organize themselves and share materials.

Interpersonal
Primary
Social Studies

Procedures:

1. Show the children pictures or examples of Masai jewelry. Pass them around and then list everything the Masai use to make jewelry, i.e., wire, straw, beads, shells, buttons, leather, tin from tin cans and thumbtacks. Ask the students where they think the Masai obtained these materials.

2. Using a world map, point out beading trade routes between Venice and India and where beads are made and traded along the Eastern coast of Africa.

3. Show students resources they will have available to complete the project:

   • head pins for making earrings

   • round-nosed pliers for bending headpins

   • monofilament for stringing the beads

   • different sizes and colors of plastic beads

   • wire

   • ear wires

4. The children are placed in cooperative learning groups. The leader's job is to make sure everyone gets to say something and ask questions. For this activity each group receives one of the following resource bags:

   • beads

   • wire and monofilament

   • head pins and round-nosed pliers

5. The children are told to begin making jewelry. It doesn't take them long to figure out they need to trade to get materials, and they make the connection with the Masai trading.

6. As the trading begins, the students experience many difficulties. They need to organize their trading so that it is fair to all. Engage the students in a discussion which allows the children to jointly resolve the problems and arrive at solutions.

7. The students practice the problem-solving strategies they have developed. Periodically the students re-evaluate their trading plans to determine what works and what doesn't.

Materials:
Head pins, round-nosed pliers, monofilament, beads, wire, ear wires, Masai jewelry (or books that contain pictures of the jewelry), scissors to cut the wires

Assessment / Reflection:
Observe how well students were able to interact in groups and get the materials they needed. Does the jewelry resemble that of the Masai?

MI Extensions:
Intrapersonal: Have the students identify their reactions and feelings toward this experience. Questions that might be asked include:

- How did you feel when everyone was taking materials and fighting?

- How did you feel afterwards?

- How might this change the way you solve problems in the future?

Bodily-Kinesthetic: Create a dance demonstrating this system of trade.

Linguistic: Create a charter regarding trade agreements.

Logical-Mathematical: Keep a daily graph of "problems" and "problems solved." Note each day how many problems were solved. Compare results of a week.

Musical: Using instruments, create music to accompany the dance.

Spatial: Draw maps indicating the countries or communities being discussed, and use string or yarn to plot the trade routes. Have students create similar trade routes within the school or neighborhood.

Spider Web

Interpersonal
Primary
Social Studies

MI Context: Interpersonal skills are used as children give positive feedback to one another.

Learner Outcomes: Children will focus on expressing positive comments to peers who they may or may not know well.

Procedure:
1. The class forms a circle while standing.

2. The teacher holds a ball of string in one hand and the loose end of the string in the other. She holds onto the loose end while she tosses the ball to a child.

3. The child catches the ball. The teacher says something that she likes or appreciates about the receiver.

4. The receiver holds onto the string that leads to the teacher and tosses the ball to someone else. When it is caught, he, in turn, compliments the new recipient of the ball of string.

5. This process continues until everyone has caught the ball of string. As the string crisscrosses the circle, a web is formed.

Materials:
A ball of string

Assessment / Reflection:
Give the students a chance to talk to the person who threw the string to them and comment on what was said, either expanding, clarifying or just showing appreciation.

MI Extensions:
Interpersonal and Intrapersonal: Use the list of qualities the students wished they had from the Linguistic extension. Seat the students in groups according to the characteristic they would most like to develop. Have the students discuss strategies to achieve this goal.

Bodily-Kinesthetic: Have the students figure out ways to get from one side of the web to the other without touching the web, i.e. crawling, rolling, stepping through the spaces.

Linguistic: The teacher leaves the web to write descriptors on the board as the students make their comments, i.e., good friend, good writer, helpful, understanding. Each child makes two lists, one containing those qualities they feel they have and the other containing the qualities they wish they had.

Students might also cluster the descriptors, linking those that are similar. Possibly they can then identify characters in literature or media who also portray these attributes.

Logical-Mathematical: On the chalkboard, represent each student in the circle with a dot with his name next to it. As the string is thrown, the teacher uses chalk to construct the path it takes. Have the students identify shapes that appear, i.e. triangles, squares, rectangles.

Musical: Construct a web a second time with one-half of the class. The other half uses found objects in the room or body sounds to create music to accompany the movement of the string as the web is constructed.

Spatial: Have the students copy the web on a piece of paper with materials such as popcorn kernels, beads or seeds.

A Structure That Will Stand

MI Context: This lesson was done in conjunction with a unit on architecture.

Learner Outcomes: The student will construct a structure that will stand and surround a group of six students.

Procedure:
1. Divide the class into groups of six or eight.

2. Each member of the class makes a minimum of six newspaper rolls by rolling a section of newspaper into a tube shape and securing the loose ends with masking tape.

3. Using the rolled tubes and tape, create a free-standing structure large enough to hold all the members of the group.

Materials:
Newspaper, masking tape

Assessment / Reflection:
After the students have assembled their structures, provide an opportunity for them to discuss their roles in planning and building the structure. How did they decide what to do? Who solved problems?, etc.

Extensions:
Intrapersonal: In their journals, describe the kind of home they would want if they could have anything at all.

Bodily-Kinesthetic: Read *What It Feels Like to Be a Building* by Forrest Wilson. Divide into groups and choose one of the structures in the book to build with your bodies.

Linguistic: Write a story about an animal who is building a home.

Logical-Mathematical: Using pattern blocks, build geometric models of buildings; for example, domes, beehives, towers, and log homes.

Musical: Turn the traditional story, "The House That Jack Built," into a song.

Spatial: Read the book *The Big Orange Spot* by Daniel Pinkwater. Design the house of their dreams.

Rain Forest Simulation

Interpersonal

Intermediate

Science

MI Context: This activity is used during a unit on biomes (grasslands, deserts, tropical rain forests, polar regions) after a study of the rain forest.

Learner Outcomes: Students will experience the diverse points of view of groups of people concerned with the rain forest. They will assume roles within their group and work to resolve conflicts with groups who have different goals.

Procedure:

1. Use the following questions as a basis of discussion with the students:

   • Why are the rain forests important?

   • Should the rain forests be cut down or protected? What are the advantages and disadvantages of each approach?

   • Should the animals be protected? Why?

   • Is there a problem with the rain forests? How would you define it?

   • Why are the rain forests being destroyed?

2. Introduce the simulation to the students by telling them it will help them understand why different groups of people in the rain forest have different points of view. They will spend time getting organized for the activity. Draw a large map of an imaginary country and have the class name it. Cover the map with a grid to be used when groups purchase land. Explain that their country is an island with two large cities, a mountain range, several rivers, and that it is mostly covered by rain forest. It is a very poor country. There are not many schools, hospitals or roads. The students will become the citizens of the country and decide what improvements need to be made.

3. Divide the class into small groups, each representing a group of people in the country. The groups are the government, villagers, industrialists, environmentalists and bankers. No one owns land at the onset of the activity. As groups buy or acquire land, they cover the land space on the map grid using a color-coded square. Each group receives a folder containing a map, goals for that group, some money and directions. The money allocation is as follows, although other values could be assigned:

   • villagers = $10,000   • bankers = $100,000

   • environmentalists = $10,000   • government = $100,000

   • industrialists = $50,000

4. Make up a chart for the class to delineate the following goals and directions. These also go into each group's folder.

- **Government Goals:** You have been elected to office by the voters. Your job is to make the best possible decisions about your country.

  Directions:
  Decide on a budget; build schools, roads, airports and/or hospitals; set land aside for forest or animal preserves; set land aside for industries to use; set land aside for villagers to farm; pass laws; tax villagers, industry, zoos and/or preserves; ask other countries for financial aid; grant permits for building.

- **Industrialist Goals:** Your job is to establish industry which will bring jobs, money, electricity and badly needed goods into the country. You also want to make some profit for your investors.

  Directions:
  Try to buy land; offer jobs to villagers to get them on your side; print books and papers about how industry will help the country; try to buy land from villagers; cut trees and sell wood; start mining for gold and minerals; ask environmentalists for advice; let hunters and zoo keepers capture animals; build roads.

- **Villager Goals:** You live in very crowded cities. You are very poor. You do not have enough food, hospitals, schools or roads. Your job is to try to improve your situation in life.

  Directions:
  Ask government for land for farming; ask government for schools and hospitals; start to cut and burn forests to plant food; look for jobs with big industry; start your own small company; sell animals to zoos and hunters; sell wood; ask environmentalists for advice.

- **Environmentalist Goals:** Your job is to protect and save as much of the rain forest as possible. There are thirty-six endangered species of plants and animals to be protected in your land.

  Directions:
  Gather information on endangered species; try to raise money; ask government for laws; organize a protest; print books and posters; buy land for preserves; pay scientists to do research; set up a zoo.

- **Banker Goals:** You are in charge of the money and land. You collect money when land is sold and mark off on the map who owns each area.

  Directions:
  Buy land as an investment; sell land to other groups; invest some money in another group; ask government to raise the price of land; build ports for shipping; ask environmentalists for advice; build large cities to attract tourists; build railroads.

5. In order for each group to work together efficiently, each group member will have a specific role to play. Each group has four roles: a president or leader, a secretary, a treasurer and a spokesperson. The class will define the duties of each role; for example, the job of the leader is not to be bossy! The leader is responsible for seeing that the group gets the job done, works and stays on task. The leader's vote is the tie-breaker. All decisions in each group are made by majority vote. Within the group the students decide which role each will have.

6. The members of the group must work together to resolve conflict. Emphasize that there are no bad guys in this game. Every member wants what is best for the group, and to an extent, the country. For example, the industrialists will bring jobs, needed goods and money into the country. The students must decide what they can do if they don't like the actions of another group. Explain the mechanics of the activity. Each group must make choices and decisions, including press releases, and methods of protest.

7. During the next several days, students begin the activity by making decisions and plans of action within their groups.

8. To evaluate progress, take a few minutes at the end of each class period to discuss what went well, what problems arose, how conflicts were solved and what individuals did that helped promote cooperation.

9. The game is scored by giving one point for each goal reached, i.e., preserves established, hospitals and schools built. Talk about the various perspectives people have on the rain forest. A hungry villager with children to feed and inadequate education might not be interested in preserving lemurs. The students begin to realize that there are no easy answers, although some solutions are definitely better than others.

Materials:
Map, folders and posters with goals and directions, fake money, posters to record laws passed

Assessment / Reflection:
Before the simulation begins, use the following discussion questions to facilitate conflict resolution before problems arise.

- Do you think everyone in your group will agree on everything?

- How will you settle disagreements in your group?

- How will you control your attitude if your choice isn't selected?

Upon completion of the exercise, discuss these questions again.

Ask if each group had the same point of view when they looked at the country. How are the goals of each group different?

MI Extensions:

Intrapersonal: Students listen to an environmental tape as they write reflections on how they feel about the activity. How is this like or unlike how their parents might feel?

Bodily-Kinesthetic: On the floor, mark off an area to represent the world's land, within this space, mark off the area of the world's rain forests. Divide the students into two equal groups. Have one group stand on the land not representing the rain forest and the other group stand in the rain forest. Over half of all known species live in rain forests. Discuss population density.

Linguistic: Students research and write paragraphs on one animal in the rain forest that is endangered. They may wish to write from the perspective of the animal.

Logical-Mathematical: Compute the percentages of land set aside for various uses by each group during the activity. Illustrate the data with bar and pie graphs.

Musical: Create a tape of rain forest environmental sounds.

Spatial: Create a rain forest within the classroom using butcher paper, construction paper, tape-recorded animal sounds, appropriate potted plants and papier-mâché animals.

Rain Forest Simulation Map

The country is a small island of 20,000 square miles surrounded by ocean. It contains a tropical rain forest and a river and there is a mountain range in the west.

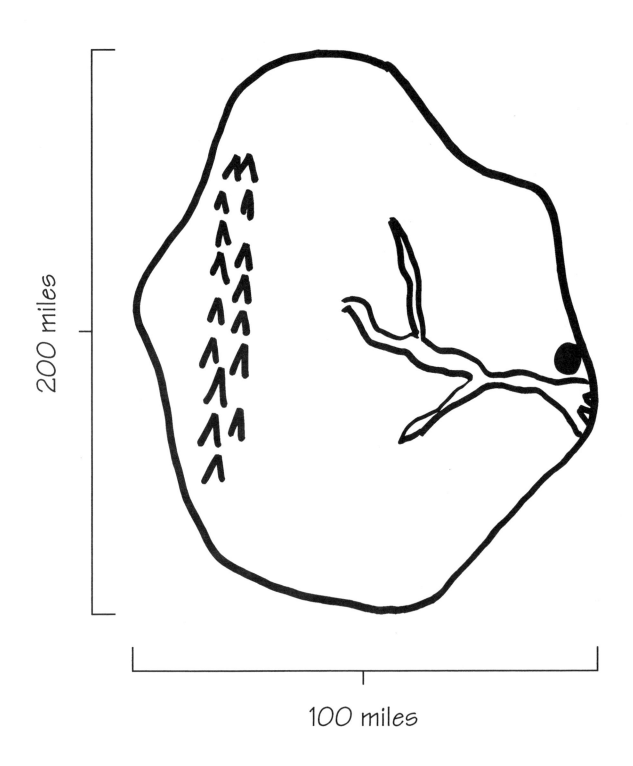

200 miles

100 miles

Unfairness on Purpose!

MI Context: This concept of "unfairness on purpose" can be adapted to any activity where materials need to be distributed. The results are wonderful insights into the Interpersonal Intelligence and how the students problem-solve. This may be a new mindset for teachers who have worked for years to keep everything in their classrooms equal for their students.

Interpersonal
Intermediate
Social Studies

Learner Outcomes: Students will experience unfairness in a controlled setting and problem-solve a solution which meets the needs of the group members. Through a guided discussion after the experience, students will gain knowledge of a variety of ways to solve the same problem.

Procedure:
1. As a celebration for finishing the first week of school, buy a couple of bags of popcorn for the class. Divide the class into groups for this activity.

2. Distribute the popcorn when the students are out of the room. Instead of taking great pains to ensure that each student has received the same amount, distribute the popcorn unfairly. Give some students lots of cheese and caramel corn. Give other students only one kind. Give one student one kernel. As the students return, tell them that this is a surprise party upon finishing the first week of school and that the party may begin.

3. The first rule in this activity is that all students must agree on the way to solve the problem before actual redistribution begins. At the beginning of the year, this type of problem solving takes longer than at the end of the year. The more you can create unfairness in a controlled setting, the more the students will learn.

4. It is very important to have the students, as they are enjoying the popcorn, share how the popcorn was divided. Some groups may actually count out the pieces, while others might combine it into one big pile and everyone just helps themselves. The children should share how they felt about the activity and process.

Materials:
Popcorn

Assessment / Reflection:
Each group must verbalize to the entire class how the problem was solved. It is important for students to see that there are many different ways to solve the same problem.

MI Extensions:

Intrapersonal / Linguistic: Students record their role in the group as problem solving took place. Were they a compromiser? Idea giver? Problem-solver? Goof off? The reflection should also include how they felt about their role. It is important for them to keep recording their role each time this problem-solving procedure takes place, and to continue to assess it each time.

Bodily-Kinesthetic: Students role-play different ways their group might solve the unfairness problem.

Logical-Mathematical: Students begin a chart entitled "How to Solve Problems," recording the method their group used as well as recording the other groups' methods. In math, students would use this chart as a reminder/guide for solving mathematical problems.

Musical: Study musical artists from the 60's. Find protest songs that have unfairness as their theme. Share these with the class.

Spatial: Instruct the students to design a new gameboard where unfairness is prominent. Students play the games and discuss how they interacted while playing.

Buttons, Buttons, Buttons

MI Context: This lesson is used with grammar lessons on adjectives and with writing assignments.

Learner Outcomes: Students will learn that some adjectives are more helpful for description than others. Students will understand that two people may describe the same object quite differently.

Procedure:

1. Each student will blindly choose a button from a bag and keep the identity of the button a secret.

2. The students are given a specified amount of time, perhaps fifteen minutes, to describe the button thoroughly by listing as many adjectives as they can.

3. At this point there are several options:

   • Have students trade buttons with one another and then repeat the listing process with their new button. Students will then get together with their button partner (the other student who has described the same buttons) and create a Venn diagram for their buttons to compare and contrast their adjectives.

   • Students hand in all of their buttons and descriptions. The teacher randomly redistributes both buttons and descriptions so that each child again has one of each. Then students must use their given adjective clues to locate the button match. When the students think a match has been found, they can place the button and its presumed description on a designated table where original owners can verify that the button and description do match. Once all matches have been found, the class can discuss what made it easy or hard to match the buttons.

   • Students are put in groups of 3-4 people. In these groups, students generate a list of adjectives that help to describe all of their buttons. That is, list those adjectives that don't really help to distinguish one button from another even though they do describe the button. Also, have children check to see how many senses they employed in describing their buttons. Could they have used more? Students should then help each other create more complete lists for each button in the group.

Materials:
A bag of buttons (old buttons seem to be more interesting), pencil and paper

Assessment / Reflection:

How detailed a list were students able to generate? Have students critique each other's lists of adjectives. Instruct them to write in their journals something they've learned about adjectives from doing this activity.

MI Extensions:

Intrapersonal: Ask the students to determine the effectiveness of their adjectives. Were others able to figure out which button they were describing? Have them add one or more adjectives to their lists to better describe the button.

Bodily-Kinesthetic: Play charades acting out the adjectives.

Linguistic: The students will write a limerick with their button as the subject using as many adjectives as possible from their list.

Logical-Mathematical: Sort and classify two handfuls of buttons by the adjectives the students developed. Use a bar graph to list the categories and record the number of buttons in that category.

Musical: Have the students create songs that utilize all the adjectives they named to describe their button.

Spatial: Use buttons to decorate a vest or shirt, or to create a mosaic "portrait."

Activities to Support the Interpersonal Intelligence

Intrapersonal
- Murphy-Meisgeier Type Indicator for Children
- Trust and team-building activities
- Partnering and Big Buddy activities with other grades
- Appreciation Statements
- Rubrics or rating sheets for activities

Bodily-Kinesthetic
- Role playing or creative dramatics
- Playing at recess
- Providing a service to another group of people
- Sending, receiving and interpreting messages through gestures, Morse Code, flags or sign language

Linguistic
- Debate or panel discussions
- Person of the Week interviews
- Partner poems or group story writing
- Peer support groups
- Reciprocal teaching or jigsawing

Logical-Mathematical
- Develop a flow chart to show classroom or playground rules the class has developed
- Chart or graph interactions during television shows
- Play strategy games-competitive and non-competitive
- Describe a pattern you have made while someone else tries to copy it
- Sort students by favorite activities or personality attributes

Musical
- Playing instruments with others
- Singing with a group
- Composing a round from a familiar song that reinforces a skill
- Creating group rhythmic patterns
- Matching music to moods

Spatial
- Design a group mural
- Make partner drawings
- Create a group quilt
- Describe a picture you have drawn while your partner tries to recreate it
- Redesign book covers for the same book or story to show different perspectives or points of view

A practical guide created by the faculty of The New City School ©1994

Identifying the Interpersonal Intelligence in Your Students

Children function at many different levels within the intelligences. Through observation of everyday activities, one can create a profile showing the level of functioning within a particular intelligence and the intelligences in relation to each other. The levels described show increased engagement and proficiency. Use this record-keeping page to obtain a richer picture of a child.

Appreciates:

YES	NO	
		Demonstrates interest in others, enjoys social interaction and is able to differentiate the moods, feelings and intention of others
		Verbally communicates needs
		Participates in group activities and discussions
		Can identify and label emotions and feelings of other people
		Understands stereotypes and prejudices
		Seeks out social interactions and situations

Performs:

		Is able to apply the intelligence to problem solve a given social situation and respond to the mood, feelings and intentions of others
		Reads, understands and empathizes with others
		Is able to confront and be assertive in appropriate situations
		Interrupts put downs, stereotyping, ethnic and gender jokes
		Accepts constructive feedback and acts upon it
		Is able to compromise and negotiate
		Volunteers help when others need it
		Solves social problems independent of assistance
		Organizes a group interaction and is able to influence others

Creates:

		Is able to apply the intelligence to generate appropriate and varied social outcomes
		Can generate positive atmosphere to help focus a group's efforts
		Exhibits leadership that enables others to work at a higher level
		Can anticipate and change the course of a conversation or comment
		Can generate solutions or find words to help others with conflict resolution
		Organizes and carries through on a large scale class project

Group: _____   Date: _____

How are We Doing?

Give 2 examples for each statement.

1. We each contributed ideas:

often___   sometimes___   not very much___

2. We listened to each other:

often___   sometimes___   not very much___

3. We encouraged each other:

often___   sometimes___   not very much___

4. We built on each other's ideas:

often___   sometimes___   not very much___

Name: _____   Date: _____

Self-assessment: Groupwork

1. I shared in my group today.

2. I encouraged others in my group to share.

3. I listened to others.

4. Others talked with me.

5. I felt supported by people in my group.

6. We worked on the task cooperatively.

Photocopy this page for student use or pull out an idea for the students to respond to in their journals

Children's Resources

Books and Recordings:

Alexander, Lloyd. *The Big Book for Peace.* Dutton Books, 1990.

Aliki. *We are Best Friends.* Greenwillow Books, 1982. ★

Baehr, Patricia. *School Isn't Fair.* Four Winds Press, 1989. ★

Buekrens, Adam. *Hi, I'm Adam: A Child's Story of Tourette Syndrome.* Hope Press, 1991.

Carl, Eric. *House for Hermit Crab.* Picture Book Studio, 1987. ★

de Paola, Tomie. *First One Foot, Now The Other.* Putnam, 1980. ★

Delton, Judy. *Two Good Friends.* Crown, 1986. ★

Ets, Marie Hall. *Play With Me.* Viking Penguin, 1976. ★

Grahame, Kenneth. *The Wind in the Willows.* David and Charles, 1992.

Havill, Juanita. *Jamaica's Find.* Houghton Mifflin, 1986. ★

Hurwitz, Johanna. *Hot and Cold Summer.* Morrow, 1984.

Johnson, Angela. *Do Like Kyla.* Orchard Books, 1990. ★

Jones, Rebecca C. *Matthew and Tilly.* Dutton Children's Books, 1991. ★

Klamath County YMCA Family Preschool. *The Land of Many Colors.* Scholastic Inc., 1993. ★

Korschunow, Irina. *The Foundling Fox.* Harper & Row, 1984.

Krementz, Jill. *How It Feels To Live With A Physical Disability.* Simon and Schuster, 1992.

Leuy, Virginia. *Let's Go to the Art Museum.* Harry Abrams, Inc., 1983. ★

Lionni, Leo. *Swimmy.* Pantheon, 1968. ★

Lobel, Arnold. *Frog and Toad Are Friends.* HarperCollins, 1970. ★

Mayhew, James. *Kate's Picture Show.* Bantom Little Rooster, 1989. ★

McLerran, Alice. *Roxaboxen.* Lothrop, 1990. ★

McLuhan, T.C. *Touch the Earth.* Dutton Books, 1971.

Miles, Miska. *Annie and the Old One.* Little, Brown and Co., Inc., 1971. ★

Pinkney, Gloria. *Back Home.* Dial Press, 1992.

★ indicates a picture book

Pinkwater, Daniel. *The Big Orange Splot.* Scholastic Inc., 1977. ★

Polacco, Patricia. *Chicken Sunday.* Philomel, 1992. ★

Polacco, Patricia. *Mrs Katz and Tush.* Bantam Books, 1992. ★

Polacco, Patricia. *The Bee Tree.* Philomel, 1993. ★

Rostand, Edmond. *Cyrano de Bergerac.* Vintage Books, 1990.

Rylant, Cynthia. *Missing May.* Orchard Books, 1992.

Smith, Doris Buchanan. *Taste of Blackberries.* Scholastic Inc., 1973.

Spier, Peter. *People.* Doubleday, 1980. ★

Spinelli, Jerry. *Maniac Magee.* Harper Trophy, 1992.

Stevenson, James. *Monty.* Greenwillow Books, 1992. ★

Taylor, Mildred D. *Mississippi Bridge.* Bantam Books, 1992.

Wilhelm, Hans. *Tyrone The Double Dirty Rotten Cheater.* Scholastic Inc., 1991. ★

Wilson, Forrest. *What It Feels Like To Be a Building.* Landmark Preservation Press, 1988. ★

Winthrop, Elizabeth. *Katherine's Doll.* Dutton Books, 1983. ★

Yashima, Taro. *Crow Boy.* Puffin Books, 1976. ★

Zolotow, Charlotte. *The Hating Book.* HarperCollins, 1969. ★

Zolotow, Charlotte. *The Quarreling Book.* Harper & Row, 1982. ★

Games:

"Friends Around the World: A Game of World Peace." Angland, Walsh. Aristoplay Ltd., 1989.

"Hidden Talents: Learn About Your Friends." Pressman, 1994.

"Max." Family Pasttimes, 1986.

"Secret Diary: The Game of Sharing Secrets and Surprises." Golden-Western Pub. Co., 1991.

"The Princess Game." Family Pasttimes, 1986.

"The Sleeping Grump." Family Pasttimes, 1981.

Teachers' Resources

Cherry, Clare. *Think of Something Quiet.* David S. Lake, 1981.

Drew, Naomi. *Learning the Skills of Peacemaking.* Jalmar Press, 1987.

Gibbs, Jeanne. *Tribes.* Center Source Publications, 1987.

Lewis, Barbara. *The Kids' Guide to Social Action.* Free Spirit Pub., 1991.

Palmer, Hap. *Hap Palmer Favorites.* Alfred Publishing Co., 1981.

Pincus, Debbie. *Interactions.* Good Apple, 1988.

Schwartz, Linda. *Think on Your Feet.* The Learning Works, 1987.

Thomson, Barbara. *Words Can Hurt You.* Addison-Wesley, 1993.

Chapter 2:
The Intrapersonal Intelligence

Contributors: Sally Boggeman, Susie Chasnoff, Linda Churchwell, Mary F. Daly, Danielle Egeling, Jean Blockhus Grover, Carla Mash, Joan Moldafsky Siwak, Monette Gooch-Smith, Christine Wallach, Denise A. Willis

"When one is a stranger to oneself, then one is estranged from others too."

Anne Morrow Lindbergh

A practical guide created by the faculty of The New City School ©1994

Web of the Intrapersonal Intelligence

"I am a sensitive person. I get my feelings hurt."

"I'm good at soccer. I'm not good at spelling."

"I like to spend time alone."

"Those are the 'by yourself' people."

- Pursues personal interests
- Sets goals
- Identifies and labels feelings
- Knows their own strengths and weaknesses
- Daydreams
- Is insightful and reflective
- Is intuitive
- Is comfortable being alone

Marva Collins knew she could teach at risk children using her own methods.

Marie Montessori developed individualized, self-correcting educational materials.

Sigmund Freud created a new area of psychotherapy based on three forms of self.

Arnold Adoff, author of *All the Colors of the Race,* wrote poetry describing his feelings and experiences.

"The kind of person you are is much more important than the kinds of things you know."

Tom Hoerr

Intrapersonal is the Key to Success

by Tom Hoerr

While all of the intelligences are important, we believe that the intrapersonal intelligence is the most important. Possessing a high degree of Intrapersonal intelligence enables an individual to capitalize on his strengths in the other intelligences. And perhaps as valuable, it allows an individual to compensate for his weaknesses in the other intelligences.

Prior to the publication of *Frames Of Mind,* educators did not think that being skilled in working with others or that knowing oneself extremely well were forms of intelligence. While we might have heard someone say that Paul has "good people skills" or Betty has "a good sense of herself," we did not equate these characteristics with intelligence. But Gardner's pragmatic definition of intelligence — the ability to solve a problem or create a product that is valued in a society — and his theory of Multiple Intelligences changed all that.

A New Way of Looking at Success

As educators, our job is to prepare kids so that they can flourish in the real world. Unfortunately, most people, including many educators, mistakenly believe that what is required to be successful in school is the same as what is required to be successful in life. In fact, however, success in these two arenas requires very different sets of skills (see *The Unschooled Mind,* Gardner, 1991 and *The Triarchic Mind,* Sternberg, 1988). It is true that the ability to read, write and compute well is important; however, in general, those who get ahead in the world — whatever your criteria — do not do so simply because they read or write or compute better than others. The people who flourish in real life do perform well in traditional academic areas, but they excel because of their ability to understand and work with others and their ability to capitalize on their strengths and compensate for their weaknesses. They excel because of their strength in the Personal Intelligences.

Most people, including many educators, mistakenly believe that what is required to be successful in school is the same as what is required to be successful in life.

Many of the difficulties which we encounter in everyday life are the result of problems that we have working with others or of problems that they have working with us. The ability to get along and work well with others has always been an essential quality for success; with our ever-shrinking world, it will be even more important in the future. Whatever the question, future technological advances will make the answers easier to find; the ability to work collaboratively with others in finding those answers will be what determines whether or not one is successful.

A high degree of interpersonal intelligence — being sensitive to the needs and moods of others, understanding them, and being able to work with them — is surely a very important component of this kind of success. Yet our belief is that Intrapersonal Intelligence — knowledge of one's own strengths and weaknesses — is the key, the starting point, the most important intelligence. Possessing a strong Intrapersonal Intelligence means that we know our strengths and our weaknesses. It also means that we know how we are perceived by others.

To the degree that we are successful in life, whatever the arena, it is because we have a sense of what we do well and what we don't do well. The things we do well, we do with vigor and aplomb. It is doing those things — selling or painting or helping others develop — that gives us our success. While we may work on the things that we don't do well — being organized or eating healthy foods or not procrastinating — it is our lack of success in these endeavors that prevents us from achieving even more.

Acting as a Result of Intrapersonal Intelligence

If we are successful, it is because we are able to find a context in which our strengths come to the fore and our weaknesses are minimized. Often we do this, particularly if we are successful, without even being aware. Perhaps we delegate the things we don't do well to others; possibly we choose our tasks so that we can succeed without mastering our weaknesses. If, for example, someone is a poor speller, that by itself is not particularly significant. Because if the individual knows that he is a poor speller, he can make accommodations. He can have his written work proofed by others who do spell well, he can present his information orally, or he can be sure to use the spell check before printing every document. His Intrapersonal Intelligence has enabled him to see this weakness and to compensate for it. However, if he is a poor speller and does not know it, his Intrapersonal Intelligence in this area is not strong, and he has a problem. Inevitably, and unfortunately, many of his good ideas will be discounted because the reader doesn't get beyond reacting to misspelled words. Improving his spelling is important; more important, however, is that he be aware of his poor spelling ability and take the necessary steps to make it less of a problem. While the spelling example is an easy one to describe, a similar case could be made for any area of weakness. Either one is aware of his weaknesses and compensates for them, or the weaknesses remain unrecognized and unaddressed, hindering growth and success.

Just as it is important that our students learn to read and write and compute, it is also important that they learn about themselves, their strengths and weaknesses along with how they are perceived by others. It is incumbent upon us to help our students improve their Intrapersonal Intelligence.

Improving Intrapersonal Intelligence in the Classroom

How do we do this at New City? First, we consciously teach the MI model and the intelligences, as developmentally appropriate, to all of our students. Understanding MI is a good entry point for helping each child begin to look at his or her intelligence profile. Children learn that there are different kinds of intelligences, not better and worse kinds. Just as some of us are African

Possessing a strong Intrapersonal Intelligence means that we know our strengths and our weaknesses. It also means that we know how we are perceived by others.

If we are successful, it is because we are able to find a context in which our strengths come to the fore and our weaknesses are minimized.

American, some Asian Americans and some Caucasian, some of us are talented linguistically, some spatially and some musically. All of us have strengths and weaknesses, and all of us need to learn what we do well and what requires more attention.

For many students, understanding their own array of strengths and weaknesses is very empowering. One example comes to mind: an intermediate-grade student who was skilled in logical-mathematical tasks had always felt inferior to his linguistically-gifted older sister. He struggled with reading while she read book after book after book. One day, however, after learning about the different intelligences and reflecting on his own intelligence profile, he told his teacher with delight, "I've got it; she's talented linguistically, but I'm strong logically-mathematically!" This awareness helped him understand the difference between him and his sister and legitimized his strength for him.

For many students, understanding their own array of strengths and weaknesses is very empowering.

Second, the Personal Intelligences have been given a great deal of attention by our faculty in our curriculum development and teaching. Because who you are is more important than what you know, we felt that it was important to begin each child's report card (and parent-teacher conference) by focusing on development in the Personal Intelligences. The first page of our report card (Progress Report) is entirely devoted to reporting student progress in the Personal Intelligences. A child's growth in attributes such as "motivation," "confidence," "appreciation for diversity," and "teamwork" is shared with parents using symbols (AC= area of concern; DA= developing appropriately; ED= exceeding developmental expectations) and narrative comments.

Who you are is more important than what you know.

Teachers everywhere work to help students understand each other and work together. We are no different. "Tell her how you feel." "Use your words." "What would you do differently?" These are typical comments made to children who are having difficulties interacting with others. Similarly, we use "Magic Circle" (a human development curriculum) with our fifth- and sixth-grade students four mornings per week and "the red chairs" (two brightly-painted chairs in which children go to sit and talk when they are having difficulties interacting) with our first graders. And the entire tone of our building is one of friendliness, casualness and respect. Everyone is on a first-name basis, everyone. Students, teachers, parents, secretaries and administrators all call one another by their first names. We all respect one another for who we are, not the titles or positions that we hold. While we used first names prior to our work with MI, I relate it here because it portrays the flavor of our school.

But perhaps the biggest change caused by our recognition of the value of the Intrapersonal Intelligence is the emphasis that we give to our students reflecting upon their own performances. Throughout the school, in all grades, students are asked to reflect upon the role that they, personally, played in learning, in the classroom and at lunch or recess. "Think to yourself," a teacher will ask, "what is the best way for you to learn this information?" or "Take a moment and think, what did you do to make this activity a success?" After a moment she might continue, "Were you a good team member? What specific thing did you do to be helpful? What could you

Throughout the school, in all grades, students are asked to reflect upon the role that they, personally, played in learning, in the classroom and at lunch or recess.

have done that you didn't? Were there things you did which were not help-ful?" Although the exact format — the kinds of questions, their specificity and whether or not the answers are shared with others — varies develop-mentally, the thrust of helping children reflect on their behaviors, the roles they played, is present at all grade levels. With the primary and intermedi-ate grades, having children write regularly in journals is often used to facili-tate children's reflection.

Teachers give time and attention to providing activities and structures for children to assess their own performance and work on areas that need strengthening. Not only do many activities conclude with children being given time to reflect and self-assess, in some classes students are given spaces on their papers or worksheets to write how they have contributed to the group's efforts and what they might do differently in the future. Some teachers use quotes from the children's reflections in their progress reports or notes to their parents. Occasionally, in some classes, children are brought together to work with others who are trying to improve similar areas. For example, one teacher created PEP ("Personal Effort Performance") Groups after having her students identify the behaviors on which they wanted to work. One group worked on reducing the times that they interrupt others; another group met to plan how they could be more assertive in speaking out in class; and others came together to share ideas and support one another in their quest to be more organized. Too, as developmentally appropriate, teachers facilitate children giving feedback to one another. Older students, in particular, learn to give one another both positive and negative feedback about their work and play performances.

Finally, our focus on the Intrapersonal Intelligence has affected us by helping our faculty become more aware of how we work with and interact with one another.

Finally, our focus on the Intrapersonal Intelligence has affected us by help-ing our faculty become more aware of how we work with and interact with one another. It has helped us improve our own Intrapersonal Intelligence. If we expect our students to constantly grow and develop, we can expect no less from ourselves. Faculty and committee meetings often have periods in which the leader asks the individuals to pause for a moment and think about what they, personally, did to move the group forward. And each August, during our week long in-service prior to the start of school, we devote a session to "being a good teammate." Part of that time is spent reflecting and part of it spent sharing and giving feedback to others. By working to improve our own Intrapersonal Intelligence, we know that not only will we be better educators and better people, our students will benefit too.

Me Bags

Intrapersonal
Preprimary
Social Studies

MI Context: This lesson can be used at the beginning of the year to help children get to know one another better. Later in the year, this lesson could be used as an oral presentation activity.

Learner Outcomes: Students will share information about themselves using items collected and brought from home. Students will identify likes, interests and facts about themselves.

Procedure:

1. Hold up a stack of ordinary brown paper grocery bags, one for each child in the room.

   Teacher: *What are these?*
   Students: Grocery bags.
   Teacher: *They may look like grocery bags now, but they are really "Me Bags."*

2. Model a "Me Bag" presentation. Explain that everything in the bag will tell them something about the teacher.

3. After the presentation, the students discuss the items in the bag and how they relate to the teacher. Students will share something they learned about their teacher that they did not know before. Have the children suggest items that would never be found in their teacher's bag.

4. Talk about the teacher's presentation. What made it good? What would make it better?

5. Tell the students they will put together a "Me Bag" at home. Have the students reflect about things they might like to include in their own bags. Remind them that everything must fit inside the bag and tell only about them.

6. Bags are given out and children write their names on them. Attach a letter to the bag informing parents about the activity and giving a deadline for having bags back to school for the student presentations. Stress a five- to six-minute time limit for the child's presentation.

7. Videotape each presentation.

Materials:
Brown paper grocery bags, teacher-completed "Me Bag," video camera, video tape for each child

MI Extensions:

Interpersonal: Students write partner poems or do portraits of each other using items in the bags.

Bodily-Kinesthetic: Students role play favorite sports, stories, or other important things while the other students guess what they are doing. Students can also pantomime favorite activities (for example, cooking, reading, dancing).

Linguistic: Students write a "Me Poem" based on the items they included in the bags. They could also create "Who Am I?" riddles with lists or drawings of the items on the top sheet, and their name or self-portrait underneath.

Logical-Mathematical: Develop time lines of the students' lives. Another activity would be to check for similarities and differences in the "Me Bags." For example, count and compare how many students brought a favorite book, a picture of their pet, a favorite collection. Graph the findings.

Musical: Students create a song about themselves. Students can also include a favorite piece of music in the bag or sing a favorite song as part of the presentation.

Spatial: Students create a poster illustrating all the items in their bags. They could also draw a self-portrait using the items as elements in their portrait. They might also draw a self-portrait of what they will look like in forty years.

I Am...

MI Context: This lesson can be used anytime as an introduction or final project to a unit on the self, the body or to introduce the Intrapersonal Intelligence.

Intrapersonal
Preprimary
Social Studies

Learner Outcomes: The student will make connections between herself and a book character followed by a reflection on herself and what makes her uniquely different.

Procedure:

1. Read the story *Quick As a Cricket* by Audrey Wood. This is a predictable book. Children will be able to "mock read" the story after listening to it once.

2. Students role play or act out the story.

3. Instruct the children to think about how they are like and different from the character in the story.

4. The child draws a self-portrait in the middle of a piece of poster board. Around the self-portrait, she draws pictures that describe components of her personality, i.e., a horse because I run fast, a pencil because I like to draw, an octopus because I can do many things at once, or marbles because I like to play them. Other possibilities include cutting out pictures from magazines, bringing in stuffed animals or making clay figures, and explaining why these things are relevant.

5. Add words to the poster as children complete their work. Each sentence should begin with the phrase "I am ...." For example, "I am fast like a horse." or "I am creative like an artist."

Materials:

Poster board, markers, scissors, crayons, other art items for poster such as yarn, fabric or paint, and *Quick as a Cricket* by Audrey Wood

Assessment / Reflection

By reading the words only, can students identify each other? Talk or write in journals about the parts of this project that were easy, difficult or enjoyable. Does the child draw an accurate picture of herself? Do the pictures reflect the child as others see her? Discuss the differences.

MI Extensions:

Interpersonal: In small groups, share the posters. Let the children brainstorm. "What else could she have added to her poster?" Talk in small groups about the reflection mentioned in the lesson.

Intrapersonal: Ask the students to reflect on what it would be like if they were one of the posters hanging in the room? What would they feel like? What would they like about being the poster? Not like? What would they hope to see or hear? Write a letter or dictate a story from the poster's perspective.

Bodily-Kinesthetic: Role play each poster. Read the words from each child's poster as the children act out the movements.

Linguistic: Share posters with the total group. Let group members say one thing they like about each poster. Assemble posters to make a big book.

Logical-Mathematical: Make up people riddles about peers. For example, "I am thinking of a person who has brown hair and brown eyes, likes to draw, is fast like a horse and is as busy as a beaver."

Musical: Let each child bring a tape, CD or record of her favorite music to play in class. Make a music collage of everybody's music. Record a portion of each child's music on one tape. Have children identify each other's music.

Spatial: Make a "Me Puzzle." Each child draws a picture of herself on a blank puzzle using markers or crayons. If puzzles are not available, use large blank index cards. Cut it into pieces. Small plastic reclosable bags make good storage containers for the puzzle pieces.

Show Us What You Can Do

Intrapersonal
Preprimary
Language Arts

MI Context: Children learn at different rates. During this lesson the students explore the differences in their development and thus build their self-esteem.

Learner Outcomes: Children will understand that everyone learns to do things at different times in their lives.

Procedure:
1. Read *Leo the Late Bloomer* by Robert Kraus and discuss how the parents felt and how Leo felt.

2. Role play the story by assigning the parts of Mom and Dad while other students all play the part of Leo.

3. Brainstorm a list of tasks they can already perform.

4. Children take turns pantomiming something they feel they do well (for example, ride a bike, throw a ball, sing, draw, or dance).

Materials:
Leo the Late Bloomer by Robert Kraus, chart paper, markers

Assessment / Reflection:
Observe how accurately the children represent the feelings of Leo and his parents when role playing. Determine the accuracy of their perceptions of what they do well.

MI Extensions:
Interpersonal: Children get together in groups and compliment each other about things they do well.

Bodily-Kinesthetic: Make Leo out of clay.

Linguistic: Write a group letter of encouragement to Leo.

Logical-Mathematical: While children pantomime, create a picture graph listing their accomplishments. Children put an "x" in the column indicating one thing they do well.

Musical: Learn the song "Sammy" by Hap Palmer from his recording "Getting to Know Myself."

Spatial: Children draw something they would like to learn to do.

Content of Their Character

Intrapersonal
Primary
Social Studies

MI Context: This lesson may be used during a unit on Civil Rights. The students focus on Dr. Martin Luther King as a person who made a difference.

Learner Outcomes: The students will identify many of the qualities in their personalities, thus strengthening the Intrapersonal Intelligence.

Procedure:

1. Through questioning, have the students review their prior knowledge of Dr. Martin Luther King.

2. Read excerpts from the "I Have a Dream Speech" by Dr. King.

3. Ask the students to describe the kind of person Dr. King was. Write these words on the board. Help the students make a connection to these words and to the words "content of his character."

4. Show the students a cut-out picture of Dr. King. Beneath this picture attach a blank silhouette of the same picture.

5. Together write the content of Dr. King's character on the blank sheet below his picture as the class reads the words on the board.

6. Ask the students to look at the content of their character. It may be necessary to create a word bank for them.

7. Distribute two blackline paper dolls to each child. On one they create a picture of themselves. On the other they will write the content of their own character.

Materials:
A copy of the "I Have a Dream Speech" by Dr. Martin Luther King, two paper doll blacklines for each student, a cut-out of Dr. King made into a "Content of Their Character" model

Assessment / Reflection:
Students will share the contents of their characters.

MI Extensions:
Interpersonal and Bodily-Kinesthetic: Use the "I Have a Dream Speech" as the inspiration for a class tapestry. Give each student a piece of different colored embroidery thread on a needle. The students can use only that thread to place their stitches on the piece of burlap. After each student has completed his stitching, he will record his idea of the picture he has created into a tape recorder. When the tapestry has been completed, students sit in a circle, listen to the tape recorder and reflect on their work.

Linguistic: Read *Happy Birthday, Martin Luther King* by Jean Marzollo.

Logical-Mathematical: Create a time line of the Civil Rights movement or the life of Dr. King.

Musical: Practice and perform protest songs from the time of the Civil Rights movement.

Spatial: Create a black tempera-over-crayon scratch drawing of Dr. Martin Luther King or scenes from his life. Similar pictures are used to illustrate the book, *Happy Birthday, Martin Luther King*.

A practical guide created by the faculty of The New City School ©1994

How Long Is a Minute?

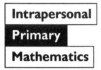

Intrapersonal
Primary
Mathematics

MI Context: This lesson is used during a unit on time. The class will discuss how to tell time and work on the concept of duration of time.

Learner Outcomes: The students will recognize which intelligences they prefer while experiencing the duration of a minute.

Procedure:

1. Predict and make a list of activities that take about one minute to perform. This list will be used later, proving or disproving the predictions related to the various intelligences.

2. Do the following activities for one minute. They could also be done in centers, but be sure the quiet spot is truly quiet or do it separately. Activities may be done in one class period, throughout the day or over the course of several days.

   • Ask classmates how many brothers and sisters they have. How many people can you talk to in one minute (*Interpersonal*)?

   • Sit quietly with your body still, eyes closed, and see if you can keep your mind from thinking about anything (*Intrapersonal*).

   • Hop on one foot or jog in place (*Bodily-Kinesthetic*).

   • Notice how far you get when reading a book silently (*Linguistic*).

   • Do a worksheet of math problems (*Logical-Mathematical*).

   • Sing "Row, Row, Row Your Boat" (*Musical*).

   • Draw a picture (*Spatial*).

3. Reflect and record which minute seemed the longest, the shortest and why.

4. Come together as a group and discuss reflections.

5. This is a good opportunity to connect their preference to the intelligences and their strengths and weaknesses. For example, students who are talented in the Bodily-Kinesthetic Intelligence will find that the time jogging passed quickly. Those who are skilled Spatially can produce a viable representation in a minute.

Materials:
Watch with a second hand or stopwatch, paper, markers, individual reading materials, math fact sheets

Assessment / Reflection:
Students make a journal entry about the intelligences they see as their strengths and weaknesses. Verify predictions made during the initial class brainstorming session.

MI Extensions:
Interpersonal: Students are given one minute to make a human clock. Provide string or rope. The rest is up to the children.

Intrapersonal: Ask the students to reflect upon what these activities tell them about themselves?

Bodily-Kinesthetic: Students design a five-minute workout with a different exercise for each minute. Each day pick a different student to lead the class in exercise.

Linguistic: Give the students one minute to speak to the class or write in their journals about their favorite time of the day and tell why. Read *The Grouchy Ladybug* by Eric Carle.

Logical-Mathematical: Graph the favorite and least favorite or shortest and longest minutes based on the activities.

Musical: Listen and compare the difference in time with a 4/4 march and a 3/4 waltz.

Spatial: Design a clock that shows the duration of a minute.

Goal Setting

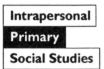

Intrapersonal
Primary
Social Studies

MI Context: This lesson is used to help children know their strengths, to help them set boundaries, and to help them focus their attention on specific behavioral or academic areas that need improvement.

Learner Outcomes: Students will gain increasing self-awareness and self-control and develop the ability to be self-directed.

Procedure:

1. Ask children what a goal is and come to a meaningful working definition.

2. Ask each child to think of something about himself upon which he wishes to focus. This will undoubtedly be difficult at first. Have him limit his goal to the school environment, for example, "I will not interrupt" or "I will keep my hands to myself in line."

3. Stress that they are all here to help support one another, and they all have room for improvement. As the children share their goals, record them on a piece of chart paper along with each child's name.

4. Allow time each day for children to reflect on individual progress. Ask each child ways in which other children have supported his progress.

5. Set a new goal on a weekly basis.

Materials:
Chart paper, markers

Assessment / Reflection:
Students reflect on their progress through discussion and self-assessment based on whether or not they have reached their goal.

MI Extensions:
Interpersonal: Classmates meet to discuss if they feel their goals have been reached, giving examples and discussing strategies.

Bodily-Kinesthetic: Each student creates a cheer that states his goal.

Linguistic: Keep a journal of goals.

Logical-Mathematical: Daily, on a scale of one to ten, each student rates his progress toward reaching his goal. Connect the points to form a line graph.

Musical: Learn the song "Wonderful Me" by Beth Pergola.

Spatial: Draw "before and after" pictures of a goal.

Dear Self

MI Context: This lesson is used to help students develop test-taking strategies. These strategies are practiced and verified throughout the year. Finally, they are applied when the student takes the standardized test given in the spring.

Learner Outcomes: Students will improve their performance on standardized tests by writing themselves a letter which will remind them of strategies they found successful from a previous standardized test.

Procedure:

1. Prior to the first test given during the year, students are asked to interview their parents on test-taking strategies that the parents felt were successful for them.

2. On chart paper, list the strategies the children collected during their interviews. These might include such things as: get a good night's sleep, never panic, don't spend too much time on any one answer, or eliminate possibilities.

3. Have the children pick one strategy that they will use on the first test and record this in their journals. Included in this entry should be how they plan to use this strategy.

4. Give the children a teacher-made test, part of which uses a format similar to the standardized tests they will be taking in the spring. Afterward, the children write a journal response indicating their test performance.

5. This procedure continues with each test. The students note in their journals which strategies have been the most successful.

6. Before the standardized test, students review their list of successful strategies and pick those they will use for the standardized test.

7. After finishing the standardized test, students write themselves a letter stating the test-taking strategies they have learned, used and felt were successful. The letters are mailed to the students the next year before the tests.

8. Another situation that would work with writing a letter to oneself is to write after report cards are issued. The student would state areas that need improvement. These letters could be mailed to the students in a month.

   Note: *If writing a letter would hinder a student from being reflective, then tape record "Dear Self."*

Materials:
Letter-writing paper, English book as a reference for letter form, journal

Assessment / Reflection:
Did the students use the strategies and were they increasingly successful on their tests? Did their confidence and test-taking attitude improve?

MI Extensions:
Interpersonal: All students who want to work on the same specific topic meet. Students could form Personal Effort Performance (PEP) groups to meet regularly to work on a common area such as relaxing during a test.

Bodily-Kinesthetic: Have the students teach and lead the rest of the class in relaxation or centering activities such as yoga or Tai Chi.

Logical-Mathematical: Students create a flow chart which tells them how to approach a test-taking situation and how to respond to the events that occur during the test. Or, students graph the various strategies reported by the parents to determine which ideas were used most and least often.

Musical: Students pick music that helps to reinforce one of their test-taking strategies. For example, if one of their strategies was to stay calm during the test, the student might pick music of Kenny G or Yanni which are very even, sedate, and without words. Students listen to the music and chart how well it helped them during their test-taking.

Spatial: Students make a mind map of the strategies they found to be successful. This is also mailed to them the following year.

Getting to Know You

MI Context: This lesson will help students examine characteristics of their personalities as well as to see the similarities and differences between themselves and their peers.

Learner Outcomes: The students will find common characteristics between themselves and objects. For example, they will find similarities between themselves and such things as the country, a city, a river, a lake or a screened-in porch.

Intrapersonal
Intermediate
Social Studies

Procedure:
1. Give each student the sheet "Which are you more like?" and explain that they will be analyzing their personalities by comparing themselves to the things on the sheet. Tell them that they are not to choose items they like best; instead, they must determine which items have similar characteristics to their personalities. The students should not discuss the questions or their responses with each other; it must be done individually or it will have an effect on the rest of the activity. Instruct them to circle their responses to the questions and to turn their papers over when they have finished.

2. When everyone has finished, spend a few minutes debriefing the exercise. For example, ask the following questions: What was the most difficult question to answer? What was the easiest question to answer?

3. The students will examine one of the items in greater depth. Instruct the students to write their response to a particular comparison, selected by the teacher, on the back of their paper. Tell the students to list all the reasons why they are like the item. For example, if a student selected river, she might write the following things: aggressive, impatient, strong, adventurous, sometimes I rush through things, don't like to sit still, or risk taker. A student who selected lake might write the following: quiet, open-minded, big heart, patient, welcome everyone, take my time to do things, laid back, or dependable.

4. After the students have recorded their thoughts, have them break into the two groups. Send the rivers to one part of the room and the lakes to another part of the room. Give each group a piece of chart paper. Instruct them to do the following: Each student shares one reason from her list. The groups discuss the ways they are like the item. Not everyone will agree. The groups record their findings on chart paper. How they choose to record the information may also reflect the word choice they made. For example, they may make a mind map or do it in a linear fashion.

5. Call the groups together after they have had enough time to get their similarities down on paper. Display the papers. Tell each group they need to concentrate only on their characteristics and not to compare themselves to the other group, i.e., the "rivers" are strong and aggressive and the "lakes" are quiet and passive. Each person in the group is given an opportunity to share and respond to questions.

6. Send the students back to their papers and choose another question to analyze. Follow the same procedure. As the posters are displayed, the students begin to make comments about the group members, the handwriting, the style of recording.

7. Three to five questions is a good number to work with in one lesson.

8. Assign the students the reflection sheet for homework. Depending on the situation, you may need to give some questions to address for the assignment, i.e., "What did you like best about the activity?" "Were you surprised by who was in your group each time?" "What did you learn about yourself?"

9. The next day, have the students share part of their reflections.

10. Then, the teacher selects the next category for comparison, i.e., motorcycle or tandem bicycle. Each student lists the people they think will be in their group. Repeat steps four and five. After the discussion, address how accurate the students were with their predictions.

Materials:
Worksheets, chart paper, markers

MI Extensions:
Bodily-Kinesthetic: As an introduction to the lesson, involve the students in a creative dramatics warm-up activity. Use items from the "Which Are You More Like?" sheet and have the students move their bodies as the teacher says, "Be a river. You're a rock band. Be a mountain. You're the future."

Linguistic: The student chooses one of the items and writes a poem, for example "I am a River."

Logical-Mathematical: Each student makes a frequency chart to display with whom they were grouped and the number of times they were grouped with each person.

Musical: Have the class distinguish between sounds of definite pitch (chanting, whistling, humming) and indefinite pitch (growls, screams, puffs). The students refer back to their "Which Are You More Like?" worksheets and assign objects sounds using both definite and indefinite pitch.

Spatial: The student makes a display (mobile, 3-dimensional model, photographic display) of one of the items that represents her personality. The similar characteristics between the student and the object need to be exhibited in the project.

Name: _____   Date: _____

Which Are You More Like?

1. The country or the city?

2. The present or the future?

3. More physical or mental?

4. More of an arguer or an agree-er?

5. A turtle or a rabbit?

6. More likely to walk on thin ice or to tiptoe through the flowers?

7. Leather or suede?

8. A computer or a quill pen?

9. A rock band or an orchestra?

10. A "No Trespassing" sign or a "Public Swimming" sign?

11. A rollerblade or a pogo stick?

12. A motorcycle or a tandem bicycle?

13. A gourmet or a fast food fan?

14. A river or a lake?

15. A screened-in porch or a bay window?

16. A mountain or a valley?

A practical guide created by the faculty of The New City School ©1994

Name: _____   Date: _____

Reflection on "Which Are You More Like?"

Getting to Know Yourself Better

Circle the ones that you picked during the class activity:

computer   quill pen

river   lake

tiptoe through flowers   walk on thin ice

present   future

arguer   agree-er

REFLECTION ON THE ACTIVITY

_____

_____

_____

_____

_____

_____

_____

_____

_____

War and Conflict

MI Context: This lesson has been used during our study of the American Civil War, its causes and outcomes. By changing the vocabulary used, this lesson can be used in the exploration of almost any conflict.

Intrapersonal
Intermediate
Social Studies

Learner Outcomes: Students will recognize the Intrapersonal and Interpersonal challenges involved in having to compromise, as they agree upon the placement of each term in the Venn diagram. Students will learn that many causes of conflict are related to people's needs, values and resources, and that these three elements overlap.

Procedure:

1. Define the terms "needs," "values" and "resources." Discuss how these words are similar and different so that everyone is working from the same perspective.

2. Provide each student with a list of vocabulary words appropriate to the conflict. This sample list is the one used during the study of the Civil War.

autonomy	capital	independence
cotton	religion	power
recognition	land	unification
labor	freedom	identity
equality	housing	shelter
segregation		

4. On a Venn diagram, each student will categorize the terms as a need, value or resource as they relate to their own beliefs.

5. Divide the class into small groups.

6. Provide each group with the same vocabulary list. In their groups, the students should analyze the terms as they relate to the Civil War and that time period. Place each word in the appropriate place on the Venn diagram. All students must be able to rationalize the placement of any word.

7. Each group transfers their draft onto chart paper. Post these around the room.

8. Students should note similarities and differences. Invite each group to defend or explain their thinking.

9. In their journals, students note the similarities and differences between their own diagrams and those generated by their group.

Materials:
Textbook or other reference books about the Civil War, dictionaries, vocabulary list, blank Venn diagrams, chart paper, markers

Assessment / Reflection:
Are students able to defend and explain their placement of words based on historical references? Students write a journal entry about their role in the group process.

MI Extensions:
Bodily-Kinesthetic: After referring to their individual diagrams, the students hold the same vocabulary word and stand in the appropriate place on a Venn diagram which has been taped to the floor. Discussion follows.

Linguistic: Students add vocabulary that also is relevant to the conflict but not provided on the prepared list.

Musical: Discuss songs from the Civil War, in particular how they express the needs, values and resources of those who sang them.

Spatial: Use magazines and newspapers to create a conflict collage organized to reflect the information presented on the Venn diagram.

Activities to Support the Intrapersonal Intelligence

Interpersonal
- Conduct a "Magic Circle" (Human Development Corporation)

- Analyze your role in a group

- Request feedback and react to it

- Describe yourself, have a class-mate describe you, then compare

- Role-play the ending to an open-ended story or situation

Bodily-Kinesthetic
- Visualize through movement a part of the story and create a story from that point of view

- Listen to a made-up situation; use body movement to react

- Assume the role of a character using voice and body language

- Do needlework that expresses a belief or feeling.

- Construct own personal space using Legos or other materials.

Linguistic
- Write "Dear Abby" letters ask-ing for advice

- Administer an interest or person-ality inventory

- Write in journals or create diary entries as a character in a story

- Record "How I feel" statements on a tape

- Act like objects that describe you

Logical-Mathematical
- Create charts and graphs of interests

- Construct Venn diagrams to show how students are similar or different

- Construct a feelings mind map

- Explain what climate you prefer and why

- Make a personal time line

Musical
- Bring in music that reminds you of a special time in your life

- Listen to a song and describe how it makes you feel

- Create body music that shows your feelings

- Share your favorite song with the class

- Construct a melody

Spatial
- Use magazine pictures to create a personal collage

- Put together a mobile that shows who you are

- Create a mind map of your likes and dislikes or interests

- Draw or paint self-portraits

- Develop a slide show or photo display to show who you are

- Design your dream room

A practical guide created by the faculty of The New City School ©1994

Identifying the Intrapersonal Intelligence in Your Students

Children function at many different levels within the intelligences. Through observation of everyday activities, one can create a profile showing the level of functioning within a particular intelligence and the intelligences in relation to each other. The levels described show increased engagement and proficiency. Use this record-keeping page to obtain a richer picture of a child.

Appreciates:

YES	NO	
		Is consistently aware of feelings and abilities and is able to differentiate among them.
		Recognizes that different feelings and abilities exist and gives them labels.
		When reading a story, can identify a given character's feelings.
		Can recognize own strengths and weaknesses.
		Knows when to ask for help and when not to ask.
		Values and enjoys time to oneself.

Performs:

		Is able to self-assess, understand feelings and abilities and use them to problem-solve in a social situation.
		Accurately recognizes a character in a story who thinks and acts similarly to the way they do.
		Through knowing strengths and weaknesses, determines what situations to avoid and those in which to become involved.
		Is able to reflect on his own feelings.
		Is willing to try something in an area which he knows is weak and not become frustrated at a lack of success.
		Accepts limits but is willing to take risks.
		Accepts responsibility for own actions.
		Actively solicits feedback from others.
		Accurately self-assesses.

Creates:

		Generates original solutions and outcomes to problems.
		Expands personal horizons and limits.
		Rather than avoiding weaknesses, tackles the situation in an original way.
		Although weak in one area, can align himself with those who are strong.

Name: _____   Date: _____

How are you feeling?

How are
you
feeling
about
school?

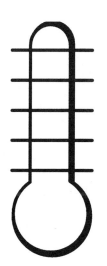

very happy
glad
half happy/sad
sad
very unhappy

How are
you
feeling
about
friends?

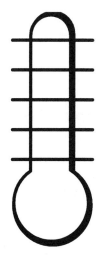

very happy
glad
half happy/sad
sad
very unhappy

How are
you
feeling
about
family?

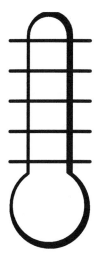

very happy
glad
half happy/sad
sad
very unhappy

Color the thermometer up to the line which best shows how you are feeling!

A practical guide created by the faculty of The New City School ©1994

Name: _____   Date: _____

What are you?

Indicate by marking on the arrow how talented you are in each intelligence.
Marking close to the "yes" end means you have a lot, toward the "no" means
you do not feel you have very much. Maybe you are somewhere in the middle.

yes   **no**

spatial   ⟵——————————⟶   not
                                               spatial

bodily-   not
kinesthetic   ⟵——————————⟶   bodily-
                                               kinesthetic

musical   ⟵——————————⟶   not
                                               musical

linguistic   ⟵——————————⟶   not
                                               linguistic

mathematical   ⟵——————————⟶   not
                                               mathematical

My goal is _____
_____
_____

A practical guide created by the faculty of The New City School ©1994

Intrapersonal Assessment

Name _____ Date _____

	Yes	Usually	No
1. I was comfortable being a leader.			
2. I was comfortable being a follower.			
3. I stayed focused on the job.			
4. I helped solve problems.			
5. I accepted responsibility for my own actions.			
6. I was an active listener.			

My intrapersonal goal is _____

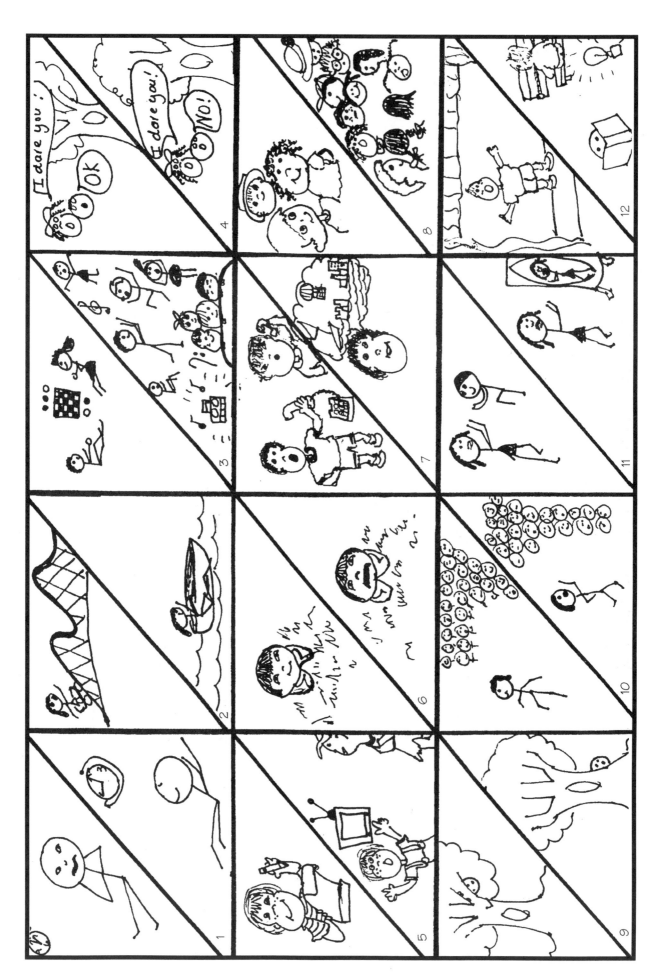

Photocopy this page for student use or pull out an idea for the students to respond to in their journals.

Intrapersonal: Introvert/Extrovert

Which statement best reflects your personality?

1. I am easily bored.
   It takes a very long time for me to become bored.

2. I love fast, scary rides.
   I love slow, easy-going rides.

3. I would rather spend an evening quietly at home.
   I would rather go to a party.

4. I almost always take a dare.
   I almost never take a dare.

5. I enjoy writing stories and books.
   I enjoy selling items to other people.

6. Sometimes I love being alone.
   I hate being alone - even for a short period of time.

7. I cherish talking, sharing my ideas, thoughts and plans.
   I cherish thinking about my ideas and plans.

8. I like having a few close friends.
   I like having bunches and bunches of friends.

9. When playing Hide-and-Seek, you'll find me
   hiding in a tree.
   Hiding behind a tree.

10. I avoid crowds.
    I like crowds.

11. I choose to dance with friends.
    I choose to mirror dance or shadow dance.

12. I crave being a star on stage.
    I crave working behind the scenes.

A practical guide created by the faculty of The New City School ©1994

Children's Resources

★ **indicates a picture book**

Books and Recordings

Adero, Malaika. *Up South - Stories, Studies, and Letters of This Century's African-American Migrations.* The New Press, 1993.

Adler, David A. *The Number on My Grandfather's Arm.* UAHC Press, 1987.

Adoff, Arnold. *Black Is Brown is Tan.* Harper & Row, 1973. ★

Aliki, *Feelings.* Greenwillow Books, 1984. ★

Allington, Richard, and Cowles, Kathleen. *Feelings.* Raintree, 1991. ★

Aneona, George. *Helping Out.* Clarion Books, 1985. ★

Bertrand, Cecile. *Mr. and Mrs. Smith Have Only One Child, But What a Child.* Lothrop, Lee and Shepard, 1992. ★

Boegehold, Betty. *You Are Much Too Small.* Bantam Books, 1990. ★

Caines, Jeannette. *Abby.* Harper Trophy, 1984. ★

Carle, Eric. *The Grouchy Lady Bug.* Scholastic, Inc., 1977. ★

Carle, Eric. *The Mixed-Up Chameleon.* HarperCollins, 1984. ★

Carlson, Nancy. *Arnie and the Stolen Markers.* Viking, 1988. ★

Carlson, Nancy. *I Like Me.* Viking, 1988. ★

Cheltenham Elementary School. *We Are All Alike, We are All Different.* Scholastic, Inc., 1991. ★

Choi, Sook Nyul. *Year of Impossible Goodbyes.* Houghton, 1991.

Christiansen, C. B. *My Mother's House, My Father's House.* Atheneum, 1989. ★

Clements, Andrew. *Big Al.* Scholastic Inc., 1991. ★

Cohen, Barbara. *Molly's Pilgrim.* Lothrop, 1983.

Cooney, Nancy. *The Blanket That Had to Go.* G. P. Putnam's Sons, 1981. ★

Curtis, Jamie Lee. *When I was Little.* HarperCollins, 1993. ★

dePaola, Tomie. *Nana Upstairs, Nana Downstairs.* G.P. Putnam's Sons, 1973. ★

Dubanevich, Arlene. *Pig William.* Bradbury Press, 1985. ★

Dwight, Laura. *We Can Do it!* Checkerboard Press, 1992. ★

Eisenberg, Lisa. *Sitting Bull: Great Sioux Chief.* Dell Publishing, 1991.

Farber, Norma. *How Does it Feel to Be Old?* Dutton, 1979. ★

Filipovic, Zlata. *Zlata's Diary: A Child's Life in Sarajevo.* Viking, 1994.

Fluek, Toby Knoble. *Memories of My Life in a Polish Village.*
    Alfred A. Knopf, 1990.

Frandsen, Karen. *Michael's New Haircut.* Children's Press, 1986. ★

Frank, Anne. *Anne Frank: The Diary of a Young Girl.* Pocket Books, 1952.

Gackenbach, Dick. *Harry and the Terrible Whatzit.* Clarion Books, 1979. ★

Gehret, Jeanne. *Eagle Eyes: A Child's Guide to Paying Attention.*
    Verbal Images, 1991. ★

Geonnel, Heidi. *Sometimes I like to Be Alone.* Little, Brown, & Co., 1989. ★

George, Jean Craighead. *Julie of the Wolves.* Harper & Row, 1972.

George, Jean Craighead. *The Talking Earth.* Harper Trophy, 1983.

Hamilton, Virginia. *Many Thousand Gone - African Americans from Slavery
    to Freedom.* Albert A. Knopf, 1993.

Henkes, Kevin. *Chrysanthemum.* Greenwillow Books, 1991. ★

Henkes, Kevin. *Sheila Rae, the Brave.* Greenwillow Books, 1987. ★

Holman, Felice. *Slake's Limbo.* Scribner, 1974.

Hudson, Nade. *I Love My Family.* Scholastic Inc., 1993. ★

Keller, Holly. *Horace.* Greenwillow Books, 1991. ★

Kherdian, David. *By Myself.* Henry Holt & Co., 1993. ★

Krasilovsky, Phyllis. *The Shy Little Girl.* Scholastic Inc., 1992. ★

Kraus, Robert. *Leo the Late Bloomer.* Simon and Schuster, 1971. ★

Leaf, Munro. *The Story of Ferdinand.* Scholastic Inc., 1964. ★

Leighton, Maxinne R. *An Ellis Island Christmas.* Viking, 1992.

Lester, Helen. *Pookins Gets Her Way.* Houghton Mifflin, 1987. ★

Mandelbaun, Pili. *You Be Me, I'll Be You.* Kane/Miller Book Pub., 1990. ★

Martin, Bill Jr. *Knots on a Counting Rope.* Henry Holt & Co., 1987 . ★

Marzolla, Jean. *Happy Birthday, Martin Luther King.* Scholastic Inc., 1993. ★

Mayer, Mercer. *All By Myself.* Western Publishing, 1983. ★

Michelson, Maureen R. *Women and Work - Photographs and Personal
    Writings.* New Sage Press, 1986.

Munsch, Robert. *The Paper Bag Princess.* Annick Press, 1980. ★

Naylor, Phyllis. *Shiloh.* Atheneum, 1991.

O'Dell, Scott. *Island of the Blue Dolphins.* Houghton Mifflin, 1960.

Pfister, Marcus. *The Rainbow Fish.* North-South Books, 1992. ★

Philips, Barbara. *Don't Call Me Fatso.* Steck Vaughn, 1991. ★

Roe, Eileen. *All I Am.* Bradbury Press, 1990. ★

Rus, Jacob. *How the Other Half Lives.* Dover Publications, Inc., 1971.

Rylant, Cynthia. *Missing May.* Orchard Books, 1992.

Say, Allen. *Grandfather's Journey.* Houghton Mifflin, 1993. ★

Scholes, Katherine. *Peace Begins with You.* Little Brown and Co., 1990. ★

Sharmat, Marjorie. *I'm Terrific.* Holiday House, 1977. ★

Sharmat, Marjorie. *Say Hello, Vanessa.* Holiday House, 1979. ★

Shyer, Marlene. *Here I Am an Only Child.* Aladdin, 1985. ★

Simon, Norma. *All Kinds of Families.* Albert Whitman, 1976. ★

Simon, Norma. *I Am Not a Crybaby.* Puffin Books, 1989. ★

Simon, Norma. *I Was So Mad!* Albert Whitman & Co., 1974. ★

Speare, Elizabeth George. *The Sign of the Beaver.* Dell Publishing, 1983.

Steig, William. *Sylvester and the Magic Pebble.* Simon and Schuster, 1969. ★

Taylor, Mildred. *Roll of Thunder, Hear My Cry.* Dial Press, 1976.

Taylor, Theodore. *The Cay.* Doubleday, 1969.

Udry, Janice. *What Mary Jo Shared.* Hale, 1969. ★

Volvavkova, Hana. I *Never Saw Another Butterfly.* Schocken Books, 1993.

Wells, Rosemary. *Shy Charles.* Dial, 1988. ★

Wood, Audrey. *Quick As a Cricket.* Child's Play, 1982. ★

Yep, Laurence. *Child of the Owl.* Harper & Row, 1977.

Zolotow, Charlotte. *William's Doll.* Harper & Row, 1972. ★

Games:

"Face It! A Fun Game to Learn About Feelings." Childswork-Childsplay, The Center for Applied Psychology, Inc. 1991.

"Feelings and Faces Game." Lakeshore, 1993.

"Mindtrap." Mindtrap Games, Inc.,1991.

"Not So Scary Things." Iron Mountain Game Company, 1989.

"Personality Probe?" Kid's Edition, N.L. Associates, Inc., 1987.

Teachers' Resources

Bissell, Harold, Ph.D. *Human Development Program: Activity Guide III.* Palomares and Associates, 1972.

Capacchione, Lucia. *The Creative Journal: The Art of Finding Yourself.* Swallow Press, 1979.

Drew, Naomi. *Learning the Skills of Peacemaking.* Jalmar Press, 1987.

Forte, Imogene. *The Me I'm Learning to Be.* Incentive Pub., 1991.

Gardner, Howard. *Frames of Mind.* Basic Books, 1983.

Gardner, Howard. *The Unschooled Mind.* Basic Books, 1991.

Graves, Donald H. and Sunstein, Bonnie S. *Portfolio Portraits.* Heinemann, 1992.

Hart, Leslie A. *Human Brain and Human Learning.* Books for Educators, 1983.

Kincher, Jonni. *Psychology for Kids.* Free Spirit Publishing Inc., 1990.

The Magic Circle Human Development Program. Palomares and Associates, 1974.

Meisgeier, Charles Ed.D. and Murphy, Elizabeth. "Murphy Meisgeier Type Indicator for Children." Consulting Psychologists Press,1987.

Palmer, Hap. "Sammy," *Hap Palmer Favorites: Songs for Learning Through Music and Movement.* Alfred Pub., 1981.

Pergola, Beth. "Wonderful Me," *Sing It Instead.* Instrumental Only, 1989.

Simon, Sidney B. *Values Clarification.* Hart Publishing, 1972.

Sternberg, Robert. *The Triarchic Mind.* Viking,1988.

Stock, Gregory Ph.D. *The Kids' Book of Questions.* Workman Pub.,1988.

Chapter 3:
The Bodily-Kinesthetic Intelligence

Contributors: Sally Boggeman, Carla Carroll, Linda Churchwell, Diane Davenport, Danielle Egeling, Joycelyn L. Gray, Susan Matthews, Lauren M. McKenna, Christine Wallach, Stephanie Cunningham Wiles

"If anything is sacred, the human body is sacred."
Walt Whitman

Web of the Bodily-Kinesthetic Intelligence

Student quotes	List of characteristics

"Bodily-Kinesthetic is my strongest intelligence because I like to run and do cartwheels."

"I learn well touching things and using things."

"I like to climb trees and repel. "

"I take Karate for five hours every Saturday."

- Coordinated
- Agile
- Good body control
- Takes in information through bodily sensations
- Hands-on learners
- Fine motor and/or gross motor skills
- A tinkerer, performer
- Demonstrates skill in crafts
- Uses body language

Marcel Marceau uses his body to communicate through mime.

Jackie Joyner-Kersey won Olympic Gold Medals in track and field.

Katherine Dunham is an accomplished modern dancer and choreographer who has founded her own dance company and school.

Dr. Christian Bernard developed methods of open-heart surgery.

"Interest and proficiency in almost any one activity- swimming, boating, fishing skiing, skating-breed interest in many more. Once someone discovers the delight of mastering one skill, however slightly, he is likely to try out not just one more, but a whole ensemble."

Margaret Mead

Famous people	Adult quote

A practical guide created by the faculty of The New City School ©1994

Out of the Gym and Into the Classroom

by Sally Boggeman and Lauren M. McKenna

It is no wonder that Physical Education class is often the highlight of many children's day. It is a place where movement is encouraged, not restrained. Collaborative efforts as a member of a team are essential, not frowned upon. Learning is active, rather than passive. Many children need to manipulate and experience to really learn and internalize something. They learn through doing and through multi-sensory experiences.

Many children need to manipulate and experience to really learn and internalize something. They learn through doing and through multi-sensory experiences.

Defining Bodily-Kinesthetic

Bodily-Kinesthetic encompasses everything and everyone who demonstrates a tendency to use their bodies to communicate or understand in a given situation. Students who are strong in the Bodily-Kinesthetic (B/K) intelligence can use their bodies in very skilled and different ways. They generally have good eye/hand coordination, balance, timing and equilibrium. The gross or fine motor skills can be well developed in a person who has strong B/K.

It is not just students who are strong in B/K who benefit from active experiences in the classroom; however, physical activities help focus many students' attention and help them to remember, which positively affects learning. Students are more motivated when they learn actively. Physical education belongs in the classroom. The more drama, creative movement, dance, manipulatives, games and exercising that can be brought into the classroom, the more that learning will be exciting and memorable.

How the PE Teacher Can Help

There are several ways the PE teacher can provide support to the classroom teacher. Sharing equipment is one small but important way. Jump ropes can be used to reinforce learning that has a pattern. Reciting a poem while "jumping" to the meter of the poem or jumping as math facts are spouted off add a B/K aspect to verbal learning. A parachute is held high by the students who each have been given half of a compound word. A riddle, which is answered by a compound word, is given by the teacher. The "halves of the word" that think they could be the answer run to the center under the parachute, say their word and exchange places before the parachute is brought down. There is also a need for cooperation when using a parachute which strengthens the interpersonal intelligence!

Hula hoops could be used as targets. They could be labeled as fractions or vowel sounds or continents, and the students answer questions by throwing bean bags into the hoops. Students can dribble a ball while learning multiples. If working with multiples of three, the student would dribble three times, lifting his leg over the ball on three, dribble, dribble, lift his leg over on six, and so on. Balls could also be used for estimation as students estimate how far they can throw the ball or how close they can throw the ball to a specific object.

The PE teacher can be invaluable to the classroom teacher by communicating with the teacher the roles that her students play in PE class. Are individual students followers? Are they leaders? Are they effective in the role they play? Team leadership is a very important quality, and the classroom teacher does not always have an opportunity to see that when on recess duty, which is perhaps the only time she sees her students playing games.

In the Classroom

There are ways to bring B/K activities into the classroom without using equipment typically found in a PE class. Scarves can by used to accompany dance movements. The mood of a scene of a book or the temperament of a character can be interpreted through dance. The water cycle can be demonstrated through dance or creative movement. Stories can be re-enacted or new chapters or endings can be created and acted out. Board games are often good extensions for literature units. Games can be made more interactive by having the students make large game boards for the floor and they, themselves, become the game pieces. Students can become cheerleaders and make up cheers, complete with actions, to reiterate a rule they have learned in class.

It is important that students who process knowledge best kinesthetically, be given the opportunity to do so in the classroom. Too often, in the interest of quiet and teacher control or because of lack of space, this intelligence, which most children feel they have great strength in, is often overlooked. If the MI theory is to be implemented, some of the PE class, B/K, has to be brought into the classroom.

Hopscotch

MI Context: This lesson incorporates learning bodily movement on a hopscotch grid.

Learner Outcomes: The students will learn to hop on one foot and jump on two feet in a series of movements.

Procedure:
1. Demonstrate a hop on one foot and a jump on two feet. Ask the children what the difference is in the two movements.

2. Allow students to practice hopping and jumping.

3. Use squares of paper or chalk or tape to outline a hopscotch grid. Demonstrate how hops and jumps are combined to go from one end to the other.

4. Encourage children to practice on the grid doing continual hopping and jumping.

Materials:
Squares or other shapes to place on the floor, chalk or tape to outline the hopscotch grid

Assessment / Reflection:
Observe the child's coordination and fluid movement while using the hopscotch grid.

MI Extensions:
Interpersonal: Have a child start at each end of the hopscotch grid. When their paths cross, they will have to work out how to get around one another without getting off the hopscotch grid.

Intrapersonal: Discuss what the children found easy and difficult about the exercise. Ask what muscles they use when you jump or hop? Is this fun? Why do (or don't) you like this activity?

Linguistic: Allow the kids to guess who invented the game and when. Then discuss how hopscotch originated.

Logical-Mathematical: Number the spaces and call out the numbers as the child jumps on them. Have children count how many jumps and hops they can do in a row.

Musical: As one child hops or jumps, another child plays rhythm sticks to the beat of the feet.

Spatial: In pairs, the students move the squares around to make a different configuration of spaces for a hopscotch grid.

Exercise With Ease

Bodily-Kinesthetic
Preprimary
Language Arts

MI Context: This lesson is used as part of the Letter of the Week. It reinforces the letter "Ee."

Learner Outcomes: The children will learn to do a variety of exercises.

Procedure:
1. Instruct the children to make the letter "Ee" using their bodies. Ask them if they can think of more than one way to do this.

2. Make the letter "Ee" with a partner.

3. Listen to a part of an exercise tape like "Aerobics for Kids" by Georgiana Liccione Stewart.

4. Using chart paper, make a list with the children of different kinds of exercises. Divide the exercises into those they can do in the classroom, e.g., jumping jacks, and those they cannot do in the classroom, e.g., swimming.

5. Have the children spread out around the room. Do some of the exercises from the list of those which can be done in the classroom. These can be done to music.

Materials:
Musical tapes for exercise, chart paper and marker, exercise tape

Assessment / Reflection:
Were students able to make suggestions for the exercise chart and participate in the exercising?

MI Extensions:
Interpersonal: Have the children make up partner exercises which require them to work in pairs.

Intrapersonal: Discuss with the children what exercise they liked the best and which exercises were easy or hard for them.

Linguistic: Have the children circle all of the "Ee's" in the list of exercises on the chart.

Logical-Mathematical: The children count how many times their heart beats in a minute before starting to exercise. Exercise for a couple of minutes and again count the heart beats for a minute. Compare the results.

Musical: Exercise to instrumental music. Half the class plays instruments while the other half exercises. Switch roles. Sing and dance the "Hokey Pokey" and "Head, Shoulders, Knees and Toes."

One Little, Two Little, Three Little Pigs

MI Context: This lesson gives the children an opportunity to act in front of a group using a familiar story.

Learning Outcomes: The students will demonstrate an understanding of the sequence of events in the story *The Three Little Pigs*.

Procedure:
1. Read *The Three Little Pigs*.

2. Discuss the main events in the story.

3. Divide the class into small groups and assign each group an event to act out.

4. Together the class decides which ensemble should perform first. After each performance, the class decides who will go next.

5. At the end, the groups take their final bow by lining up in front of the room in the correct sequence from the story.

Materials:
A copy of *The Three Little Pigs*

Assessment / Reflection:
Teacher observes the extent to which the children are involved in determining the sequence.

MI Extensions:
Interpersonal: Working in pairs, one child tells an event that happened in the story. The partner has to tell an event that occurred later in the story. This strategy game continues until one child cannot add another event.

Intrapersonal: If you were the wolf, what two things would you have done differently? What if you were the pigs?

Linguistic: Read a different version of the story. Have the class discuss ways in which the order of events is different in the two stories.

Logical-Mathematical: Each child draws and cuts out one of the pig's houses. Sequence all the houses from the smallest to the largest.

Musical: Sing the song "Who's Afraid of the Big, Bad Wolf?" Add a verse that corresponds to the story.

Spatial: Have the children create the pigs' houses with red rectangles, tooth picks and brown grass. Glue them down on paper.

Everybody's Jumping

Bodily-Kinesthetic
Primary
Language Arts

MI Context: This lesson is used as an extension for the book *Oliver Button Is a Sissy* by Tomie dePaola.

Learner Outcomes: Students will not only improve their skill at jumping rope but also recognize that it is valuable exercise for both boys and girls.

Procedure:

1. Read *Oliver Button Is a Sissy* by Tomie dePaola.

2. Discuss the things Oliver did that were considered unusual for a boy, i.e., not liking ball games, walking alone, jumping rope. Brainstorm a list of activities that both girls and boys enjoy.

3. Provide different ropes for jumping and let the children practice different types of jumping including double dutch, singles, group and skip jumping.

4. Teach the children to count their breath rate. Compare rates before and after jumping.

5. Time the children and encourage them to improve on the length of time they can jump without missing.

Materials:
Oliver Button Is a Sissy, ropes, stopwatch or a watch with a second hand

Assessment / Reflection:
With practice, are the students able to jump for a longer time without missing? Can they name and perform different jump rope techniques?

MI Extensions:
Interpersonal: Jump rope with a partner. Establish together when the positions will change and take turns being the turner and the jumper.

Intrapersonal: Discuss stereotypical girl games and boy games. Ask if they have ever been teased about their interests in a certain activity. How do they react to being teased?

Linguistic: Discuss jump rope jingles and have students write one of their own. Use the book *Anna Banana: 101 Jump-Rope Rhymes* by Joanna Cole to familiarize the students with other rhymes.

Logical-Mathematical: With a partner, students record how many times they can jump without missing. Do this three times. Find the average number of jumps. Graph the class's jump average. Check again a week later and note and discuss any changes.

Spatial: Students decorate their own plastic jump ropes.

Continental Twister

MI Context: This lesson is used prior to studying any continent.

Learner Outcomes: Students will be able to locate and identify the seven continents.

Bodily-Kinesthetic
Primary
Social Studies

Procedure:
1. Write the word "continent" on the board and elicit a working definition from the class.

2. Give each student a map of the world and ask them to find the seven continents. Write them on the board.

3. Form groups of four or five. Give each group a large laminated map of the world for the floor and two stacks of game cards. One stack shows pictures and the names of the continents. The other stack has cards that say "right hand," "left hand," "right foot," "left foot."

4. One child in each group is the "caller." The players follow the directions of the "caller" as she draws a card from each stack. When someone falls, the game is over and one of the standing players becomes the new "caller."

Materials:
Individual world maps, a large laminated world map for each team, game cards for each team, small world maps of continent outlines for each child

Assessment / Reflection:
Students will label the continents on the blank maps of the world. They may need to refer to the game board map for assistance.

MI Extensions:
Interpersonal: Play the game "Twenty Questions" about the continents.

Intrapersonal: Students talk or write about which continent they would like to visit and explain why. How might they be different today if they had grown up on each of the other continents, i.e., how would they be affected by the climate and kinds of available food?

Linguistic: Design a travel brochure for a specific continent.

Logical-Mathematical: Find the longitudinal and latitudinal lines that define the outer most parts of each continent. Are there any similarities? Use atlases to create topographical maps of each continent.

Musical: Create a song about the seven continents and perform it for the class. Learn "The Continent and Ocean Song."

Spatial: Tear pieces of construction paper into the shapes of the continents. Glue them on large paper to create a map of the world.

The Continent and Ocean Song
(to the tune of "He's Got The Whole World In His Hands")

Chorus:
I've got the seven continents
in my hands.
I've got the four oceans
in my hands.
I've got the oceans and continents
in my hands.
I've got the whole world in my hands.

I've got Africa and Australia
in my hands.
I've got Europe and Asia
in my hands.
I've got North and South America
in my hands.
I've got Antarctica in my hands.

(Chorus)

I've got the four oceans
in my hands.
I've got the Atlantic and the Pacific
in my hands.
I've got the Indian and the Arctic
in my hands.
I've got the oceans in my hands.

(Chorus)

Shadows

MI Context: This lesson is used during a study of shadows.

Lesson Outcomes: Students will learn that when light is blocked by their bodies, shadows result. They will refine their cooperative skills while improving their sense of balance, coordination and perception.

Procedure:

1. For this activity, the class will go outside on a hardtop area in the morning or late afternoon. It must be a sunny day. The students will explore the shadows their bodies make. Instruct them to make a shadow with a hole in it, a round shadow, a square shadow and a shadow with an angle.

2. Divide the class into an even number of small groups. Each group designates one member as the tracer. Outside, the other group members create a sculpture with their bodies. The tracer uses a piece of chalk to trace around the shadow cast by the bodies.

3. When the groups have completed their shadow sculptures, they move to another group's work and try to replicate the outline of the shadow with their bodies. The tracer joins the group and another group member becomes the engineer, directing the movement and position of the students to recreate the shadow.

Materials:
Chalk, sun

Assessment / Reflection:
Discuss how the students made their shadow shapes. Explore the difficulties in creating the exact same sculpture shadow, i.e., the sun has moved, the children in the groups are different sizes and shapes and the cooperation level may be different among the groups Were the students able to problem-solve ways to block the light to make a particular shadow?

MI Extensions:
Interpersonal: In their small groups, have the students list at least five things that members did which helped the group accomplish the task of creating and then recreating a shadow sculpture.

Intrapersonal: Ask the students to think about their role within the group using the Shadow Puzzles Reflection sheet.

Linguistic: Read *Bear Shadow* by Frank Asch. Take the students outside again on a sunny day to see if they can make their shadow disappear.

Logical-Mathematical: Use sheets of notebook-sized paper to determine the area of each group's shadow sculpture.

Musical: Play several different kids of music (for example, a march, soft environmental music, classical and jazz). Hang a sheet in the classroom. Behind the sheet place an overhead projector with its light shining on the sheet. Student take turns moving and dancing between the sheet and the light source. Other students have to guess who the performer is.

Spatial: Design a sun dial.

A practical guide created by the faculty of The New City School ©1994

Name: _____ Date: _____

Shadow Puzzles Reflection

Names of the people in my group:

The person it was easiest to work with:

Because:

The person it was hardest to work with:

Because:

I was a leader in my group.	yes	no
I was a follower in my group.	yes	no
I was happy being the leader or the follower.	yes	no
I gave some ideas to the group.	yes	no
The group used my ideas.	yes	no
I tried to help someone who was quiet.	yes	no

One way we cooperated was:

One thing that didn't work was:

Next time I work in a group I will try to:

A practical guide created by the faculty of The New City School ©1994

Recipe for a Dance

MI Context: To explore the elements of creative movement as they reinforce the Bodily-Kinesthetic Intelligence.

Learner Outcomes: The students will be able to create a dance that involves some or all of the elements of movement as it illustrates a character, the plot, setting or some other aspect of a book the students have studied.

Procedure:

1. Explain to the students that creative movement, when organized, becomes dance. It speaks in movement phrases. The sequencing of movement phrases involves energy, intensity, direction, dimension and level.

2. Experience the elements of movement by investigating the definitions. As the definitions are explained, the students experiment by pretending they are an object like a power drill and explore the element by moving.

   • Energy is the force which initiates, controls and stops movements.

   • Intensity describes the movement in terms of strong and weak.

   • Direction is going from one place to another.

   • Dimension means that movement looks and feels different based on the size of the movement.

   • Level is the position, high, medium, low or in-between.

3. As a class, choose a character from the book that has just been studied. Choose movements, directions, dimensions, and levels that reflect the character and write them on the board.

4. With music in the background, have students work for a few minutes organizing some of the actions into a dance. Although the movements will not be polished, have some students share what they have created with the class so everyone has an understanding of what to do and can see the variety of ways the same movements can be interpreted.

5. Next, give the students the options of plot, setting, climax or any part of the book they would like to interpret through dance. Once a subject has been chosen by each student, she makes her own list of the elements to include.

6. Allow time for the students to plan their dances. Have them select three or four ideas that they want to use and begin to explore and improvise. Arrange the ideas in the order in which they want to do the movements. They need to determine the dimension, level, direction, intensity and energy of each movement. After there has been ample time for practice, have the students perform them for the class.

Materials:
Taped musical selections, tape recorder

Assessment / Reflection:
Were the students able to apply their understanding of the elements of movement to a finished piece? Was it difficult to make choices? Did the dance accurately reflect the part of the book they chose?

MI Extensions:
Interpersonal: Rather than create a dance independently, do it with a partner or in a small group.

Intrapersonal: After the students have planned their dance, give them a check list that will help them assess the following:

- Do the movements express your ideas?

- Is the movement interesting?

- Are all the movement elements included?

- Are you satisfied with the order of the movements?

- Should the order or actual movements be changed?

Linguistic: Students can build a word file of "movement" words in the classroom that describe different movements related to different activities, i.e., sports, cooking, acting, etc.

Musical: The students can explore different elements of music as they apply to movement by choosing appropriate instruments or sound compositions to accompany their dances.

Spatial: Students create a notation system for recording their dances. How does the piece look when drawn? Students can draw each other's dance compositions.

Prepositional Charades

MI Context: This lesson is used during grammar study to help reinforce students' ability to identify prepositional phrases.

Learner Outcomes: Students will successfully act out and identify prepositional phrases.

Procedure:

1. Prepare strips of paper for the charades by writing a prepositional phrase on each, i.e., *through the window, on the carpet, under the sun.* Be sure there is one for every student in the class.

2. Students are divided into teams numbering three or four and decide on the order in which each member will rotate into the game.

3. Charade rules vary, so, as a class, decide what is "legal."

4. The first player draws a strip and has ten seconds to start acting it out for her team to guess.

5. Once a player has begun her charade, only that player's team members guess for fifty seconds, trying to identify the correct prepositional phrase. If a team member guesses correctly, that team receives two points.

6. Once the minute has elapsed and no team member has guessed correctly, the next team in line gets ten seconds to consult, and then may take one guess. If they guess incorrectly, the opportunity to guess goes to the next team. The team that does guess correctly earns one point.

7. No team may talk, comment or consult while it is another team's turn. By doing so, that team loses a point.

8. If no team succeeds in guessing correctly, the phrase strip is returned to the basket.

9. Continue play until all students have had a chance to act out a phrase. Total up team points.

Materials:
A basket from which the players can pull phrase strips, phrase strips

Assessment / Reflection:
Observe whether or not the students' guesses are prepositional phrases, even if not correct.

MI Extensions:

Interpersonal: Charades are acted out in pairs with each person having an active part. More than ten seconds will be needed to prepare.

Intrapersonal: In prepositional phrases, students list all the activities they do in one day, i.e., *out of bed, down the stairs, in the car, in my backpack.*

Linguistic: In teams, students think of common phrases that start with a prepositional phrase. In three minutes, list as many as possible, i.e., *by the way, in a minute, under the influence.* Share the lists and score by either the longest list, or give a point for each phrase that no other team has on their list.

Logical-Mathematical: Keep track of how long each player acts before her team guesses correctly. Add up the times for each team to see which took the least amount of time.

Musical: Have groups think of song titles that contain prepositional phrases, i.e., "Tiptoe Through the Tulips," "Somewhere Over the Rainbow." Have the students act them out for the class to guess.

Spatial: Rather than act out the prepositional phrases, draw them on the board for the team to guess, in a manner similar to the game "Pictionary."

Everything and the Net

Bodily-Kinesthetic
Intermediate
Mathematics

MI Context: Students are given the opportunity to practice shooting baskets while working on the skills of percent and probability.

Learner Outcomes: The student will be able to calculate the probability of making baskets given a finite number of attempts using the percent data collected during earlier trials.

Procedure:

1. On a basketball court (if no basketball court is available, a trash can and ball could also be used), give the students time to practice shooting baskets.

2. After the students are warmed up, tell them they will each be shooting ten baskets from a fixed position on the court. Students estimate how many baskets they will make.

3. As one student shoots, another tallies the number of shots taken and made. When the students have completed the task, this information is used to figure the percentage of successful shots made. At least three opportunities for data collection should be provided, preferably on different days.

4. Students look at all the data they have collected and predict the probability of success given ten more shots.

Materials:
Basketball, hoop, pencil and paper

Assessment / Reflection:
Students take ten more shots and see how closely their prediction matched the outcome. If given twenty shots, is their percentage prediction more accurate?

MI Extensions:

Interpersonal: Divide into small groups to make teams and determine the probability of the team making baskets based on the data collected. What team behaviors might be used to improve the percentage probability, given that each team member must make the same number of shots?

Intrapersonal: Have students observe the attitudes of the other students as they shoot. How could their behavior be characterized? Ask the student where she fits in. Where would she like to fit in?

Linguistic: Have the students each write a sports article detailing the outcome of the basketball activity. Compile the articles into a sports section of a newspaper.

Logical-Mathematical: Students have been determining the probability of success for all ten shots, for example, they will make six out of ten shots. Have the students figure the probability of success as each shot is attempted. If a student has made six of ten shots in the past, for example, and now makes the first six shots, is the student likely to miss the last four shots or will the student's chances of making more than six be increased.

Musical: How many different sounds can be made with a basketball hitting the surfaces that it would hit during a game? Turn that into a song.

Spatial: Design a ball that would ensure a greater probability of success when shooting baskets.

Activities to Support the Bodily-Kinesthetic Intelligence

Interpersonal
- Role playing

- Drama, mime, and charades

- Athletics or sports

- People as game pieces during floor games like chess or checkers

- Facial expressions

Intrapersonal
- Acting techniques that require the artist to become a character

- Individual sports

- Meditation and yoga

- Hobbies like gardening or cooking

- Activities to avert anger or frustration (for example, hitting pillows, tearing paper or squishing playdough)

Linguistic
- Play a game to practice content (for example, catch the ball and answer a question or juggle while spelling words)

- Use sign language

- Prepare demonstrations

- Write or make letters using the body

- Practice spelling words by writing words with a paintbrush and water or drawing the words in the sand or on someone's back

Logical-Mathematical
- Solve problems using manipulatives

- Create floor graphs using bodies

- Solve story problems by acting them out

- Practice Chisanbop and other finger counting systems

- Use body math to reinforce patterning, estimating, shapes, and counting

Musical
- Dancing

- Playing a musical instrument

- Jogging, jumping rope, and exercising to music

- Story telling through musical performances

- Creating rhythms using one's body

Spatial
- Using tools while cutting or taking apart machines

- Creating play dough and clay sculptures

- Building

- Hair braiding

- Sewing, quilting and weaving or other craft activities

Identifying the Bodily-Kinesthetic Intelligence in Your Students

Children function at many different levels within the intelligences. Through observation of everyday activities, one can create a profile showing the level of functioning within a particular intelligence and the intelligences in relation to each other. The levels described show increased engagement and proficiency. Use this record-keeping page to obtain a richer picture of a child.

Appreciates:

YES	NO	
		Consistently demonstrates interest, respect and enjoyment within the intelligence.
		Enjoys movement activities as an observer or participant.
		Enjoys fine motor activities as an observer or participant.
		Collects sports cards
		Enjoys tactile experiences like clay, sand and water
		Talks about, attends, writes or reads about sporting events

Performs:

		Is able to apply the intelligence to re-create an exhibit or demonstration or problem solve within a given situation.
		Demonstrates skill in fine motor (i.e., knitting, sewing, Origami) or gross motor activities
		Participates in plays, puppet shows, sports, and dance
		Enthusiastically uses playground equipment
		Is skillful in taking apart and putting objects together (i.e., Legos, toasters, models)
		Is able to use tools effectively to solve a problem, make an object
		Plays jacks, pickup sticks, string games, and handclaps rhymes
		Voluntarily moves body, does work standing up, prefers movement to sitting still
		Has inner sense of where one is in space, kinesthesia
		Forms letters and numbers well

Creates:

		Is able to apply the intelligence to generate original work, to develop unique solutions to problems or create prototypes.
		Choreographs a dance or invents a new game
		Demonstrates new dramatic style
		Designs and constructs with a novel recognizable style (i.e., jewelry, dance)

A practical guide created by the faculty of The New City School ©1994

Evaluation of the Field Trip

Name: _____

Before you go, what do you think you'll see.

1. Before I left on the trip, I thought...

2. Three good things about the trip were...

3. The part I didn't like about the trip was...

4. Something during the trip that surprised me was...

5. What one thing would you change about the trip, and how would you change it?

Children's Resources

Books and Recordings:

Adoff, Arnold. *Sports Pages.* Harper & Row, 1990.

Allard, Harry. *Miss Nelson Has a Field Day.* Houghton Mifflin, 1985. ★

Asch, Frank. *Bear Shadow.* Prentice Hall, 1985. ★

Christopher, Matt. *The Dog That Pitched a No-Hitter.* Trumpet Club, 1988.

dePaola, Tomie. *Oliver Button Is a Sissy.* Harcourt Brace Jovanovich, 1979. ★

Dodds, Dayle Ann. *Wheel Away.* Harper & Row, 1989. ★

Galdone, Paul. *The Three Little Pigs.* Clarion Books, 1970. ★

Glenbock, Peter. *Teammates.* Harcourt Brace Jovanovich, 1990. ★

Isadora, Rachel. *Max.* Macmillan, 1976. ★

Jay, Allen. *The Bicycle Man.* Houghton Mifflin, 1982. ★

Kalon, Kalan. *Jump, Frog, Jump.* Greenwillow Books, 1981. ★

Krementz, Jill. *The Very Young Dancer.* Knopf, 1976. ★

Marzollo, Jean. *Pretend You're a Cat.* Dial Books for Young Readers, 1990. ★

McAully, Emily. *Mirette on the High Wire.* G.P. Putnam's Sons, 1992. ★

Parker, Kristi. *My Dad The Magnificent.* Dutton Children's Books, 1990. ★

Pinkney, Andrea Davis. *Alvin Ailey.* Hyperion Books for Children., 1993. ★

Rabe, Berniece. *The Balancing Girl.* Dutton, 1981. ★

Ungerer, Tomi. *Crictor.* Harper & Row, 1983. ★

Games:

"Azuma : The Game of Reckless Abandon." Parker Brothers, 1992.

"Dance Party." Golden: Western Publishing Co., 1991.

"Guesstures." Milton Bradley, 1990.

"Hammer and Nails Game." Creative Toys Ltd., 1991.

Jacks, a traditional game

"Jumpin' Monkeys." Pressman Toy Co., 1991.

"Kids On Stage: The Charades Game For Kids." University Games, 1988.

Marbles, a traditional game

"Spoon and Egg Coordination Game." Lakeshore, 1991.

"Tricky Fingers: A Skill Game for the Whole Family." Reger Games, 1990.

"Twister." Milton Bradley, 1986.

"Unimax : Moveable Mazes." Inimax Toys Ltd., 1990.

Teachers' Resources

Beall, Pamela, and Hagon, Susan. "Head, Shoulders, Knees, and Toes." *Wee Sing and Play*. Price, Stern, Sloan, 1981.

Caney, Steve. *Steven Caney's Invention Book*. Workman Publishing, 1985.

Cassidy, Nancy and John. "Whole World In His Hands." *Kids Songs*. Klutz Press, 1988.

Cole, Joanna and Calmerson, Stephanie. *The Eentsy, Weensty Spider*. Morrow Junior Books, 1991.

Cole, Joanna. *Anna Banana, 101 Jump Rope Rhymes*. Scholastic Inc., 1989.

Daray, Maya. *J is for Jump*. Fearon Teacher Aids, 1982.

Fluegelman, Andrew. *New Games Book*. Dolphin Books/Doubleday, 1981.

Gregson, Bob. *The Incredible Indoor Games Book*. Pitman Learning, 1982.

Macaulay, David. *The Way Things Work*. Houghton Mifflin, 1988.

Macfarlan, Allan and Paulette. *Handbbook of American Indian Games*. Assn. Press, 1958.

Rubin, Rosyln, and Wathen, Judy. "Hokey Pokey," *The All Year-Long Songbook*. Scholastic Inc., 1980.

Stewart, Georgiana Ciccione. "Aerobics For Kids". Lakeshore, 1980 tape #KM7043.

Weissman, Julie. *Kids in Motion*. Alfred Publishing Co., Inc., 1993.

Wirth, Marian Jenks. *Teacher's Handbook of Children's Games*. Parker Publishing Co. Inc., 1976.

Chapter 4:
The Linguistic Intelligence

Contributors: Carol Beatty, Carla Carroll, Mary F. Daly, Bonnie L. Frank, Jean Blockhus Grover, Carla Mash, Julie Stevens, Susie Tenzer, Stephanie Young

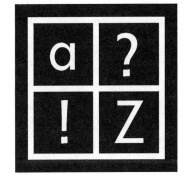

"Language is magic: it makes things appear and disappear.
Nicole Brossard

Web of the Linguistic Intelligence

"My greatest intelligence is Linguistic because I read a whole lot and I write a whole lot.'

"I like it when everyone has to be quiet and it is my turn."

"I'm linguistic because I have a good vocabulary."

- Appreciates the subtleties of grammar and meaning
- Spells easily
- Enjoys word games
- Understands puns, jokes and riddles
- Has developed auditory skills
- Can use descriptive language
- Memorizes easily
- Is a good story teller
- Enjoys the sounds and rhythms of language

Maya Angelou has written poems and stories that communicate to generations.

Abraham Lincoln wrote and developed speeches that defined the culture.

Jerry Seinfeld has developed a unique comedy style.

Mary Hatwood Futrell is an international teacher/leader whose oratory inspired others in the profession.

Jackie Torrence is a nationally acclaimed story teller and recording artist.

"The limits of my language stand for the limit of my world."

Ludwig Wittgenstein

The Library: We're More Than Linguistic!

by Nancy Solodar

Traditionally, elementary school libraries have focused on stories and library skills instruction to the virtual exclusion of music, dance, art and math activities. Thanks to Multiple Intelligences (MI), however, while still retaining a story-based curriculum, it is possible to use MI to enrich the library program and pull in a variety of interests by exploring "new" areas of study previously reserved for the math class or the gym. Additional benefits also accrue as closer ties are forged with the science, music, art and PE specialists. All of the specialists' areas can be brought closer into the mainstream of the school-wide curriculum through the library.

All of the specialists' areas can be brought closer into the mainstream of the school-wide curriculum through the library.

Bringing Other Intelligences Into the Library

When I first started incorporating MI into the library program, I decided to focus on one intelligence at a time to make it easier to gather materials and plan new activities. I realized that I needed foremost to shift my linguistic mindset and open myself to new possibilities. Not being a math person, I decided to tackle math first, because I felt that it would be the most difficult. I quickly discovered how rich an area it is, and it continues to be my favorite way to explore children's literature.

Each month I focused on a different intelligence, but I followed the same pattern of starting with a story, then planning an activity, game, discussion, center or project that utilized the targeted intelligence.

Each month I focused on a different intelligence, but I followed the same pattern of starting with a story, then planning an activity, game, discussion, center or project that utilized the targeted intelligence.

Logical-Mathematical:

Two favorite books in the kindergarten classes were *Anno's Counting House* and *The Doorbell Rang*. Anno's book features ten kids who move from one house to another on opposite pages. The puzzle is to figure out how many kids are in each house at any one time, including the hidden ones. One kindergarten girl, who had been rather unresponsive to fantasy and make-believe, came to life and manipulated the numbers faster than anyone else. She insisted on reading that book every week for several months and moved on to other Anno math concept books.

In *The Doorbell Rang*, twelve cookies are divided among an increasing number of children as the story progresses. With paper plates and cut out chocolate-chip cookies, the story can be re-enacted innumerable times. *12 Ways to Count to 12* becomes a game of adding and subtracting. After reading *Inch by Inch,* we measured objects all over the library. *Much Bigger Than Martin* prompted a discussion and comparison of sizes of people and objects in the room. Counting books abound. *Moja Means One* and *The Afro-Bets 1,2,3* add cultural diversity as well. *Alexander Who Used to Be*

Rich Last Sunday involves problems with money. *How Much Is a Million* and *If You Made a Million* are good for giving kids a better understanding of large numbers.

With the fifth and sixth graders, I combined some library skills and math skills in a project to examine the cultural, ethnic and gender diversity in the History, Geography and Biography collections.

With the intermediate classes (third grade and up), the *Young Math Series* offers many possibilities. I used *Rubber Bands, Baseballs and Doughnuts* to explore topology. With the fifth and sixth graders, I combined some library skills and math skills in a project to examine the cultural, ethnic and gender diversity (or lack thereof) in the 900 (History and Geography) and Biography collections. Working in small teams with an assigned shelf, the students recorded the ethnic and cultural affiliation of the person or the culture depicted. They collected their findings, graphed the results and drew conclusions in the form of recommendations for future library purchases.

Math centers were also set up using games and activities from Marilyn Burns' *I Hate Mathematics* and *Math for Smarty Pants*. Chess instruction books and game pieces were put out and have continued to be a popular activity three years later.

Musical:

To utilize the Musical Intelligence to explore literature, I used three stories set to music - two symphonic and one vocal - *The Sorcerer's Apprentice*, *Merry Pranks* and a version of *How the Leopard Got His Spots*. In each case, we read the story together, then listened to the musical version. In the discussions that followed, we compared and contrasted the mood, feelings and ambience of the stories as written words and as musical performances.

In the discussion that followed, we compared and contrasted the mood, feelings and ambience of the stories as written words and as musical performances.

Working with the Performing Arts specialist, we created our own sound story based on *Nicholas Cricket*. Students used found materials (sticks, cans full of rocks, rubber bands), as well as an autoharp, to create rhythm instruments. Using our voices in chorus and solo readings, we recreated the story.

During the Musical month, I played tapes of traditional Native American, Caribbean and African music to accompany and set the mood when reading stories from those cultures. The music would be playing before school, as the students entered the library and during the story.

Spatial:

During Spatial month, the primary children were introduced to a number of Caldecott Award-winning books and authors. We read stories and biographies of the artists and played a game of matching book covers and illustrations with the author's picture and name. Each class chose a book to illustrate, with each child responsible for at least one original drawing. The resulting books were spiral-bound, displayed in the library, and placed in circulation. Parents attending our Specialists' Open House also made a book.

After doing research in the library, the students used the space and materials in the art room to recreate King Tut's tomb, complete with a mummy, art objects, and hieroglyphs.

Several activities were coordinated with the Art specialist. The fifth grade mummy project started by watching the video of the opening of Tutankhamen's tomb and reading some stories from Egyptian mythology. After doing research in the library, the students used the space and materials in the art room to recreate King Tut's tomb, complete with a mummy, art objects, and hieroglyphs.

A quilt project also involved working cooperatively with the Art specialist. We started in the library by reading Faith Ringgold's *Tar Beach* and *Dinner at Aunt Connie's* and Flourney's *The Patchwork Quilt*. We made small story quilts using paper and glue. In the art room, the older students sewed twelve-inch square quilt pieces.

Centers for the Spatial Intelligence included exploring optical illusions, modeling clay to depict the story of the day, drawing materials to work on additional pages of the class book, using "Print Shop" by Broderbund on the computer, making quilt squares with patterns to copy or materials to create one's own quilt story square and hieroglyphic rubber stamps.

Bodily-Kinesthetic:
How to bring sports into the library (other than putting out sports related books and magazines) was a real challenge. Focusing on the Olympics, mime and dance allowed me to bring in large muscle activities in a controlled manner.

Focusing on the Olympics, mime and dance allowed me to bring in large muscle activities in a controlled manner.

I introduced the unit with a videotape of the highlights of the most recent summer Olympics, then set up a tumbling mat for somersaults, flips and simple gymnastics. We read *Casey At The Bat* and acted out the story in mime. The primary kids enjoyed forming the letters of the alphabet and numbers using their bodies, while reading *Afro-Bets ABC* and *Afro-Bets 123*.

We watched video tapes of Merce Cunningham designing a production from the ground up - choreography, costumes, and John Cage's music composition. We also watched a video tape of the Alvin Ailey Dance Company and read his biography. The dance tapes had a powerful impact on the students. For most of them, it was their first experience with this form of modern dance.

In the future, I would include some small muscle activities as well, sewing, model building, and crafts using wood, string and wire. Perhaps the quilt project could be a bridge between the Spatial and Bodily-Kinesthetic units.

Linguistic:
The primary classes explored their Linguistic Intelligence by retelling stories like Remy Charlip's *Fortunately* in large and small groups. We discovered new words for groups of animals in *Herds of Words*. We did some choral reading using Fleischman's *Joyful Noise*. We read MacLachlan's *Three Names* and Steptoe's *The Story of Jumping Mouse* and imagined what names we would have if we could choose a new one and why.

We did some choral reading using Fleischman's **Joyful Noise.**

The intermediate students participated in the Junior Great Books reading and discussion program - an exercise in shared inquiry designed to develop the critical thinking skills of interpretation, analysis and synthesis. In addition to the traditional discussion groups, we used different intelligences to get at the meaning of the stories including journal writing, role-play and a mock-trial. Intermediate students were also encouraged to expand their reading horizons and read a variety of different types of books including Newbery Award winners, adventure, mystery, animal stories, science fiction and fantasy.

The library is a great set-
ting for working on the
Personal Intelligences too.

Interpersonal and Intrapersonal

The library is a great setting for working on the Personal Intelligences too. Having students reflect about the books they have read — Why do you like the book? Which character reminds you of yourself and why? —helps students improve their Intrapersonal Intelligence. The Interpersonal Intelligence can be focused upon in Junior Great Books discussions and as students share what they have read with one another, and work on presentation skills and understanding others.

Libraries can be more than Linguistic. Certainly in this age of exploding technology, libraries are truly information centers. Just as the image of the storyteller doll with many children sitting on her lap reminds us of the rich diversity and variety of children and stories, so too it reminds one of the many ways to tell a story — through words, art, music and active participation.

Librarians and teachers need to put on Katy No-Pocket's apron with its multiple pockets to have all facets of MI immediately at hand.

The Little Red Hen

MI Context: This lesson gives students an opportunity to retell a story that they have heard.

Learner Outcomes: The student will listen to a story and then retell it to demonstrate an understanding of the main idea and some supporting details by role-playing.

Procedure:

1. Read *The Little Red Hen* to the class, having the students listen for the patterns of the Little Red Hen's friends' lines and the sequence in which things happen.

2. After reading the story, review the main points:

   A. She finds the wheat.

   B. She plants the seed.

   C. She harvests the wheat.

   D. She takes it to the mill.

   E. She grinds it into flour.

   F. She makes the bread.

3. Assign the parts of The Little Red Hen and her friends. Have the children act out the story saying their own lines as they are able with minimal guidance from the teacher. Add additional "friends" if the group is large. Act the story out more than once so everyone has a chance to perform.

Materials:
A copy of the folk tale *The Little Red Hen*

Assessment / Reflection:
Ask the class if it was easy or hard to remember all the parts and the order in which they came. How did they feel while acting? What strategy did they use if they forgot a line or couldn't remember the order? Record how accurate their perceptions were to what you observed while they were acting.

MI Extensions:

Interpersonal: Discuss ways the Little Red Hen could have gotten her friends to help her.

Intrapersonal: Have the children discuss which character in the story they are most like and explain why.

Bodily-Kinesthetic: Have a child pantomime a part of the story while the rest of the class guesses which part it is.

Linguistic: Do the same activity with another story like *The Three Bears* or *The Little Gingerbread Man.*

Logical-Mathematical: Follow a recipe and make bread.

Musical: Use a familiar tune and make up words to a song the Little Red Hen could have sung while she was doing all the work.

Spatial: Draw a map showing the path the Little Red Hen traveled in the story from beginning to end.

A practical guide created by the faculty of The New City School ©1994

Inquiring Minds Want to Know

Linguistic
Preprimary
Language Arts

MI Context: This lesson is used to develop questioning skills and to introduce letter writing on a preprimary level.

Learner Outcomes: Students will dictate and illustrate a letter to a fictional character. Students will develop one or two appropriate questions for the character of their choice.

Procedure:

1. Read *The Jolly Postman* by Janet and Allan Alhberg. Discuss the different letters in the story.

2. Discuss the main parts of a letter — greeting, body, signature — as is appropriate for the age level.

3. Brainstorm a list of book characters with which the children are familiar.

4. Working in small groups, have children discuss what questions they would like to ask the characters.

5. Write a letter to one of the fictional characters, asking at least one appropriate question. The letter can be dictated to the teacher or written, using "inventive" spelling, by the children; or the children can draw a picture illustrating their question and the teacher can add words later. This can also be done in several small groups; one child does the writing, another dictates and another could illustrate. Make sure that all the letters have the three elements introduced in the lesson— greeting, body and signature.

6. Ask students in older classes to answer the students' letters by becoming the character to whom the letter was written. "Mail" the letters to those students.

Materials:
A copy of *The Jolly Postman by* Janet and Allan Ahlberg, paper, pencils, board and markers

Assessment / Reflection:
Were the students able to write letters with appropriate questions? Did the letters include a greeting, body and a signature?

MI Extensions:
Interpersonal: Write group letters to thank someone, to get information or to invite someone to visit. Someone could come in character from a favorite story to visit the class and answer questions in person. Invite a local author to talk to the class.

Intrapersonal: Which book character are you most like? Why? Which character would you like to be? Why?

Bodily-Kinesthetic: Develop pantomimes of the stories or nursery rhymes used by the children in their letter writing.

Linguistic: Many nursery rhymes and story characters have only one name. Make up some last names for them, i.e., Goldilocks Bushey, Jack and Jill Jimmerson, Rapunzel Richie.

Logical-Mathematical: After "mailing" the letters, count how many hours, days or weeks it takes to get an answer.

Musical: Sing nursery rhymes. Create sound effects when reading the stories. Sing the repeating lines from the story *The Jolly Postman.* Create an opera of a familiar nursery rhyme or story; instead of speaking the lines, children sing them. The fairy tale *Goldilocks and the Three Bears* works well with young children.

Spatial: Students draw a picture of their character on a small piece of poster board, being careful to fill the entire piece of board. The teacher can cut the picture into puzzle pieces (preprimary children have a tendency to cut too many pieces) and put them in reclosable bags. Freezer bags have a place to write the student's name.

Caterpillar to Butterfly

MI Context: This lesson shows the process of a caterpillar changing into a butterfly.

Learner Outcomes: Students will be introduced to metamorphosis.

Linguistic
Preprimary
Science

Procedure:
1. Decorate a knee-length sock to look like a caterpillar, complete with wiggle eyes. The toe of the sock is the head of the caterpillar. Make a butterfly out of felt. Holding the wadded up butterfly in your hand, put your hand inside the sock and pull the sock up to your elbow. Make the caterpillar "eat" by moving the mouth with your hand inside the sock.

2. Read *The Very Hungry Caterpillar* by Eric Carle. While reading it, the caterpillar "eats" through the pages. Turn the sock inside out as the cocoon opens, thus hiding the caterpillar and exposing your hand with the butterfly that unfolds.

2. Discuss the sequence of the story.

3. Look at real pictures of caterpillars and butterflies.

4. Discuss characteristics of caterpillars and butterflies. The students generate a list of descriptive words for each.

Materials:
The Very Hungry Caterpillar by Eric Carle, pictures of caterpillars and butterflies, paper, and markers, sock, wiggle eyes, felt

Assessment/Reflection:
Are the students able to describe the stages in the cycle in the correct order?

MI Extensions:
Interpersonal: Working in small groups, children make their own metamorphosis posters.

Intrapersonal: Discuss how it might feel to change from a caterpillar to a butterfly.

Bodily-Kinesthetic: Act out the stages of metamorphosis.

Logical-Mathematical: Count how many times each fruit appears in the book. Make a chart of the fruits so the children can see the relationship of the numbers.

Musical: Crawl like caterpillars and fly like butterflies to fast/slow music.

Spatial: Children make their own sock caterpillars.

"Ai" Centers

Linguistic
Primary
Language Arts

MI Context: This lesson is used when teaching the letter combination "ai." During these centers, which reflect all the intelligences, the students learn that "ai" has the sound of long "a."

Learner Outcomes: The students will say a long "a" when they see the "ai" letter combination.

Procedure:

1. The class spends several days bringing in words from home or looking through books and observing printed material like signs to find words with the "ai" combination. Write these words on a chart.

2. Read through "ai" chart words with the class. Discuss the vocabulary and point out exceptions to the pattern, such as in the word "said."

3. Children will reinforce the sound of "ai" through centers:

   • **Interpersonal:** Children work with a partner to fill in blank Bingo boards with "ai" words. Make cards with all the words that are used and play Bingo.

   • **Logical-Mathematical**: Using rulers, children create mazes with straight lines.

   • **Musical:** Use rain sticks and tin pans of water to create rain music.

   • **Spatial:** Paint a picture of an "ai" word and give the painting a title.

   • **Intrapersonal:** Choose an "ai" word and write a poem on chart paper beginning with "I'm an (ai word)." Illustrate the poem and share it with the class.

   • **Bodily-Kinesthetic:** Play charades using prepared cards with "ai" words.

   • **Linguistic:** Have the children create a word search using "ai" words.

Materials:
Chart paper, blank Bingo sheets that children can fill in with "ai" words, paper for mazes, rulers, rain stick, water, tin pans, paints, charade cards of "ai" words, large graph paper to be used for word search

Assessment / Reflection:
In a few days, come back to the chart and see how many words are remembered. When reading, are the children able to pronounce the words with an "ai"?

MI Extensions:
The same centers can be used to reinforce other vowel combinations.

Trees

MI Context: This activity is designed to be used during the study of the Northeast Woodland Indians and the environment in which they lived. It could also be adapted to a unit on plants or animals.

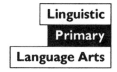

Learner Outcomes: The students will use a field guide to determine the names of various kinds of trees found within the school neighborhood. This information will be used to create a class field guide.

Procedure:
1. The students walk around the neighborhood and by referring to field guides, identify the trees.

2. Using paper and crayons, the students make bark and leaf rubbings and collect several leaves and other tree samples. Each rubbing and sample should be labeled with the kind of tree from which it came.

3. The students make observations and write field notes incorporating their observations, i.e., physical characteristics, fruit, animal nests and cavities in the tree, and the surrounding area.

4. The students use their field notes, rubbings, and samples to create a class field guide.

Materials:
"Tree identification books, paper, crayons

Assessment / Reflection:
Are other students able to use the field guide to identify trees?

MI Extensions:
Interpersonal: During the publication process, students will make decisions about the order of the trees in the book, page layout, the depth of the information to be covered, and establish criteria for including pages in the book.

Intrapersonal: At different points during the project, allow the students to reflect on how sensitive they are being to the abilities, knowledge and feelings of others. Create a rubric which includes the following statements. Students rate themselves as good, fair, or need improvement.

- I think about the feelings of others before I choose my words.

- I share ideas instead of telling others what to do.

- I am helpful without making others feel I am better than them.

- I listen so I can use the ideas of others.

Bodily-Kinesthetic: Create models of trees with toothpicks and clay, paying particular attention to the branching and form of the tree. Label each tree with its name.

Musical: Go outside and listen to the wind or rain in the trees.

Logical-Mathematical: Make a caliper-like instrument using two popsicle sticks with a thumbtack as the hinge. Hold the sticks at arm's length and match the angle made by the branches of a tree. Lay the instrument onto a protractor to measure the angle. Do all trees have similar angles or do they vary according to the type of tree?

Spatial: Take photographs for the book or to include in the display.

A practical guide created by the faculty of The New City School ©1994

The Talking Earth

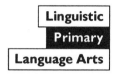

MI Context: This lesson is used after reading *The Talking Earth* by Jean Craighead George in conjunction with the study of the Seminole Indians.

Learner Outcomes: Students will show their understanding of *The Talking Earth* by completing a project using an intelligence of their choosing.

Procedure:
1. The children read the book and discuss it with the class. Some skills that might be highlighted are adjectives and the use of descriptive language.

2. Upon completion, the students have the option of working by themselves or with other students. They may choose one of the following:

   • **Musical:** Write and perform a theme song for *The Talking Earth*. Using musical instruments, produce sounds of *The Talking Earth*.

   • **Spatial:** Create a board game that relates to the book. Create a crossword puzzle using words from the book. Build a model of one of the structures in the book, i.e., the houseboat or cave.

   • **Bodily-Kinesthetic:** Act out a scene from the book. Pantomime the animals from the story for the other students to guess.

   • **Linguistic:** Rewrite the ending of the book or add another chapter.

   • **Logical-Mathematical:** Draw a map of Billie Wind's trip using a legend and a scale of miles. Draw the cave to scale.

   • **Intrapersonal:** Pretend you are a companion of Billie Wind's. Make five journal entries of things you saw and felt.

   • **Interpersonal:** Divide the class into pairs. Have one child be Billie Wind and the other a TV news reporter who interviews Billie Wind upon her return to Florida.

Materials:
The Talking Earth by Jean Craighead George, a keyboard, music paper on which to compose songs, art materials

Assessment / Reflection:
After each chapter, students will write responses to these questions:
   • What strategies did Billie Wind use to solve the problems she encountered in this chapter?
   • What would you have done to solve the problem?
   • If you had been on the trip with Billie Wind, describe, from your point of view, what happened.

Sincerely Yours: Parts of a Letter

Linguistic
Intermediate
Language Arts

MI Context: This lesson is used when students are writing friendly letters to pen pals.

Learner Outcomes: The students will learn the order and purpose of the following five parts of a letter: heading, greeting, body, closing and signature.

Procedure:
1. Divide the class into five groups and assign each one to be part of a letter.

2. Each group will define its role in the letter and demonstrate its purpose and function by acting it out. For example, the closing could be asked where it came in a friendly letter, what kinds of words it might be, how it felt being all by itself.

Materials:
English text book to be used as a reference, props the groups might need, i.e., a fake microphone for an interview.

Assessment / Reflection:
Students write a friendly letter using correct letter format.

MI Extensions:
Interpersonal: Debate which letter part is the most important. Students draw cards telling them which parts of a letter they need to support.

Intrapersonal: Which part of a letter are you most like and why?

Bodily-Kinesthetic: Pantomime the parts of a letter or "sign" the letter on video.

Logical-Mathematical: Determine the fraction representing each of the five parts of their letter. It could be calculated by fifths for the five parts of the letter or it could be divided by the number of lines, words or syllables in each part.

Musical: Listen to a piece of music and decide which sections might be the parts of a letter. The introduction in the music would be the heading in a letter. Provide sheet music or piano books and find the correlation between the parts of a piece of music and the parts of a letter.

Spatial: Using geoboards and bands, show the parts, sizes and positions of the parts of a letter.

Which Book Is in the Lead?

MI Context: This lesson is used during a literature unit. It may also be used as a book report introduction.

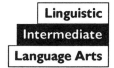

Learner Outcomes: Students will utilize newspaper lead elements- Who, What, When, Where, Why and How (five W's and H)- to write articles about particular parts/chapters of a book. These articles should exhibit an understanding of the book, as well as appropriate newspaper-writing techniques.

Procedure:

1. Review the five W's and H- elements present in every newspaper lead. Explain that each of these questions should be answered within the first two paragraphs of every well-written newspaper article.

2. Read the first two paragraphs of a newspaper article to the class. Ask students to identify the five W's and H. Discuss how these six elements let the reader know what will be covered in the rest of the article.

3. Provide the students with copies of the article and have them individually circle or mark the five W's and H in the lead.

4. Divide the class into pairs or groups of three. Give each group copies of two different articles from a daily newspaper. Have groups circle or mark each of the five W's and H within the lead. All group members must agree on the five W's and H before marks are made on the copies.

5. Groups then discuss what the article is about, based on information given in the lead. Was enough information given?

6. Bring the class together and go over the groups' answers for the five W's and H in each article. Discuss different responses and determine correct answers. Students record correct answers.

7. Instruct students to write newspaper articles summarizing a chapter in a book they are studying. Review the importance of a well-written lead.

Materials:
Copies of three different newspaper articles from a daily newspaper, pencils, writing paper

Assessment / Reflection:
Each student should read through his own article and determine the effectiveness of the lead. Did the lead encompass one or two paragraphs? Were there particular words which helped to make a good lead?

Point This Way, View That Way

Linguistic
Intermediate
Language Arts

MI Context: This lesson is used when students are reading and writing short stories.

Learner Outcomes: From the point of view of non-living things, students will role-play situations and write short stories.

Procedure:

1. Create an area in the room where students can move about. Designate an instrument or sound that will signal when they are to stop moving and "freeze." The students will act out words, "freezing" after each word.

2. Prepare a list of words of living and non-living things, ie., a washing machine, roller blades, a dog, jello, glue, a tree, President Clinton, a football, an elephant, a computer, water, a telephone. Explain that you will tell them what object to be and then say "Go." The students move around the room imitating the object in any way they choose. After a short period, they are told to "freeze" and are given another object to act out. Do several objects in this manner.

3. Bring the students together and make a list on the board of the objects they were asked to act out. Ask for suggestions of how to categorize the list, stopping when "living and non-living things" is suggested.

4. Discuss what makes the categories "living" and "non-living" different. Focus on non-living things and talk about feelings these things might express if they were able to speak. Students will look at their environment from another point of view as they do this.

5. The students break into groups of two or three and assume the role of non-living things. They role-play a conversation between these objects and exhibit the point of view of the object they are enacting.

6. After fifteen minutes or so, have the small groups perform for the class. Students are to guess what objects are being depicted, i.e., milk and a cereal bowl, paper and a pencil, popcorn and a popper, candy and a mouth. Discuss the performances.

7. Each student creates a short story in which he writes from the point of view of non-living things.

Materials:
Instrument to signal "freeze," paper, list of living and non-living things

Assessment / Reflection:
Students share their short stories with the class.

MI Extensions:

Interpersonal: If the groups were going to show these to a much younger or much older audience, what would need to change?

Intrapersonal: List eight similarities and differences between the objects used in their writing and themselves. Decide if you are writing from the perspective of a living or non-living item and finish these sentence starters: "I would rather be a living/non-living item because…" and "The one thing people don't understand about living/non-living is…"

Logical-Mathematical: In groups of two or three, the students make Venn diagrams using the objects from their stories to represent different circles. The focus should be on point of view rather than physical characteristics, i.e., a football and a piece of luggage can both get lonely when no one is using them; pens and gum get sore because people chew on them.

Musical: Assign sounds to each of the living and non-living items. Perform a sound symphony program for the other groups, or make up a musical notation for each sound.

Spatial: Design and construct their objects three-dimensionally. Attach their stories and display them.

Activities to Support the Linguistic Intelligence

Interpersonal
- Oral presentations or story telling
- Collaborative writing
- Panel discussions or debates
- A persuasive article or "how to" story
- Partner and choral reading

Intrapersonal
- Show and Tell activities and Person of the Week interviews
- Books for choice reading
- Personal narratives, journal writing or experience charts
- Tape recorded reflections
- Questionnaires

Bodily-Kinesthetic
- Scavenger hunts
- Keyboarding on the word processor and handwriting
- Finger plays and puppet shows
- Charades and pantomime
- Dramatic play

Logical-Mathematical
- Story mapping
- Reasoning skills like analogies, palindromes, and comparing and contrasting
- Crossword puzzles
- Logical humor; for example, riddles, puns and jokes
- Flow charts

Musical
- Creating poetry
- Writing lyrics to songs
- Detecting meter and pattern in poetry (limerick, haiku)
- Performing an opera
- Using a Karaoke machine and lip-synching

Spatial
- Book making
- Alphabetizing
- Playing games, such as Scrabble and Boggle
- Labeling diagrams
- Cartooning

Identifying the Linguistic Intelligence in Your Students

Children function at many different levels within the intelligences. Through observation of everyday activities, one can create a profile showing the level of functioning within a particular intelligence and the intelligences in relation to each other. The levels described show increased engagement and proficiency. Use this record-keeping page to obtain a richer picture of a child.

Appreciates:

YES	NO	
		Consistently demonstrates interest, respect and enjoyment within the intelligence and is able to differentiate qualities
		Enjoys expressive/receptive language
		Enjoys listening to stories, poems, plays
		Asks questions about words, sounds or definitions
		Asks "What does this say?" making the connection between meaning and the written word

Performs:

YES	NO	
		Is able to apply the intelligence to recreate an exhibit or demonstration or problem-solve with a given situation
		Uses language to solve problems and convey meaning in other disciplines
		Is adept at learning languages
		Uses figurative/descriptive language in speaking and writing
		Is able to make oral presentations
		Understands and responds to puns, riddles, jokes
		Memorizes easily

Creates:

YES	NO	
		Is able to apply this intelligence to generate original work, to develop unique solutions to problems or create prototypes
		Develops an author's voice
		Modifies an existing form of communication
		Has distinctive writing/speaking style

Name: _____   Date: _____

Video Viewing Criteria

Rate yourself on a scale of 0-10 (10 highest)
on the following:

___ voice quality - comment:_____

___ eye contact - comment:_____

___ costume/props - comment:_____

___ content of speech - comment:_____

Estimate of average score:_____ Actual:_____

Write yes or no on the line:

___ I included in my speech how my person
made a difference.

___ My speech was between two and
three minutes. (Please time accurately.)

My favorite part of this project was _____

_____

If I were going to do this project again, I would ____

Name: _____   Date: _____

Research Evaluation

On a scale of 1 - 10, rate yourself.
(1 = very easy, 10 = extremely hard)

1. Taking notes   _____

2. Keeping track of note cards/folder, etc.   _____

3 Writing the report   _____

4. Creating main idea sentences   _____

5. Keeping everything organized   _____

6. Completing the introduction
   and summary   _____

Average: _____ guess _____ actual

This is what I learned about writing a research
paper: _____
_____
_____

If I were going to do it again I would _____
_____
_____

I would like to thank _____for_____
_____

A practical guide created by the faculty of The New City School ©1994

Reader: _____   Date: _____

Reading Survey

Do you like reading?_____

Do you read at home?_____

Do you visit the library?_____

Are you a good reader?_____

Do you think it is important to be a good reader?

_____

Do you like speaking in front of people?_____

_____

What is your favorite book?_____

_____

What do you like reading about?_____

_____

What would you like to learn about this year?_____

_____

A practical guide created by the faculty of The New City School ©1994

Writer: _____   Date: _____

Writing Survey

Do you write at home?_____

Are you a good writer?_____

Do you think it is important to be a good writer?

_____

Do you like to write stories?_____

What do you like writing about?_____

Are you a good listener?_____Why/Why not?_____

_____

What is something you are good at?_____

_____

What do you need to work on?_____

_____

What do you like to do when you are not at school?

_____

Children's Resources

Books and Recordings

Ahlberg, Janet P. and Allan. *Jolly Postman*. Little, Brown and Co., 1986. ★

Aliki. *How a Book Is Made*. Crowell, 1986. ★

Anno, Mitsumasa. *Anno's Counting House*. Philomel, 1982. ★

Arnold, Tedd. *The Signmaker's Assistant*. Dial Books, 1992. ★

Balsam, David and Kahn, Martin, "The Print Shop." Broderbund Software, 1993.

Baylor, Byrd. *The Desert Is Theirs*. Aladdin, 1987. ★

Beisner, Monika. *Monika Beisner's Book of Riddles*. Farrar Sraus Giroux, 1983. ★

Brisson, Pat. *Your Best Friend, Kate*. Bradbury Press, 1989. ★

Carle, Eric. *The Very Hungry Caterpillar*. Philomel, 1970. ★

Charlip, Remy. *Fortunately*. Four Winds, 1980. ★

Cohen, Miriam. *When Will I Read*. Dell Publishing, 1983. ★

dePaola, Tomie. *Andy*. Prentice-Hall, 1973. ★

Elting, Mary and Folson, Michael. *Q is for Duck*. Clarion Books, 1980. ★

Feelings, Muriel. *Moja Means One*. Dial Publishing, 1971. ★

Galdone, Paul. *Little Red Hen*. Clarion Books, 1973. ★

Gorey, Edward. *Amphigorey-Fifteen Books*. Pedigree, G.P. Putnam's Sons, 1972. ★

Heller, Ruth. *A Cache of Jewels*. Grosset and Dunlap, 1987. ★

Heller, Ruth. *Kites Sail High*. Grosset and Dunlap, 1988. ★

Heller, Ruth. *Merry-Go-Round, A Book About Nouns*. Putnam, 1990. ★

Heller, Ruth. *Up, Up and Away: A Book About Adverbs*. Grosset and Dunlop, 1991. ★

Hennessy, B. G. *Jake Baked the Cake*. Viking Penguin, 1990. ★

Hopkinson, Deborah. *Sweet Clara and the Freedom Quilt*. Alfred A. Knopf, 1993. ★

Hudson, Cheryl Willis. *Afro-Bets ABC Book*. Just Us Books, 1987. ★

Hutchins, Pat. *The Doorbell Rang*. Greenwillow Books, 1986. ★

Hutchins, Pat. *The Tale of Thomas Mead*. Mulberry Books, 1980. ★

Kalman, Maria. *Max Makes a Million*. Viking Penguin, 1990. ★

Keller, Charles. *Tongue Twisters*. Simon and Schuster, 1989. ★

Kellogg, Steven. *Much Bigger Than Martin*. Dial, 1986. ★

Kipling, Rudyard. "How the Leopard Got His Spots," *Just So Stories*. Doubleday, 1972.

Lepscky, Ibi. *William Shakespeare*. Barron's Educational Series, Inc., 1988. ★

Lester, Alison. *Imagine*. Houghton Mifflin, 1990. ★

★ **indicates picture book**

Levine, Ellen. *I Hate English*. Scholastic, 1989. ★

Lionni, Leo. *Inch By Inch*. Astro, 1960. ★

MacLachlan, Patricia. *Three Names*. HarperCollins, 1991. ★

Maxner, Joyce. *Nicholas Cricket*. Harper & Row, 1989. ★

McMillan, Bruce. *One Sun: A Book of Terse Verse*. Holiday House, 1990. ★

Merriam, Eve. *12 Ways to Get to 11*. Simon and Schuster, 1993. ★

Most, Bernard. *There's an Ant in Anthony*. Mulberry Books, 1992. ★

Osborne, Mara Pope. *American Tall Tales*. Scholastic Inc., 1991.

Pallotta, Jerry. *The Icky Bug Alphabet Book*. Children's Press, 1991. ★

Patterson, Francine, Dr. *Koko's Kitten*. Scholastic Inc., 1985. ★

Patterson, Francine, Dr. *Koko's Story*. Scholastic Inc., 1987. ★

Paulson, Jim. *The Beanstalk Incident*. Carol Publishing Group, 1990. ★

Purviance, Susan and O'Shell, Marcia. *Alphabet Annie Announces an All-American Album*. Houghton Mifflin, 1988. ★

Rankin, Laura. *The Handmade Alphabet*. Dial Books, 1991. ★

Ringgold, Faith. *Dinner at Aunt Connie's House*. Hyperion Books for Children, 1993. ★

Ringgold, Faith. *Tar Beach*. Crown Publishers, 1991. ★

Rockwell, Anne. *The Story Snail*. MacMillan, 1974. ★

Roehrig, Catherine. *Fun With Hieroglyphs*. Metropolitan Museum of Art, 1990.

Roop, Peter and Connie. *Ahyoka and the Talking Leaves*. Lothrop, Lee and Shepard Books, 1992.

Schwarz, David M. *How Much Is a Million?* Lothrop, Lee & Shepard Books, 1985. ★

Schwarz, David M. *If You Made a Million*. Lothrop, Lee & Shepard Books, 1989. ★

Scieszka, Jon. *The True Story of the 3 Little Pigs*. Scholastic Inc., 1991. ★

Sharmat, Marjorie Weinman. *My Mother Never Listens to Me*. Albert Whitman & Co., 1984 ★ .

Stanek, Mureil. *My Mom Can't Read*. Albert Whitman & Co., 1986. ★

Steptoe, John. *The Story of Jumping Mouse*. Lothrop, Lee and Shepard Books, 1984. ★

Terban, Marvin. *The Dove Dove: Funny Homograph Riddles*. Houghton Mifflin, 1988.

Terban, Marvis. *Mad as a Wet Hen*. Clarion Books, 1987.

Waber, Bernard. *Dear Hildegarde*. Houghton Mifflin, 1980.

Williams, Jay. "The Wicked Tricks of Tyl Uilenspiegel," *Junior Great Books, Series 4*. The Great Books Foundation, 1987.

Poetry:

Feelings, Tom. *Something on My Mind*. Dial Books for Young Readers, 1978.

Ferris, Sean. *Children of the Great Muskeg*. Black Moss Press, 1985.

Fleischman, Paul. *Joyful Noise: Poems for Two Voices*. Harper and Row, 1988.

Giovanni, Nikki. *Spin a Soft Black Song*. Farrar, Straus and Giroux, 1985.

Lee, Dennis. *The Ice Cream Store*. Scholastic Inc., 1991.

Lesser, Carolyn. *Flamingo Knees*. Oakwood Press, 1988.

Mathis, Bell Sharon. *Red Dog/Blue Fly Football Poems*. Viking, 1991.

Prelusky, Jack. *The New Kids on the Block*. Greenwillow Books, 1986.

Silverstein, Shel. *A Light in the Attic*. Harper & Row, 1974.

Silverstein, Shel. *Where the Sidewalk Ends*. Harper & Row, 1984.

Sullivan, Charles. *Children of Promise*. Harry N. Abrams Inc., 1991.

Thayer, Ernest. *Casey at the Bat*. Raintree, 1985.

Withers, Carl. *A Rocket in My Pocket*. Scholastic Inc., 1948.

Games:

"Alphabet Soup: The Letter Matching Game." Parker Brothers, 1992.

"Balderdash: The Hilarious Bluffing Game." Gameworks Creations, 1984.

"Boggle: Three Minute Word Game." Parker Brothers, 1992.

"Brainquest." University Games Corporation, 1993.

"Electronic Dream Phone Game." Milton Bradley, 1991.

"Guess Who?" Milton Bradley, 1987.

"Hangman." Milton Bradley, 1988.

"Holly Hobbie: Wishing Well Game." Parker Brothers, 1976.

"Outburst Junior." Hersch & Company, 1989.

"Read My Lips, Kids." Pressman, 1991.

"Scattergories Junior." Milton Bradley, 1989.

"Scrabble." Milton Bradley, 1989.

"Scrabble: Sentence Cube Game." Selchow & Richter Co., 1983.

"See and Read Dominoes." Random House, Inc., 1989.

Teachers' Resources

Bullock, Doris. *Designed to Delight.* The Library, 1977.

Burns, Marilyn. *The I Hate Mathematics Book.* Little Brown, 1975.

Caduto, Michael. *Keepers of the Earth.* Fulcrum, 1989.

Caudron, Jill M. *Alphabet Activities.* Fearon Teacher Aids, 1983.

Caudron, Jill M. *Alphabet Fun and Games.* Fearon Teacher Aids, 1984.

Caudron, Jill M. *Alphabet Stories.* Fearon Teacher Aids, 1983.

Hamilton, Virginia. *The People Could Fly - American Black Folktales.* Knopf, 1985.

Sebranek, Patrick. *Writers Inc.* Educational Publishing House, 1989.

Smith, Havilan and Lyn. *Easy Plays for Preschoolers to Third Graders,*
    Quail Ridge Press, Inc., 1985.

Zimmerman, Bill. *How to Tape Instant Oral Biographies.* Banton Books, 1992.

Chapter 5:

The Logical-Mathematical Intelligence

Contributors: Bonnie L. Frank, Joycelyn L. Gray, Jean Blockhus Grover, Elizabeth King, Susan Matthews, Suzy Schweig, Christine Wallach, Stephanie Cunningham Wiles, Denise A. Willis

"Every solution to a problem is a new problem."

Goethe

A practical guide created by the faculty of The New City School ©1994

Web of the Logical-Mathematical Intelligence

Student quotes

Student quotes

List of characteristics

"I do a lot of math projects."

"I'm Logical-Mathematical because I like to do lots of things with computers and the sciences."

"I'm Logical-Mathematical because I like to figure things out, like puzzles."

- Notices and uses numbers, shapes and patterns
- Is able to move from the concrete to the abstract easily
- Enjoys computer games and puzzles
- Thinks conceptually
- Explores patterns and relationships
- Organizes thoughts
- Has systematic approach during problem solving

Stephen Hawking created an explanation of the universe.

Albert Einstein discovered scientific relationships related to matter.

Marilyn Burns is an innovative math educator who is in the forefront of educational reform.

Alexa Canady was the first black woman neurosurgeon in the United States.

"A mathematician, like a painter or poet, is a maker of patterns."

G. H. Hardy

Famous people

Adult quote

A practical guide created by the faculty of The New City School ©1994

The Logical-Mathematical Intelligence: Identification and Implementation

by Bonnie L. Frank

Keisha likes creating patterns with her art supplies; Leonard enjoys organizing his collection of baseball cards; Paul seems to question everything around him; and Barbara would spend all day in front of the computer if you'd let her. What do all these children have in common? Do they exhibit qualities similar to those found in your students or other children you know? What is the best way to teach them?

Each of the students above is utilizing, among others, Logical-Mathematical intelligence. This intelligence, according to Howard Gardner, author of *Frames of Mind* (1983), is just one of the seven intelligences that an individual possesses. These four children may each have a particular strength in the Logical-Mathematical realm, yet they also possess the Interpersonal, Intrapersonal, Linguistic, Spatial, Musical, and Bodily-Kinesthetic Intelligences in varying degrees.

Characteristics of Strong Logical-Mathematical Students

Children strong in the Logical-Mathematical Intelligence will display many common characteristics: they enjoy showing relationships and patterns; they learn information easier when it is presented in an orderly way and they are given opportunities to question; they will often categorize or classify information; they like computer activities, logic puzzles, and strategic games like chess. These types of girls and boys are in every classroom and every population. At The New City School, we feel the best way to teach them is not through an additive approach where the instructor only provides more Logical-Mathematical activities in the classroom, but by consciously including other intelligences within each Logical-Mathematical activity or lesson and, likewise, consciously including Logical-Mathematical activities in as many other lessons as possible.

At The New City School, we feel the best way to teach is not through an additive approach...but by consciously including other intelligences within each Logical-Mathematical activity or lesson ...

In my efforts to accomplish this implementation in each of the subjects I teach (reading, language arts, social studies, math), I realize that students who do well in a particular subject area may not be utilizing their strongest, or favorite, intelligence at all. For example, during social studies one day, a boy from my top math group offered some statistics to enhance our discussion of World War I. This didn't surprise me because this particular child was very interested in World War I; however, as I began to look at the rest of the students in the top math group, I realized that many of these students would approach the topic from a Linguistic, Spatial, or Musical perspective if given the opportunity. I utilized this discovery as a framework for restructuring many of my standard lessons, several of which I will share in this article.

As I began to look at the rest of the students in my top math group, I realized that many of these students would approach the topic from a Linguistic, Spatial, or Musical perspective if given the opportunity.

Bringing Logical-Mathematical Into the Other Intelligences

Restructuring began with book reports in reading. My students are required to read and report on a specific number of books each year. They often viewed these reports as tedious and time consuming; even my avid readers dreaded them. Student interest and enthusiasm began to increase, however, as I implemented various intelligences within the book report formats. For example, when reading a mystery or adventure, students were asked to summarize the book as well as create an interest, tension, or excitement graph. Here they charted "their personal level" in these categories as they read each chapter or section of the book. When these reports were turned in and displayed around the room, students began to compare and contrast the results, thereby continuing to utilize the Logical-Mathematical Intelligence.

Student interest and enthusiasm began to increase as I implemented various intelligences within the book report formats.

In language arts, I had been integrating vocabulary words into the weekly spelling lists. Spelling continued to be difficult for the students and I was constantly looking for new ways to teach it. I handed out pieces of graph paper and asked them to print three of their spelling words on the paper (one letter per box) and connect them by common letters. They continued to do this until all of the twenty words were used. One student intrigued by the activity, challenged the class to "beat him" by connecting the list of words using fewer boxes than he used. The race was on and the interest accelerated with it!

During social studies, I continued to utilize statistics within each unit of study, but I gave the students more time to work with them and make sense of them. For example, when we were studying The Civil War, we researched the life spans of many of the key figures such as "Stonewall" Jackson, Abraham Lincoln, Harriet Beecher Stowe, Frederick Douglas, and Robert E. Lee. We determined an average life span for this time period and then compared and contrasted it to our findings from the colonial period in order to look at advancements in health and medicine. Students had the opportunity to write a report on this topic for extra credit.

Math, ironically, proved to be the biggest challenge. Once again I looked at my math group. It was filled with artists, writers, singers, and dancers, who, through both nature and nurture, happened to also be talented mathematically. How could I alter my lessons to focus on the Logical-Mathematical Intelligence? The tool, I decided, was the students' math journals.

Math Journals

My students wrote in their math journals three to five times a week for many reasons, including exploration, reflection and explanation.

My students wrote in their math journals three to five times a week for many reasons, including exploration, reflection and explanation. Each time they wrote an entry, they needed to write as mathematicians, clearly communicating each idea, theory, or step to solving a problem. Communication is one of the standards that The National Council of Teachers of Mathematics views as crucial for mathematical literacy, and one on which I focus. As I worked with the students on writing explanations to mathematical problems, I noticed that some of my brightest math students had the most difficulty explaining their answers. (This also occurred with oral explanations.) These students often said to me, "I got the right answer; why do I have to explain it?" By the end of the year, however, these same students, along with the rest of the class, voiced feelings of increased confidence and ability in their mathematical communication. I have provided an example of a word problem and three student responses to illustrate the importance of communication in mathematics.

Problem: Suppose that you are driving on the highway and you approach a tollbooth. As you open your coin tray, you see 8 coins totaling 74 cents. The toll is 30 cents. Can you go through the exact change lane? What coins do you have? Explain your answer in writing.

Susie: "I have 4 pennies, 2 dimes, and 2 quarters. That's 8 coins and if you add them up it's 74 cents. To figure this out, I started with the 4 cents of 74 cents, that can only be made in pennies so you have 4 coins there. I made 70 cents, then I took 50 cents (2 quarters) out of 70 cents. I had 2 coins and 20 cents left, that was easy, 2 dimes! (By the way, you can try and try every combination of coins, but I still cannot go through the exact change lane at the tollbooth!)"

Pedro: "I will not be able to use the exact change tollbooth. To make 74 cents using 8 coins, you would have 2 quarters, 2 dimes, and 4 pennies. To make 30 cents out of that would be impossible, because if you tried to use 1 quarter and the 4 pennies you'd get 29 cents. You'd need one more penny. Two dimes and 4 pennies is 24 cents...to get 30 cents you could do 1 quarter and a nickel (5 pennies), 3 dimes, 30 pennies, 6 nickels, or a mixture of those."

Lauri: "I have 8 coins - 2 quarters, 4 pennies, and 2 dimes. I have 74 cents. When I had to pay 30 cents, I did not have exact change because 1 quarter and 4 pennies would equal 29 cents. One quarter and 1 dime would equal 35 cents, and 2 quarters equal 50 cents."

Genuine Understanding in Math Class

Although each of these students arrived at the correct answer, they justified and communicated their work in very different ways. Different levels of understanding were, therefore, exhibited and could be used for assessment or evaluation. For example, of the three students, Pedro was the only one to list various ways to equal 30 cents. (He failed to say, however, that each of the five possibilities listed would not work because he did not have those combinations of coins.) Susie alluded to the combinations but did not give any examples, and Lauri chose to give only combinations of coins that she had and showed that none of those equaled 30 cents. Providing students with writing opportunities in mathematics is also providing teachers with windows to students' thinking and understanding.

Providing students with writing opportunities in mathematics is also providing teachers with windows to students' thinking and understanding.

Students do not all learn in the same way yet for many years teachers have given them "recipes" for understanding, each one receiving the same portion of a given subject regardless of their level of starvation or sense of fullness. Implementation of any of the seven intelligences into the curriculum requires restructuring. It does not mean, however, simply providing "logical-mathematical time" or throwing out lessons that are well-founded and enjoyable for the students. As with any mechanism for change, this work requires patience and time. Too often educators run out of both of these elements as they abandon one reform model for another. Let us not make this mistake again, one which harms teachers and students alike.

Numbers

Logical-Mathematical
Preprimary
Mathematics

MI Context: This lesson is used to teach number skills through the seven intelligences. It can last as few as two or three days or as long as five or six days depending on class size and time constraints.

Learner Outcomes: Children will learn number skills such as counting using one-to-one correspondence, writing numbers, recognizing and identifying numbers and matching numbers to a set.

Procedure:
1. Set up a variety of number learning centers in the classroom. These centers can include the following:

   • Number Songs (Musical): Children can listen to a cassette tape that includes songs about numbers, e.g., "One, Two, Buckle My Shoe" or "Ten Little Fingers" from Learning Basic Skills Through Music Volume I by Hap Palmer.

   • Body Numbers (Interpersonal and Bodily-Kinesthetic): Children will make numbers by using their bodies. This can be done with a partner or in a larger group. Photograph the body numbers and display them.

   • Writing Numbers (Spatial): Children will practice writing numbers as high as they can using different media, i.e., chalk, markers, crayons, colored pencils.

   • Number Books (Linguistic): Provide a variety of books about numbers. Have the children look through them. Then, they can make their own number book.

   • Number Puzzles (Spatial): Children can put together a variety of puzzles that deal with numbers.

   • Matching Number to Set (Logical-Mathematical and Spatial): Provide a variety of folder games in which the children need to match numbers to a set. In the "Dog Bone Game," a teacher-made game, one-half of the bone has the set while the other half has the number. They need to match them.

2. Write instructions for each activity to post in each center. Be sure to include pictures for non-readers (for example, rebus instructions).

3. Explain each activity thoroughly before sending the children out to the various centers. It is best to limit the number of children who can work in each center at one time. A list of students' names can be put in each center so the children can put a check by their name as they complete each center. In this way, the teacher can keep track of student progress.

4. The students can check their work with the teacher as they complete the task.

Materials:
Various number songs on cassette, number puzzles, number books, folder games, paper, crayons, markers

Reflection / Assessment:
Assess progress by observing the children and checking the children's work as they work through the various centers.

Have the children reflect on what they did by asking what centers they liked and disliked. Discuss their responses.

MI Extensions:
Intrapersonal: If I could be any number...

Interpersonal/Bodily-Kinesthetic: Write numbers on a partner's back with fingers and have them guess the numbers.

Linguistic: Make a number book entitled "What Can You Do With..." Each child is assigned a number. What can you do with one person, two people, three people and so on?

Musical: Turn the story-poem *Over in the Meadow* by Ezra Jack Keats into a song.

Spatial: Make numbers with geoboards, rubber bands, play dough or clay.

Number Book List
Count Your Way Through China by Jim Haskins

Count Your Way Through Africa by Jim Haskins

My First Counting Book by Lilian Moore

Two Is for Dancing by Woodleigh Hubbard

Ten, Nine, Eight by Molly Bang

The Icky Bug Counting Book by Jerry Pallotta

How Much Is a Million? by David M. Schwartz

One Gorilla by Atsuko Morozumi

Shapes Galore

MI Context: This lesson is part of a study of geometric shapes.

Logical-Mathematical
Primary
Mathematics

Learners Outcomes: Children will identify shapes and practice seeing the relation of part to whole.

Procedure:
1. Glue rectangles, squares, circles, triangles and diamonds randomly on blank pieces of paper. Make sure each child has one page for each shape.

2. Have the children use crayons to turn the shapes into different things (for example, a square–truck or a triangle–ice cream cone).

3. Assemble all of the pages into a classroom copy of a book about shapes.

4. Look through Tana Hoban's book *Shape*.

Materials:
Construction paper cut into shapes, glue, paper, crayons, *Shapes* by Tana Hoban

Assessment / Reflection:
Can the students tell you the name of each shape and what they turned the shape into in their picture? Can students recognize shapes on classmates' sheets?

MI Extensions:
Interpersonal: Play "Color Bingo" and "Shape Bingo" by Trend.

Intrapersonal: Ask the children to explain what shape they would be if they were happy, mad or scared. Follow each with the question, "Why?" Follow with other feelings as time allows.

Bodily-Kinesthetic: Make shapes with their bodies. Go on a shape walk around the school building.

Linguistic: Write a story about a shape.

Logical-Mathematical: Create a pattern with attribute blocks.

Musical: Have the children clap a steady beat while one child at a time gives clues to the beat. An example is, "I have four corners and four equal sides; I look like a window or the side of a box."

Sizing Up the Three Bears

MI Context: This lesson uses a flannel board story to introduce and reinforce the mathematical concept of size, specifically big, medium and small.

Learner Outcomes: The students will learn to differentiate big, medium and small.

Procedure:
1. Read the book *The Three Bears,* varying voice pitch for the size of each bear.

2. As a group, retell the story using the flannel board and cut outs.

3. Ask the children questions about the story that relate to size, i.e, Whose bowl is this? Is this the medium sized bear? Is this the big, medium or small bed? How can you tell whose chair this is?

Materials:
The Three Bears storybook; flannel board cut outs including Goldilocks, the bears, bowls, chairs, beds in various sizes; a flannel board

Assessment / Reflection:
Observe whether or not the children can match the bowls, chairs and beds with the appropriate bear. Can they identify the sizes in terms of big, medium and small?

MI Extensions:
Interpersonal: Act out the story as a group.

Intrapersonal: Ask the students, "If you had been Golidlocks, which size bowl, chair and bed would you have chosen?" "Why?"

Bodily-Kinesthetic: Have the students make their body the sizes of the different bears and show how they would move. Pretend they are carrying the different-sized bowls and sitting in the different-sized chairs.

Linguistic: Read another book, such as *The Three Billy Goats Gruff,* that has characters of different sizes.

Musical: Practice chanting the refrains the bears said, i.e., "Who's been sitting in my chair?" using different-sized voices.

Spatial: Have the children draw the bears in ascending or descending order.

Taping the Buffalo

MI Context: This lesson was used while studying the Plains Indians' relationship with the buffalo. It is a component of a year-long Native American theme. By using different resources, this lesson could relate to any theme.

Logical-Mathematical
Primary
Social Studies

Learner Outcomes: The students will develop a frame of reference with which to comprehend the size of a buffalo. The students will work in groups to complete the task of creating a life-sized outline of a buffalo.

Procedure:
1. Display a picture of a buffalo on an overhead transparency.

2. Using the article "Bison Americanus: America's Great Shaggy Beast," by Sue Macy, ask students to determine the height and length of a male (bull) and female (cow) buffalo. Write the information on the transparency under the picture.

3. Divide the class into two groups. Assign the bull to one group and the cow to the other group.

4. Pass out masking tape and rulers.

5. Give each group the task of creating a life-sized outline of a buffalo on the floor using masking tape. Remind them to refer to the picture and the measurements on the overhead for dimensional accuracy.

Materials:
A copy of "Bison Americanus: America's Great Shaggy Beast," overhead transparency of a buffalo, a ruler for every student, one roll of masking tape for every two students

Assessment / Reflection:
Students will discuss how their group completed the task and which parts of the task were the easiest and most difficult. Students will share their reactions to seeing the actual size of a buffalo.

MI Extensions:
Interpersonal: In small groups, agree on three things that are similar in size to the buffalo.

Intrapersonal: In their journals, students reflect upon their role in completing the task. Did they become a leader or follower in their group? What would they have done differently if the group had or had not agreed with them? Did they enjoy it? Did the size of the buffalo surprise them? What can they compare to the size of a buffalo?

Bodily-Kinesthetic: After the figures of the buffalo are completed, the students determine how many students can fit end to end or side by side in the buffalo by actually placing themselves in the figure.

Linguistic: Students compose a poem using the information they have learned about the buffalo.

Logical-Mathematical: Students write word problems based on their own height, width, and weight as compared to that of the buffalo. Using the average length of a buffalo as a "unit of measure," how long is their classroom? How tall is the school?

Musical: Students turn the poem they wrote during the Linguistic activity into a song or rap about the buffalo and perform it for the class.

Spatial: Students may create a watercolor painting of a buffalo. They may superimpose a poem onto the painting. (See Linguistic above.)

Scaling the Miles

MI Context: This lesson is used during a unit on Lewis and Clark. Because map skills are a major component throughout our study of Lewis and Clark's journey, the students must learn to use an atlas' scale of miles in a variety of problem-solving situations.

Learner Outcomes: The students will learn to use the scale of miles on a map to determine distances.

Procedure:

1. Prepare, in advance, slips of paper with a city and its state printed on each one. Make a different city/state slip for each student.

2. Each student picks a slip and, using the atlas or U.S. map, finds his hometown (St. Louis, for instance) and the location of the city on his slip. The city on his slip of paper will be called the destination.

3. Each student will then cut a piece of string equal to the distance between their hometown and their destination.

4. Guide students through the process of using the scale of miles. Have them use a ruler to determine what scale is being used, (for example, one inch is equal to one hundred miles). Use both the standard English and the metric system of measurement.

5. Demonstrate how to measure the length of string on the ruler.

6. Ask students to divide into small groups to discuss how knowing the length in inches can help determine the actual distance in miles.

7. The children should determine the distance from their hometown to their destination and share the method they use to solve the problem. Each student records the strategy used to determine the distance.

8. Tape the length of string next to their written explanation.

9. Using the same method, the students determine which of the following routes was shorter for fur traders. How many miles were saved by choosing the shorter route?

   • From St. Louis to the Gulf of Mexico (down Mississippi River) around the southern tip of South America to Portland, Oregon.

   • From St. Louis to Portland, Oregon (by way of the Missouri and Columbia Rivers).

Logical-Mathematical
Primary
Social Studies

Materials:
String, scissors, atlases or maps, rulers, paper

Assessment / Reflection:
After determining which route is shorter, the students will present their findings to the class for discussion.

MI Extensions:
Interpersonal: Divide the class into two groups and debate whether mileage or terrain is a bigger factor in determining how long it would take to travel a route.

Intrapersonal: Ask the students to think about what they have learned about a scale of miles as a result of this activity. Individually, students make a list of at least five things they know now that they didn't know before.

Bodily-Kinesthetic: Divide the class into two groups to create two scales of miles. Each group decides how it will form the scale. Predict how far it is from one end of the hall to another for each group's scale. Measure, discuss and compare the results.

Linguistic: Write a postcard or letter to a friend telling them how to use a scale of miles.

Musical: In what way is a staff for music like a scale of miles for a map?

Spatial: Using the scale of one inch equals one foot, draw a "blueprint" of the classroom and its contents.

Rap That Place!

MI Context: This lesson and the extensions are a group of activities which will help students develop an understanding of the concept of place value, learning the names of the places and the procedural knowledge. For example, the students will trade ones for tens, tens for ones, tens for hundreds, and hundreds for tens.

Logical-Mathematical
Primary
Mathematics

Learner Outcomes: The students will use the "Place Value Rap" as a mnemonic to remember that there are ten digits in our number system and that place determines the value of the digit.

Procedure:

1. Introduce the song to the students after they have already been introduced to the concept of place values and the vocabulary of the song, for example, the word "digit."

2. Sun glasses and a baseball cap set the mood when the teacher performs the rap for the students!

3. Teach the rap to the class moving to the rhythm and keeping the beat. Perform it regularly during the study of place value.

Place Value Rap
The number of digits in our system is ten.
You will learn their value if you just begin.
There's a zero, there's a one, two, three, four,
Five, six, seven, eight, nine, no more.
Every digit has a value on its face;
And each digit has a value in its place.
Two can be two ones or two can be two tens.
Either way its two, the value just depends
On where you put it,
On where you put it.
The value just depends on where you put it.
Two tens are twenty and two ones are two.
When you use the proper place it's easy to do.

(Repeat)

That's a rap!

Materials:
Baseball cap, copies of the song for every student, sunglasses

Assessment / Reflection:
Do the students use the song on their own when working on place value?

MI Extensions:

Interpersonal: Students work in pairs and try to reach a sum of one hundred. Together they get five rolls on a die. After each roll, they must decide if they want the value of the digit on the die to be in the ones or the tens place.

Intrapersonal: Students write in their math journals and share what they think they understand and what they find confusing. If they are in the prewriting stage they can draw pictures and then explain their drawings.

Bodily-Kinesthetic: Use a sheet of butcher paper to create a large place value board. With a large die, roll a number. That many children are placed in the one's column. As more children are added, group them into tens by instructing them to link arms. When they become a ten, they move to the ten's column. Count forward and backward to zero asking questions along the way.

Linguistic: Read the book *101 Dalmatians* by Fran Manushkin to the class. Make one hundred and one little Dalmatians using the illustrations in the book as a guide. You can make them for the overhead or run them off. As you read each page, place the cut-out dogs on a place value board and count them. A piece of black construction paper would work or an overhead transparency. All the Dalmatians are found when you reach one hundred and one. The children practice trading ten ones for one ten and ten tens for one hundred.

Spatial: Using base ten blocks, build structures. After the structure is complete, the students tell their classmates about the structure and determine its value.

Here a Fraction, There a Fraction

Logical-Mathematical
Intermediate
Mathematics

MI Context: This lesson is used as an introduction to a unit on fractions, or after a preliminary introduction or exploration has occurred.

Learners Outcomes: Students will understand and analyze fractions through research at home, fraction statements and Venn diagrams.

Procedures:

1. Briefly discuss and draw pictures of various fractions in class. Encourage students to notice fraction situations all around them, such as one-half of the students are girls; one-fifth of the dictionaries are upside-down; three-sevenths of the people wearing blue jeans also have black hair.

2. Divide the students into pairs or small groups. Give each group ten minutes to create as many fraction statements as possible representing fractions in the classroom. Students may also illustrate these statements.

3. Bring the class together and share the groups' fraction statements. Discuss similarities and differences among the types of fractions used (tenths, fifths, thirds) and the items in the room (windows, lights, chairs). Reproduce student responses as examples for the following homework assignment:

   • Look around your house tonight.

   • Make at least ten observations about fractions in your home.

   • Draw a picture of each item you observe.

   • Write the fraction represented next to each item.

   • Use the fractions to create fraction statements.

   • Note the room or area of the house in which you discovered your fractions.

   Teachers may want students to complete this assignment in their journals or, in colored pencil, marker or crayon on white paper.

4. During class the next day, students read over their fraction statements and share their pictures.

5. Students create a table, chart or organized list of the items used in their fractions in relation to the room or area of house in which the fractions were located. For example, how many items were found in the kitchen? How many were in the bathroom and the kitchen? Were any fractions located in the hall?

6. Ask for volunteers to discuss the items and the rooms involved in their fraction statements. Record the corresponding number of people also having this same information on the overhead projector or chalkboard.

7. Ask students to analyze the data, focusing on the following questions:

   • What statement(s) can you make from analyzing these data?

   • Are there any areas of the home not represented in this list? Why?

   • Are there any items found in most homes which are not represented? Why?

   • Could you create the mean (average), mode (occurs most often) and median (middle) from this data? Are the numbers accurate? Why or why not?

8. Divide the class into partners or small groups to create Venn diagrams. Each Venn diagram should represent information from each group members' fraction statements and research. All diagrams must include, a title and label for each circle, several pictures, at least three true fraction statements referring to information on the Venn diagram and group members' names. Students must share ideas among group members and determine the format of their group's Venn diagram. Things to consider are the rooms or areas of the house that should be represented in the Venn diagram, the number of circles, the best title for the diagram, items to be placed outside the circles, pictures to be included and the fraction statements to be included.

9. Groups will present the "Fractions in Your Home" Venn diagrams and fraction statements to the class, allowing each group member to discuss a portion of the presentation. Students are given an opportunity to ask other groups questions about their Venn diagrams.

10. Display the groups' work once the presentations have taken place.

Materials:
Pencils, notebook paper, construction paper, markers

Assessment / Reflection:
Students will write a journal entry in their math journals evaluating their group's diagram and presentation, as well as their personal contribution to the group.

MI Extensions:
Interpersonal: Share your journal entry (assessment/reflection) and/or your responses to the intrapersonal extension with another classmate. Discuss any similarity and difference the two of you had.

Intrapersonal: Determine your present level of understanding about fractions, having done this activity, versus your level of knowledge prior to the activity.

Bodily-Kinesthetic: Exhibit body movements for fractions (for example, one and one-half steps forward, four hops to the right).

Linguistic: Write and illustrate a story which includes as many fraction statements as possible.

Musical: Compose a song about the fraction statements you've written.

Spatial: Draw or paint a picture showing a fraction room or fraction house.

The Westing Game
Fractions

Logical-Mathematical
Intermediate
Language Arts

MI Context: This lesson is used during the study of the novel *The Westing Game* by Ellen Raskin. There are sixteen people in the story who are playing a game, a number which lends itself nicely to the exploration of fractions.

Learner Outcomes: Each student will identify fractions as part of a whole, add and subtract fractions with like denominators and explore equivalent fractions.

Procedure:

1. After all sixteen characters have been introduced, each student takes a 12" X 18" sheet of paper to evenly divide into sixteen pieces. Once the paper has been divided and cut, each of the sixteen names is written on a separate small section of paper. These cards will be manipulated by the students throughout the remainder of the fraction activities.

2. Small group exploration will take place with students using each *Westing Game* card to represent one-sixteenth of the group of characters. Students will be encouraged to use fraction language, being introduced to such terms as the groups generate them. They will discover what happens when the sixteen cards are put into groups of various sizes (equivalent fractions), and figure out the total size of the group, in relation to the entire group, when cards are added or taken away.

3. For homework, students will be given story problems to solve about the story characters. Each student chooses one story problem to solve and prove independently in at least two ways.

4. During the next class, solutions and proofs to problems are shared in small groups. Students work with others who chose the same problem. Each group writes on chart paper a list of strategies that were used to solve the problem. They will also be asked to make generalizations about fractions from their explorations to this point. Charts are displayed around the room, and the information from the small groups is shared with the class.

5. Homework is to create five story problems using *The Westing Game* characters.

6. In class the following day, stories will be shared and solved. Some stories can be given as homework, again including a variety of levels of difficulty.

Materials:
12" X 18" sheets of construction paper, chart paper, scissors, copies of *The Westing Game,* paper

Assessment/Reflection:
Informally, observe explorations and interactions while the students work in small groups. Evaluate the homework assignments. Have each student write about her explorations including information about insights gained, parts that were difficult and parts that were easy.

MI Extensions:

Interpersonal: On the day the students dress as a character from the story, pair the students up and have them create a scene, interacting as the characters would have in the novel.

Intrapersonal: Each student chooses one *Westing Game* character and compares herself to that character by means of a Venn Diagram.

Bodily-Kinesthetic: Each student becomes a *Westing Game* character for the day. She comes to school dressed as that character and acts as that character would act. Others guess who each student is by observing actions and clothing and listening to dialogue.

Linguistic: Each student creates "Who Am I?" riddles about the *Westing Game* characters. Riddles are exchanged, answered and shared by classmates.

Musical: Choose a concert or radio station that the student's favorite character would listen to and explain why that character would make that choice.

Spatial: Create a mind map to show connections between the characters.

Westing Game Fractions

Use your **Westing Game** fraction cards to solve these story problems. Write all your equations in fraction language.

1. Mrs. Crow went to a restaurant. Otis followed her, Sandy followed him, Sydelle followed him and Denton followed her. A half-hour later, Chris joined them. All the Wexlers had gone to James Shin Hoo's restaurant. All of the Hoo family was also at Shin Hoo's restaurant. The Theodorakis family sat in their restaurant wondering where Chris was. Everyone else was home in their rooms. What fraction of the heirs were in their rooms?

2. James Hoo and Gracie W. catered a party in Hoo's on First. Everyone in Sunset Towers came. Flora Baumbach and Turtle left because they were going to find out about the stock market. Then Sandy and J.J. left. What fraction of the heirs were left in the restaurant?

3. James Shin Hoo was having a big party in his restaurant. Everyone came. Angela, Theo, Madame Hoo, Doug Hoo, and Jake Wexler left. Doug came back right when Turtle left. What fraction of the heirs were in Shin Hoo's restaurant?

4. Doug was running laps when Theo joined him. Then Chris came to wheel himself around the track. Chris left after half an hour because his arms were tired. If Sandy, Jake, and Otis came, what fraction of the heirs would be running?

5. Angela, Grace, and Turtle were at Angela's party with some of Grace's friends. Suddenly a bomb went off, and eight of the heirs rushed over to help them. Then four of the heirs left. What fraction of the heirs were still at the party?

Restaurants and Percents

MI Context: The students have been exposed to numerous activities to help them with conceptual understanding and the relationships of fractions, decimals, and percentages. Preceding this lesson, the students have been involved with an activity that requires them to discuss reasonable and unreasonable tips, and to use mental math and estimation for finding the tips, the concept being to find the percent of a number.

Learner Outcomes: Students will design attractive menus which contain food items with descriptions and logical prices. They will order from different restaurants, trying not to spend more than $125. Students will calculate the bills from their own restaurants, finding tax and tip. Students find the totals for their expenses and profits. Students write checks out to the restaurants where they ate.

Procedure:
1. The teacher needs to take time to give a quick overview of the outcomes and clearly state instructions for the first step, that of creating the menus. As homework, each student must design a menu for a restaurant. The food items on the menu must have descriptions. The importance of this part is stressed. There is discussion about adjectives and attractive words versus plain words, and the students generate examples so everyone has a clear understanding about the expectations before leaving the class. The prices need to be realistic; however, it's the students' choice if they want to have inexpensive or expensive restaurants. (See the example of a student's menu at the end of this lesson.)

2. Students bring their menus to class. The class divides into groups of six. Each student has $125 to spend, and will order from the five restaurants represented in his group. Students may also order from their own restaurants, and it's free.

3. Students must order at least one thing from each of the five restaurants, leave no less than a ten percent tip at each one, pay tax at each restaurant (an amount that the class has determined ahead of time) and spend as much of the $125 as possible without overspending. There are penalties for those students who spend over the amount. This is figured at the end when the students find the total amount of money spent at other restaurants and the amount of money spent at their own restaurant.

4. Students break into their groups and begin ordering from each others' restaurants. They must write the quantity and name of item on the order form. They also need to write the tip percentage they want to leave at each

place on an order form for each restaurant. This usually takes one or two class periods. As they are ordering, they are also writing down estimates of their spending on a piece of scratch paper to help them keep track of their total expenditure.

5. When the students are finished ordering, they give all the order forms back to the restaurant owners. The owners complete the forms by writing the prices of the food items, and then they use calculators to figure the sub-total, tax, tip, and grand total. The owner then completes the order form summary sheet.

6. You may want to have the customers recheck the bills to make sure they agree with the owners' calculations before moving on. This step takes a con-siderable amount of time and some confusion on the students' part if clear instructions on how to deal with the errors aren't given. To prevent students from rushing through calculating the bills, inform them there is a penalty of two dollars for each bill that has an error. This money is taken from their profit, not from their $125 they started with to use at the restaurants.

7. The students complete the profit and expense sheets.

8. Students write checks out to the restaurants from which they ordered.

Materials:
Worksheets, paper, pencil, art supplies

Assessment / Reflection:
How many students were assessed penalties for overspending? In their jour-nals, have the students list strategies they could have used to avoid penalties.

MI Extensions:
Interpersonal: The students must share the $125 with a partner so all the decisions are being made jointly.

Intrapersonal: Students complete a self-reflection page. They critique their menus and discuss the positive and negative aspects of the activity.

Bodily-Kinesthetic: Transform the classroom into a restaurant complete with cooks, waiters, waitresses, and bus boys.

Linguistic: Explain on paper using words rather than numbers how one calculates the tip or the tax for one of the menus.

Logical-Mathematical: Students bring in one item from their menus and divide it into enough servings for everyone in the class. The students choose what samples they want to eat, and the whole class computes the bill for what was eaten, including the tax and tip. Assume that each serv-ing is a full serving and use the prices off their menus.

Musical: Students create a jingle to go along with their restaurant and sing it before the ordering begins in each group.

Spatial: Design a billboard for your restaurant.

ANDY'S VEGETARIAN DELIGHT

Solid Appetizers

Cold Veggie Medley	$2.25
Mushroom Caps in Garlic & Soy Sauce	$3.50
Cold Noodle Spoodle (Andy's Special)	$3.00
Hot Noodle Spoodle (Andy's Hot Special)	$3.00

Liquid Soups

Chilled Idaho Swimmers	$3.75
Drowned Hot Potato	$3.75
Leeking Coconut	$4.00
Vegetable (Of course!)	$3.25
No Bologna Minestrone	$3.95
Squashed Yellow (Splat!)	$3.50

Leafy Salads

Blooming Salad With Fresh Wild Flowers	$4.75
Nutty Evergreens (Greens With Pine Nuts)	$5.75
No Chicken Chef Salad (Ask your server for ingredients of the day.)	$5.50
Dinner Salad	$2.25

Dressings: Ranch, 1000 Island, Creamy Italian, Oil & Vinegar, Honey Dijon or Poppy Seed.

Dinners

Zucchini Linguine Sliced fresh zucchini served over a bed of linguine noodles topped with a yummy sauce	$11.50
Eeny Meeny Tortellini Stuffed with good healthy veggies; mozzarella, provel and romano cheeses	$12.25
Teeny Weeny Fettuccine Baby carrots, baby snap peas, baby corns and other youngin's snoozing in a fettuccine cradle	$12.50
Wheel of Wonder A pizza topped with 7 wondrous vegetables of your choice (9")	$8.50
Fat Spud An overweight potato stuffed with all your favorite brainless foods	$6.75

Liquids (not soups)

Coffee or tea (hot or not)	$1.00
Soft Drinks: Cola, Diet Cola or Andy's Favorite Root Beer	$1.25
V-8 (a drinker's salad)	$1.50
Cow Juice (with/without chocolate)	$ .50

Desserts

Frozen Mozen	$3.50
Frozen Applesauce	$2.75
Apple Pie (just like mom's)	$2.50
With a huge scoop of ice cream	$3.50

A practical guide designed by the faculty of The New City School ©1994

Name: _____   Date: _____

Restaurants and Percents

Order Form - Summary Sheet	
Restaurant:	
Owner:	
Customer 1	
Customer 2	
Customer 3	
Customer 4	
Customer 5	
Total Amount of $ Collected:	

Name: _____   Date: _____

Restaurants and Percents

Order Form		
Restaurant:		
Customer:		
QUANTITY	ITEM	PRICE

SUB-TOTAL:_____

TAX:_____

TIP:_____

TOTAL:_____

A practical guide created by the faculty of The New City School ©1994

Name: _____   Date: _____

Restaurants and Percents

Expense Sheet	
Customer:	
Bill 1	
Bill 2	
Bill 3	
Bill 4	
Bill 5	
Total Amount of $ Spent	
Balance:	

Name: _____   Date: _____

Restaurants and Percents

Penalty Sheet

PENALTY 1
(over spending)

$ .01 - $10.00   = 10%
$10.01 - $20.00   = 15%
$20.01 - $30.00 = 20%
$30.01 and up   = 30%

Amount over $125   _____

Penalty Amount   _____

PENALTY 2
(calculation errors)
$2.00 for every bill that had errors.

Number of errors   _____

Penalty Amount   _____

A practical guide created by the faculty of The New City School ©1994

Name: _____ Date: _____

Restaurants and Percents
Profit Sheet

NAME:

Profit
From Restaurant . . . . _____

Dining Account Balance . . . . . _____

BALANCE: _____

Less Penalty 1
(over spending) . . . . _____

Less Penalty 2
(calculation errors) . . . . _____

BALANCE: _____

Activities to Support the Logical-Mathematical Intelligence

Interpersonal
- Plexirs

- Board games

- Strategy games

- Cooperative skill building

- Problem-solving

Intrapersonal
- Estimate/Predict

- Use deductive reasoning

- Write in math journals

- Create your own story problems from your life experiences

- Identify math problems you deal with in your own life

Bodily-Kinesthetic
- Orienteering

- Duration activities

- Building and constructing with blocks

- Using your body for constructing graphs, Venn diagrams, patterning and people sorting

- Determining probability by shooting basketballs or rolling dice

Linguistic
- Thinking strategies (for example, *Mind Benders* by Anita Harnadek)

- Time lines

- Statistical analysis to create story problems

- Computer programming

- Students make up the problem when given the answer

Musical
- Create your own time signatures and musical notations

- Put number problems to music

- Turn logic stories into chants or raps

- Play instruments by following different time signatures

- Clap patterns and rhythms

Spatial
- Manipulatives like Unifix cubes, Cuisenaire rods, pattern blocks, geo-solids and geo boards

- Puzzles and mazes

- Story mapping

- Tessellations

- Tangrams

Identifying the Logical-Mathematical Intelligence in Your Students

Children function at many different levels within the intelligences. Through observation of everyday activities, one can create a profile showing the level of functioning within a particular intelligence and the intelligences in relation to each other. The levels described show increased engagement and proficiency. Use this record-keeping page to obtain a richer picture of a child

Appreciates:

YES	NO

Consistently demonstrates interest, respect and enjoyment within the intelligence and is able to differentiate qualities

Shows curiosity about numbers, shapes, patterns and relationships

Shows an interest in how things work

Listens to math stories and notices numbers

Sees patterns and relationships in the environment (for example, brick walls or spelling patterns)

Performs:

Applies the intelligence to recreate an exhibit or demonstration or problem solve within a given situation

Demonstrates skill in the use of numbers, shapes, patterns and relationships in problem solving

States the problem

Demonstrates "How to..."

Takes a survey and incorporates the data into a graph

Uses information to solve a problem

Notices and counts the children who are absent

Independently gets and uses resources to solve a problem

Creates rhythm patterns

Recognizes math concepts outside the math context

Creates:

Applies this intelligence to generate original work or to develop unique solutions to problems or create prototypes.

Develops a new problem or strategy

Designs a new game format

Forms hypotheses and develops own experiments and proofs

Creates a new type of graph to show information

A practical guide created by the faculty of The New City School ©1994

Math Journal

Something I learned today...

Something I did well...

Something easy...

Something hard...

Something I didn't understand...

Something I did to help...

I wish I...

I found the right tool to...

I saw a pattern...

I predicted...

I estimated...

I organized...

I graphed...

I measured...

I explored...

I made...

I found...

I explained...

I completed...

I made a connection...

I cooperated...

I thought of a new strategy...

When I find an answer I feel...

My plan for tomorrow is...

Something I learned recently in math...

Math is easy when...

Math is hard when...

I wish my teacher would...

I wish my teacher wouldn't...

Something in math I don't understand...

Something in math I'd like to learn...

I feel best about math when...

Skill(s) that I enjoyed learning:

Skill(s) that I had to work harder to learn:

A practical guide created by the faculty of The New City School ©1994

Children's Resources

Books and Recordings:

Aker, Suzanne. *What Comes In 2's, 3's and 4's?* Simon and Schuster Books for Young Readers, 1990. ★

Allen, Pamela. *Who Sank the Boat?* Coward-McCann, 1983. ★

Anno, Mitsumasa. *Anno's Counting Book.* HarperCollins, 1992. ★

Anno, Mitsumasa. *Anno's Counting House.* Philomel, 1982. ★

Anno, Mitsumasa. *Anno's Math Games.* Philomel, 1987.

Anno, Mitsumasa. *Anno's Mysterious Multiplying Jar.* Philomel, 1983. ★

Anno, Mitsumasa. *Topsy-Turvies.* Walker/Weatherhill, 1970. ★

Bang, Molly. *Ten, Nine, Eight.* Scholastic Inc., 1983 ★

Base, Graeme. *The Eleventh Hour.* Harry N. Abrams, Inc., 1989. ★

Blocksma, Mary. *Reading the Numbers.* Penguin Books, 1989.

Brett, Jan. *Goldilocks and the Three Bears.* Dodd Mead, 1987 ★ .

Briggs, Raymond. *Jim and the Beanstalk.* Coward-McCann, 1970. ★

Carle, Eric. *Rooster's off to See the World.* Picture Book Studio, 1972. ★

Carle, Eric. *The Secret Birthday Message.* Harper Trophy, 1986. ★

Carle, Eric. *Very Hungry Caterpillar.* Philomel, 1987. ★

Crew, Donald. *10 Black Dots.* Greenwillow Books, 1986. ★

Crews, Donald. *School Bus.* Mulberry Books, 1993. ★

Dee, Ruby. *Two Ways to Count to Ten.* Henry Holt and Co., 1990. ★

Dunbar, Joyce. *Ten Little Mice.* Harper Brace Jovanovich, 1990. ★

Ehlert, Lois. *Planting a Rainbow.* Harcourt Brace Jovanovich, 1988. ★

Feelings, Muriel. *Moja Means One.* Dial Books for Young Readers, 1976. ★

Galdone, Paul. *The Three Billy Goats Gruff.* Seabury, 1973. ★

Giganti, Paul Jr. *How Many Snails.* Greenwillow Books, 1988. ★

Goldberg, Hirsch M. *The Book of Lies - History's Greatest Fakes, Frauds, Schemes, and Scams.* Quill/William Morrow, 1990.

Gretz, Susanna. *Teddy Bears Go Shopping.* Puffin Books, 1983. ★

Haber, Louis. *Black Pioneers of Science and Invention.* Harcourt, Brace & Jovanovich, 1970.

Hague, Kathleen. *Numbears.* Henry Holt and Co., 1986. ★

Hartman, Gail. *As the Crow Flies: A First Book of Maps.* Bradbury Press, 1991.

Haskins, Jim. *Count Your Way Through Africa.* Carolrhoda Books, 1992. ★

★ indicates a picture book

Haskins, Jim. *Count Your Way Through China.* Carolrhoda Books, 1987. ★

Haskins, Jim. *Count Your Way Through Italy.* Carolrhoda Books, 1989. ★

Hoban, Tana. *Shapes, Shapes, Shapes.* Greenwillow Books, 1986. ★

Hoffman, Mary. *Amazing Grace.* Dial Press, 1991. ★

Hubbard, Woodleigh. *Two Is for Dancing.* Chronicle Books, 1991. ★

Humez, Alexander and Humez, Nicholas and Maguire, Joseph. *Zero to Lazy Eight - The Romance of Numbers.* Simon and Schuster, 1993.

Hutchins, Pat. *1 Hunter.* Greenwillow Books, 1982. ★

Hutchins, Pat. *Changes, Changes.* Collier Macmillan, 1987. ★

Hutchins, Pat. *The Doorbell Rang.* Mulberry Books, 1989. ★

Kitamuro, Satoshi. *When Sheep Cannot Sleep.* Farrar, Straus, Giroux, 1986. ★

Langstaff, John. *Over in the Meadow.* Harcourt Brace Jovanovich, 1957. ★

Lepscky, Ibi. *Albert Einstein.* Barron's, 1992. ★

Lionni, Leo. *Inch by Inch.* Astor-Honor, 1960. ★

Lord, John. *Giant Jam Sandwich.* Houghton Mifflin, 1972. ★

MacDonald, Suse. *Numblers.* Dial Books for Young Readers, 1988. ★

Mack, Stan. *Ten Bears in My Bed.* Pantheon, 1974. ★

Manushkin, Fran. *101 Dalmatians: A Counting Book.* Disney Press, 1991. ★

Marzolla, Jean. *I Spy.* Scholastic Inc., 1992. ★

McKissack, Patricia. *A Million Fish More or Less.* Alfred A. Knopf, 1992. ★

McMillan, Bruce. *Eating Fractions.* Scholastic Inc., 1991. ★

McPhail, David. *Lost.* Little, Brown and Co., 1990. ★

Mohy, Margaret. *17 Kings and 42 Elephants.* Dial Books for Young Readers, 1990. ★

Moore, Lilian. *My First Counting Book.* Golden Book, 1956. ★

Morozumi, Atsuko. *One Gorilla.* Farrar, Straus, Giroux, 1990. ★

Munsch, Robert. *Moira's Birthday.* Annick Press Ltd., 1987. ★

Numeroff, Laura. *If You Give a Mouse a Cookie.* HarperFestival, 1992. ★

Oppenheim, Joanne. *Left and Right.* Harcourt Brace Jovanovich, 1989. ★

Pallotta, Jerry. *The Icky Bug Counting Book.* Charlesbridge, 1992. ★

Pinczes, Elinor J. *One Hundred Angry Ants.* Houghton Mifflin, 1993. ★

Raskin, Ellen. *The Westing Game.* Puffin Books, 1992.

Sachar, Louis. *Sideways Arithmetic From Wayside School.* Scholastic Inc., 1989.

Saunders, Hal. *When Are We Ever Gonna Have to Use This? - Updated Third Edition.* Dale Seymour, 1988.

Schwartz, David M. *How Much is a Million.* Lothrop, Lee and Shepard Books, 1985. ★

Schwartz, David M. *If You Made a Million.* Lothrop, Lee and Shepard Books, 1989. ★

Shannon, George. *Stories to Solve: Folktales From Around the World.*
   Beech Tree, 1991.

Tompert, Ann. *Grandfather Tang's Story.* Crown Publishers, 1990. ★

Tudor, Tasha. *Bedtime Book.* Platt and Munk, 1977. ★

Viorst, Judith. *Alexander, Who Used To Be Rich Last Saturday.*
   Aladdin, 1988. ★

Games:

"Abalone Galoob." Abalone Games Corp., 1989.

"Body Bingo." Lakeshore, 1993.

"Boggle Junior Math." Parker Brothers, 1993.

"Candyland Bingo." Milton Bradley, 1984.

"Chess." Pavillion, Geoffry Inc., 1989.

"Chinese Checkers: Classic Game." Golden: Western Pub. Co., Inc., 1989.

Color and Shape Bingo." Trend Enterprises, Inc., 1984.

"Color and Shape Lotto." Trend Enterprises, Inc., 1985.

"Little, Big, Medium: Discovering Opposites." Creative Toys, 1990.

"Mastermind." Invicta, 1976.

"Perfection." Lakeshore, 1975.

"Somebody: The Human Anatomy Game." Artistoplay, Ltd, 1990.

"The Original Memory Game." Milton Bradley, 1989.

"What's for Dinner?" Rapid Mounting and Fishing Co., 1989.

"Where in the USA is Carmen Sandiego?" University Games, 1993.

Teachers' Resources

Anderson and Bereites. *Thinking Games.* Fearon, 1980.

Baker, Ann and Baker, Johnny. *Raps and Rhymes in Math.* Heinemann, 1991.

Baratta-Lorton, Mary. *Mathematics Their Way.* Addison Wesley, 1976.

Braddon, Kathryn and Hall, Nancy and Taylor, Dale. *Math Through Children's Literature: Making the NCTM Standards Come Alive.* Teacher Ideas Press, 1993.

Burk, Donna. *Box It or Bag It Mathematics.* Basset Press, 1988.

Burnam, Tom. *The Dictionary of Misinformation.* Harper and Row, 1975.

Burns, Marilyn. *A Collection of Math Lessons.* Math Solutions, 1988.

Burns, Marilyn. *Math for Smarty Pants.* Little, Brown and Co., 1982.

Burns, Marilyn. *The Book of Think.* Little Brown and Co., 1976.

Burns, Marilyn. *The I Hate Mathematics Book.* Little Brown and Co., 1975.

Butzow, Carol. *Science Through Children's Literature.* Teacher's IdeasPress, 1989.

Grimm, Gary and Mitchell, Dan. *The Good Apple Math Book.* Good Apple, 1975.

Harnadek, Anita. *Warm-Up Mind Benders.* Midwest Publications, 1979.

Macy, Sue. "Bison Americanus: America's Great Shaggy Beast." Cobblestone, Vol. 2, Number 8, August 1981.

Moscovich, Ivan. *Fiendishly Difficult Math Puzzles.* Sterling, 1991.

Palmer, Hap. *Learning Basic Skills Through Music, Vol. I.* Educational Activities, AR 514.

Read, Ronald C. *Tangrams - 330 Puzzles.* Dover Publications, Inc., 1965.

Reimer, Luetta and Reimer, Wilbert. *Mathematicians Are People, Too; Stories From the Lives of Great Mathematicians.* Dale Seymour Publications, 1990.

Russell, Stone. *Used Numbers.* Dale Seymour Publishing, 1990.

Sloane, Paul. and MacHale, Des. *Challenging Lateral Thinking Puzzles.* Sterling Pub., 1993.

Stenmark, Jean. and Thompson, U. and Casson, R. *Family Math.* Lawerence Hall of Science, 1986.

Thiessen, Diane. *The Wonderful World of Mathematics- A Critically Annotated List of Children's Books in Mathematics.* NCTM, 1992.

Welchman-Tischler, Rosamond. *How to Use Children's Literature to Teach Mathematics.* NCTM, 1992.

Whitin, David and Wilde, Sarah. *Read Any Good Math Lately?* Heinemann, 1992.

Chapter 6:
The Musical Intelligence

*Contributors: Sally Boggeman, Joe Corbett, Mary F. Daly,
Diane Davenport, Bonnie L. Frank, Monette Gooch-Smith,
Christine Wallach, Denise A. Willis*

*"Where there's music
there can be no evil."*
Miguel De Cervantes

A practical guide created by the faculty of The New City School ©1994

Web of the Musical Intelligence

Student quotes

"I think my greatest intelligence is Musical because I like to act, sing and put on shows."

"I'm Musical because I play a few instruments and every day I sing a song in my head."

"I hum and dance all the time, everywhere."

List of characteristics

- Remembers melodies
- Enjoys listening
- Keeps beats
- Makes up their own songs
- Mimics beat and rhythm
- Notices background and environmental sounds
- Differentiates patterns in sounds
- Is sensitive to melody and tone
- Moves body when music is playing

Famous people

Henry Mancini wrote musical themes for television and movies.

Marian Anderson is considered the greatest contralto of her generation and one of the golden voices of the century.

Midori is an international violinist and recording artist.

Paul McCartney changed the direction of modern music during the sixties and continues to perform internationally.

Adult quote

"Music expresses that which cannot be said and on which it is impossible to be silent."

Victor Hugo

Musical Intelligence... Sounds Good to Me!

by Diane Davenport

Picture this...an inservice session dealing with implementation of the Multiple Intelligences (MI) Theory. One of the new components of the assessment related to the classroom is an MI Profile for the students. The teacher evaluates the students' involvement with all of the intelligences as they are displayed in the classroom or at recess. Many teachers feel comfortable assessing most of the intelligences except, yes—you guessed it—musical! As the performing arts teacher, my mission is to help teachers understand that they can foster the musical intelligence in their students even though the teachers may think, "I can't carry a tune." or "I am not musical."

Musical Intelligence in the Classroom

Opportunities for offering musical experiences in the classroom connect very naturally with many components of the curriculum. Musical Intelligence means the ability to produce and appreciate rhythm, pitch and timbre; to appreciate forms of musical expression; to be sensitive to melody and time; to be able to hear and remember, to master and produce musical sequence; to notice background and environmental sounds; to sing well; to play instruments; and to recognize and recall many songs or melodies. Do not be afraid of these descriptors, because music can be more simply understood by looking at a very simple definition. Consider: "Music is organized sound. It is the interaction of sound and silence in time and space." How can we apply this definition to the classroom and our daily activities? The mind map may assist in helping one see the relationships to the other intelligences. (See following page.)

Opportunities for offering musical experiences in the classroom connect very naturally with many components of the curriculum.

All Curriculum Can Be Related to Music

Music can be easily connected to the language arts and social studies curricula. When used to enhance experiences in listening, awareness, vocabulary development and language in the oral and written tradition, we can enhance the Musical and Linguistic Intelligences. Music is a natural component of social studies, especially when the expressions of many cultures are explored. Sound, vibration, meter, pattern...what is the connection? As we explore, let us use these connections; let us look at the following elements of sound: dynamics, rhythm, form, pitch, harmony and melody. To understand each element is to be able to apply the world of sound to our creative classroom. A lack of musical background need not be an obstacle. Teachers can still introduce students to these elements in their classroom. Here are some activities to begin using as connections:

When used to enhance experiences in listening, awareness, vocabulary development and language in the oral and written tradition, we can enhance the Musical and Linguistic Intelligences.

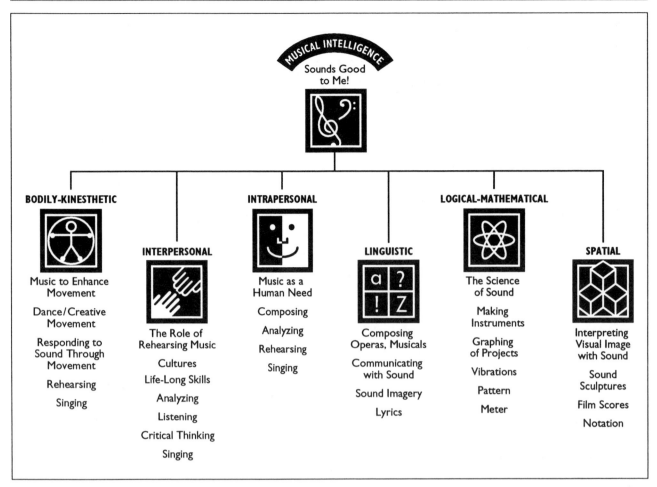

1. The teacher plays a drum, gradually varying the dynamic levels. A circle of children responds by moving closer to the center as the sound get softer (smaller) and widening out as the sound gets louder (bigger).

2. One child goes out of the room and a small object is hidden. She is called back and the classmates guide her to the object with handclaps. When close, they clap louder; as she moves farther away the claps get softer.

3. Choose different styles of music for the children to listen to. As they listen, have them demonstrate the changes in dynamics by moving their bodies in a strong or weak manner.

Rhythm: Pulses Organized Into Regular and Irregular Groupings

1. The teacher, and later a child, begins to walk in a steady rhythm and the children clap an accompaniment to the steps. If the child changes to a faster or slower pace, the clapping must adjust quickly to match it. Small percussion instruments can be used to accompany the steps.

2. This activity helps the child to understand pattern related to rhythm. Each child is given a piece of grid paper. They are to create a visual pattern by placing an "x" in different squares. Remind them that they are to create a pattern with the placement of their "x's." When they are finished, each child will then perform his own pattern by first clapping each x and

being silent in the empty squares. They can then choose percussion instruments with which to perform their compositions. (With smaller children, I would have the squares drawn out on a large piece of paper and have the group design a pattern together.)

3. Have the students bring in empty food containers that have rhythmical names, i.e. cereal boxes, pasta boxes, soup labels, or juice cans. Have them create rhythmic chants or raps based on these products. This could be recorded and an instrumental accompaniment could be added.

Form: Similar and Contrasting Segments

1. The repetitive pattern in music and literature can be explored for its particular "form." As you read a story to the children, emphasize the recurrence of certain words or portions of the story. Listen then for repeated melodic or rhythmic patterns in music. Some examples are "Chicka Chicka Boom Boom," "Follow the Drinking Gourd," and "Get Along, Little Dogies."

2. The students will listen for examples of ballad style in songs. Discuss what a ballad is by having the students think of a favorite story. They should pretend they are singing the story just as the old minstrels did a long time ago. In free or rhyming verse, the story can be retold, some listening examples are "Bojangles," "The Cat's in the Cradle," and "My Dolly."

Pitch: The Highness or Lowness of Sound

1. One or more children sit in the center of a circle with a pile of blocks, small boxes or a stacking toy. The teacher strikes high or low pitched tones on a melody instrument, pausing after each one. A block is added to the tower when a high note is heard, then removed when a low tone is heard. Alternate, choosing among the children often, encouraging those who are waiting to observe carefully for practice.

2. A piece of thick yarn or a jump rope is held, stretched out between two children who must react to the high or low tones played by moving the rope up or down. The rest of the children walk under the high tones and jump over the low ones.

Timbre: The Quality of Sound Determined by the Source

1. The children sit in a circle. They are told to close their eyes. The teacher will make three different sounds. The children are to name the sounds as they were heard in order. This activity can be expanded very easily.
2. Make sound cards by collecting and mounting pictures of objects that have interesting sound qualities on individual oak tag boards. Show these pictures to the children and ask them to make a sound as if the picture were to come alive. Encourage the children to make sound compositions by organizing the cards.
3. Explore your voice by sending it into a bottle or through a brick wall, an electric fan or a narrow tunnel. Use your voice to write your name, blow out a candle, conduct an orchestra, knock over a chair, stampede an elephant or quiet a baby.

Harmony: Two or More Sounds Happening Simultaneously

1. Create a soundscape to enhance a mood, poem or place. Experiment with different sound sources to create different effects. If you have time you can notate your composition.

2. List the sounds you might hear in a Brazilian rain forest, in a space shuttle, at a rock concert, in a desert, at a basketball game, at the zoo at night, at the beach, in the ocean, at the grocery store, or in the Grand Canyon.

There are many ways for children to explore sound. These suggestions are just a taste, something to whet your appetite. One activity that is easy is for the children to have the opportunity to "Play the Classroom." In this, the students are encouraged to use some type of beater and walk around the room striking it on different surfaces in the environment. After they have had some opportunity to explore, give them time to reflect on all of the different sounds they heard, discovered, and created. Each child should have an opportunity to share a sound. These sound sources could then be categorized, labeled and filed away as a creative resource in using sound images. This activity also reinforces their ability to differentiate between the sounds in their environment. Keep your ears open and your many intelligences will give you cues on ways to connect. Enjoy; there is so much to explore with children. Sounds good to me!

Sing One, Two, Three!

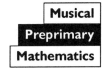

MI Context: This is a song that introduces the concept of counting forward and backward. It is also a song that can be used as a time-filler during transitions.

Learner Outcomes: Through number songs, students will develop the skill of counting forward and backward automatically.

Procedure:

1. Discuss with children what numbers are, why people need them, how they are used, where they can be found. Look for numerals around the room.

2. Make a list of all the number songs the class knows. Children can work in groups or independently. The songs can contain the word *number* or actual numbers. Post the list in the room.

3. Teach the song, "I Can Count" to the tune of "Are You Sleeping?"

   I Can Count

I can count.	*I can count,*
I can count,	*In Spanish,*
One, two, three,	*Uno, dos, tres,*
One, two, three.	*Uno, dos, tres.*
I can count backward,	*I can count backward,*
I can count backward,	*I can count backward,*
Three, Two, One,	*Tres, dos, uno,*
Three, Two, One.	*Tres, dos, uno.*

   Other options: French: *un, deux, trois.*
   Swahili: *moja, mbili, tatu.*
   Japanese: *ichi, ni, san.*

4. Add movement or motions while singing the song (for example, stand and stoop or hold up fingers).

5. Divide the class into small groups. Several groups play an instrument, such as rhythm sticks or bells, while one group sings the song. Switch. If you don't have access to instruments, children can snap, clap, hum, rub hands or use other body instruments.

6. Review the original number song list and encourage students to add more songs. Add to the list throughout the week.

Materials:
Chart paper, marker, musical instruments are optional

Assessment / Reflection:

Are children able to learn the song? Can they transfer the tune to other languages? Can they count forward and backward and sing the song as a solo, duet, trio.

MI Extensions:

Linguistic: Can you think of stories and games with numbers in the title? Make a number or counting book - one for each language.

Spatial: Make number collages. Write a number on a sheet of paper, then incorporate the number into a picture.

Musical: Record the songs from the number song list.

Interpersonal: Play Silent Pass. Form a circle and hold hands. Pass a ball from one person to the next until it goes completely around the circle. This game only has three rules. No talking, you must continue to hold hands and you must not let the ball touch the floor. How many people can pass the ball before it falls? Do the same activity with a very large ball and a small ball. It can also be played with a hula-hoop.

Bodily-Kinesthetic: Use your body to form the numerals one, two and three. This can be done with a partner. Make giant numbers with string or yarn. Make numbers on the sidewalk with chalk.

Intrapersonal: Write the numbers one, two and three on slips of paper. Each child selects one. Of what do you have one, two, or three?

Logical-Mathematical: Act out story problems that use the numbers one, two and three.

Digestion Song

MI Context: This lesson is part of the year long theme called "Busy Bodies." Throughout the year students explore units on body characteristics, the brain, the skeletal system, the muscular system, the respiratory system, the circulatory system and general physical well-being.

Learner Outcomes: Children will learn names and functions of some parts of the body's digestive tract.

Procedure:
1. Write the word "digestion" on the board and have the children try to pronounce it. To establish prior knowledge, brainstorm the answers to such questions as, "What is digestion?" "What could it be?" "What does it sound like?" Record the children's answers.

2. Teach the class the song about digestion using the tune to "The Wheels on the Bus." Tape record the children singing the song. After singing it a couple of times, again ask what they think digestion is.

3. Use other musical and movement activities to reinforce the song. Play musical instruments while singing the song and have part of the class dance while others sing the song. The dancers move like the parts as they are mentioned, i.e., tongue, teeth. Pantomime a piece of food as it moves through the digestive tract.

4. Children think about the song and movement activities and tell something they learned about digestion. Go back to the original brainstorming list and compare what they now know to what they knew then.

Materials:
Chalkboard, words to song written on chart paper, copy of the song for each child, musical instruments, tape recorder, crayons and paper

Assessment / Reflection:
As the children listen to the tape of their song, they draw the parts of the body as they are mentioned. Look at the drawings for content and accuracy. The children reflect and write about the movement and musical components of the activity.

MI Extensions:
Interpersonal: Working in pairs, use a stethoscope to listen to your partner's digestive tract as he eats a carrot. Listen at the cheek, throat and stomach. Discuss what the sounds bring to mind.

Intrapersonal: Each child chooses a part of the digestive tract. If that part could talk, what would it talk about and to whom? What does it like and dislike about its job and why?

Bodily-Kinesthetic: Play the Digestion Relay Race game. Players select a piece of plastic food to carry as they move from one place to another on a digestive tract placed on the floor.

Linguistic: Read the story *What Happens to Hamburger?* by Paul Showers. Discuss the carrot experiment mentioned in the book.

Logical-Mathematical: Give each pair or small group of children a hand held mirror. Children take turns counting their teeth. Does each child have the same number? How many teeth are there in the whole group? Sort the children by teeth!

Musical: Find other songs related to eating (for example, "Today is Monday"). Have children compose a song about their favorite food.

Spatial: Let children individually, or in groups, select one part of the digestive tract to paint and cut out. Bring together all the parts and display them or laminate them and use them as a floor puzzle.

Digestion Song

The teeth in my mouth chew, grind, tear,
chew, grind, tear, chew, grind, tear.
The teeth in my mouth chew, grind, tear,
whenever food is there.

The glands in my mouth squirt saliva,
squirt saliva, squirt saliva.
The glands in my mouth squirt saliva,
all day long.

The tongue in my mouth moves food down,
moves food down, moves food down.
The tongue in my mouth moves food down,
down the esophagus.

Esophagus takes it to my stomach,
to my stomach, to my stomach
Esophagus takes it to my stomach
and breaks down food much more.

The stomach takes food to my intestine,
to my intestine, to my intestine.
The stomach takes food to my intestine
the small, then the large.

That's how my body digests food,
digests food, digests food.
That's how my body digests food,
Every time I eat. YUM! YUM!

A practical guide created by the faculty of The New City School ©1994

Body Music

MI Context: This lesson is used during a study of instruments in the orchestra. The students practice rhythms and a symbolic representation of sound.

Learner Outcomes: Students will create a rhythm and develop a method, representing it on paper. Students will use their bodies to make sounds.

Procedure:

1. Read the story *I Like the Music* by Leah Komaiko. Discuss all the different ways of making music that were used in the story.

2. Challenge the students to think of ways to make sound with their bodies. Have them think of a way to illustrate the action. List the methods, i.e., draw hands for clapping, fingers for snapping, feet for stomping.

3. Use symbols to represent pauses and stops, i.e., X = stop, # = pause. Demonstrate a rhythm. Clap, clap, stomp, pause. Clap, clap, stomp, stop. This translates into Hands, hands, feet, #. Hands, hands, feet, X.

4. Take suggestions from students for rhythms and write them on the board. Children will read symbols and play body music. Children can take turns composing and recording music. After doing several rhythms, students will write their own patterns and the class will become an orchestra by playing body music.

Materials:
I Like the Music by Leah Komaiko, writing implements, paper, chalk board

Assessment / Reflection:
Were students able to write and play music using the symbols?

MI Extensions:
Interpersonal: Form a quartet and play a song on your body instrument.

Intrapersonal: Which instrument are you the most like and why? If you could learn to play any instrument, which one would it be and why? What did you feel like when you were playing the rhythms?

Bodily-Kinesthetic: Perform well known songs, i.e., "Happy Birthday" and "Twinkle, Twinkle Little Star" using body instruments.

Linguistic: Read *Orchestranimals* by Vlasta van Kampen. Tell the story while students use their bodies to create sound effects to interpret the story.

Logical Mathematical: Create repeating rhythms using body music.

Spatial: Write your own music using the symbols.

Sounds of the City

Musical
Primary
Language Arts

MI Context: Students from diverse communities need to develop an awareness and appreciation for the unique nature of the urban environment.

Learner Outcomes: Student will recognize the sounds of the city.

Procedure:
1. Elicit from students the sounds that are unique to an urban area and list these sounds on chart paper. Show pictures of different urban settings to enhance the activity. Some sounds that might be included in this list are airplanes, traffic, emergency sirens and street vendors.

2. Have students record city sounds on their empty playground if the school is located in an urban area. For homework, they could record city sounds from their neighborhoods or from the television.

3. Instruct the students to create a rhythm chant based on the sound word list created earlier and use the taped examples to enhance the mood of the chants. Percussion instruments may be used to accompany portions of the chants. Students perform their musical numbers for the class.

Materials:
Pictures of city scenes, tape recorders, cassette tapes, percussion instruments, chart paper, markers

Assessment / Reflection:
Are the students able to identify urban sounds? How are the sounds the students collected from the various locations the same and different? What generalizations are the students able to make from this information?

MI Extensions:
Interpersonal: Help the students develop an awareness of how these city sounds affect their relationships with others.

Intrapersonal: How do city sounds affect moods?

Bodily-Kinesthetic: Use movement to complement the compositions.

Linguistic: Read *Apt. 3* by Ezra Jack Keats. List all the sounds that are heard within the story and who made those sounds. Use the sound hints to determine who lives on each floor.

Logical-Mathematical: Collect data on the number of times specific sounds can be heard within a community. Interview people and graph their reactions to these sounds. Propose a hypothesis as to how the frequency of sounds might affect the lives of the people they interviewed.

Spatial: Create cityscape murals that capture the city and its sounds.

Pollination

MI Context: During a unit on plants and flowers, students explore pollination, photosynthesis, life cycle, seed dispersion. After extensive study, the students are given opportunities to demonstrate their understanding.

Musical
Primary
Science

Learner Outcomes: Students will use music and movement as a way to communicate their understanding of concepts associated with plant life.

Procedure:

1. Inform the students that they will use instruments and dance to create a performance that communicates one of the concepts they have been studying concerning plants, and that their performances will be videotaped.

2. Divide students into small groups. Have students discuss what concept they wish to communicate. Give each group a piece of chart paper which they are to use to create a movie poster that tells their title and lists the group members as actors and their roles in the drama. As they work on the poster, the students discuss their parts, create a performance plan and talk about the resources they will need to complete the project.

3. Students make or choose musical instruments that will accompany their performance and begin practice sessions.

4. When all groups are ready, or after an appropriate amount of time, the groups come together to perform. Each performance is captured on video tape.

Materials:
Chart paper, markers, musical instruments, junk to create instruments, video camera, video tape

Assessment / Reflection:
How accurately are the students able to communicate the concept they are portraying?

MI Extensions:
Interpersonal: On a scale of one to ten, students rate how well they contributed to the group. In addition, other group members rate each individual member of their group using the same scale. Each student compares the ratings for consistency.

Intrapersonal: Before the performance, each student creates a Likert scale. On one end is recorded what a performance would look and sound like if it was the student's personal best. At the other end is recorded what the performance would look and sound like if it was the worst. After the performance, each student rates his performance on the scale and looks for ways to improve. Students share their scales with one another and discuss strategies.

Bodily-Kinesthetic: Students do a performance using only their bodies to communicate a concept about plants.

Linguistic: Students write a review of their performance which explains how their movements and sounds represent the concept they are trying to communicate.

Logical-Mathematical: Are there certain instruments which lend themselves more to a particular concept? Classify the instruments with this idea in mind. Discuss the reasons for placing an instrument in a particular category.

Spatial: As the students watch the performances, have them draw the plant concept that they see and hear.

African Ceremonies

MI Context: This lesson is part of a focus on Swahili-speaking countries on the African continent.

Musical
Primary
Social Studies

Learner Outcomes: Children will gain insight into African ceremony and ritual by developing beats, rhythms, movements and chants. By using color, texture and design, they will create their own ceremonies.

Procedure:
This lesson occurs over a period of several days.

1. Read *Dancing Masks of Africa* by Christine Price. Have a child beat a drum as the story is being read.

2. Brainstorm ceremonies with which the students are familiar and list them on chart paper.

3. Look at real African masks or photos of masks.

4. Discuss such qualities of movement as sway, sustained and shake. Use percussion instruments to emphasize these movements.

5. Refer to the list of ceremonies that the students generated. Have students decide how percussion instruments and movement could convey the mood of the ceremonies on the list.

6. In "clans" of three or four, children choose a ceremony to enact. They decide what type of music, dance and chanting they want to incorporate.

7. Construct masks by tearing earth tone colored construction paper. Examine the rough edges of the paper and talk about how this gives the masks a primitive look. Embellish with shells, raffia and jingles. Tape sticks to the back of the masks so they can be held in front of the child's face.

8. Have "clans" perform their ceremonies for the rest of the class.

Materials:
Percussion instruments, markers, crayons, earth tone colored construction paper, glue, sticks, shells (cowy if possible), raffia, jingles, scissors, paper, pencils, chart paper, *African Designs of the Congo* by Caren Caraway, *Dancing Masks of Africa* by Christine Price

Assessment / Reflection:
Students ask questions and give feedback to the "clans" after each performance.

MI Extensions:

Interpersonal: Students fill out a reflection sheet about their role in the "clan." Each student will determine if he was cooperative, an active listener, willing to share, nice, helpful in solving problems and focused. Each is to be checked "yes, no, usually." After each child has filled out the form, he records how the students in his group perceived him. Using a crayon, he reads the list and marks where the group would have "rated" him without the group seeing his original markings. From this rating sheet, the child can set a goal for group work.

Intrapersonal: Each child chooses an event for which to create a ceremony. He develops music, movement and symbols that are meaningful.

Linguistic: Children keep a written record of their chants. All the chants are collected and made into a class book. Photos taken during the ceremonies are used to illustrate the chants.

Logical-mathematical: Students record the musical movement in the ceremony using color and shape patterns.

Spatial: To get a feel for lines, designs and colors, students color pictures as found in *African Designs of the Congo* by Caren Caraway.

When Words Sing

Musical
Intermediate
Language Arts

MI Context: This lesson can be used during the study of any historical period.

Learner Outcomes: The student will be able to see the relationship of pop music to current social needs. The student will be able to analyze the lyrics of popular songs.

Procedure:

1. As a group, have the students list contemporary social issues, i.e., material-istic values, ecology, love and commitment, loneliness and alienation, war and peace, respect for individual differences, technology.

2. After the list is made, display it prominently and ask students to bring in musical examples that focus on any of these issues. Students are told that the music must be appropriate for the classroom, and that the teacher will make the final decisions as to what is appropriate if there is a question.

3. Each student leads the group in a listening activity related to the music examples or the music can be placed in listening centers where the students individually respond by answering questions on a reflection sheet.

   • What is the title of the song?

   • Tell what the song is about?

   • Use phrases or sentences to write down poetic language from the song.

   • Listen for some colorful or strong words in the song.

   • Did you hear many rhyming words?

   • Could this song have another title? Is so, what?

   • What was the style of the musical example (blues, hip-hop, alternative, ballad, reggae, rap, zydeco)?

4. This lesson can be repeated throughout the year. Has the focus of issues changed?

Materials:
Chart paper, tape recorder or CD player, reflection sheets, musical examples

Assessment / Reflection:
Were the students able to match a social issue to a musical example? Was it valuable to analyze the words of a song? Did the students respect different musical styles?

MI Extensions:

Interpersonal: The students organize a panel discussion or debate to deliberate the issue of censorship of lyrics in pop music and freedom of speech.

Intrapersonal: Ask the students to determine which music speaks to them concerning social issues about which they are concerned. Do some artists and some types of music have a greater impact on their willingness to become involved in an issue and to begin action to make changes?

Bodily-Kinesthetic: Instruct the students to use their bodies to produce the images that songs bring to their minds.

Logical-Mathematical: Chart the top ten songs in the pop category over a period of time. Use newspapers or a news magazine to determine what social issue was most prevalent during that time. Create a frequency graph to show how often popular music addressed the concerns of the day.

Musical and Linguistic: The students compose a song related to a social issue. This could be done as a large group, small group or as an individual activity. Some students create the lyrics while others do the composing. The result is a collaboration of the two intelligences.

Spatial: Illustrate a song by creating a design for a CD or cassette cover or jacket.

The Music of Poetry

MI Context: This lesson is used during a unit on poetry.

Learner Outcomes: Students will explore the use of repetition, rhyme scheme and hard/soft sounds in poetry. They will also utilize these techniques in creating poems or music.

Procedure:

1. Read *An Invitation to the Butterfly Ball - A Counting Rhyme* by Jane Yolen to the class.

2. Discuss the effectiveness of the author's use of repetition, rhyme and hard/soft sounds.

   Identify the rhyme scheme used throughout the book, A-A-B-B...every two lines rhyming.

   Encourage students to explain the importance of repetition in the poem. At what point did they notice the refrain? When did they begin memorizing those lines?

   Determine which hard and soft sounds were used. Create a list and post it in the room. Which sounds were used most often?

3. Re-read the poem in its entirety, or just parts if necessary, for students to analyze these writing techniques.

4. Explore ways to create these hard/soft sounds with one's mouth, body, or through the use of common objects in the classroom, e.g., eraser, pencil, chair, computer keyboard, paperback book.

5. Ask which sounds are more pleasant to listen to and which are disturbing? Why? When and why would an author or musician incorporate these hard and soft sounds? What moods or tones are evoked?

6. Elicit responses to these questions and record answers on chart paper. Students may mention the use of hard sounds to describe a terrible, depressing, gloomy or dark situation, while soft sounds could be used to signify happy, light, free, whimsical or beautiful experiences.

7. Provide students an opportunity to use hard and soft sounds in writing poems or creating music. Musicians may be given the opportunity to work with musical instruments as they create their music.

Materials:
A copy of *An Invitation to the Butterfly Ball-A Counting Rhyme* by Jane Yolen, chart paper, markers, writing paper, pencils, crayons, instruments

Assessment / Reflection:
While students read their poems or perform their musical compositions, other members of the class give feedback about the mood created through these sounds.

MI Extensions:
Interpersonal: Work with another student and put a poem to music, concentrating on evoking a particular mood or tone.

Intrapersonal: Write a journal entry reflecting two or three various situations that you would describe by using all hard or all soft sounds. Include reasons for your choices.

Bodily-Kinesthetic: Act out a poem or move your body to a particular piece of music. Can you use hard and soft movements?

Linguistic: Read other poems or music and determine the mood created by hard/soft sounds. Do certain authors/musicians utilize particular hard or soft sounds repeatedly? Why?

Logical-Mathematical: Gather statistics on the types and frequency of hard/soft sounds used in your classmates' poems and musical compositions. Compare these data to that of another class.

Spatial: Draw a picture of something you think of while listening to a musical piece or reading a poem. How does the picture reflect the sounds used?

The Incredible Journey Soundtrack

MI Context: This lesson is used as students are learning plot development while reading *The Incredible Journey* by Sheila Burnford. Each student will have the opportunity to become a musical director and choose the music that will accompany one of the chapters in the novel.

Learner Outcomes: The student will identify the introduction, rising action, climax, falling action and conclusion of a chapter in the novel and will choose music to accompany each component.

Procedure:

1. Plot development will be introduced after the class has read Chapter Three. In small groups, students will be asked to compare the events in the chapter to a roller coaster ride, i.e., How does the roller coaster ride/chapter begin? When does the tension begin to mount during the ride/chapter? What is the most exciting and tense moment during the ride/chapter? How does the ride/chapter end? As each comparison is made, groups share their ideas with the rest of the class. This model can be used with other chapters with students working individually or in small groups.

2. Ask the students to imagine that a new movie is going to be made of *The Incredible Journey*, and they have been asked to be the musical directors. Their job is to develop the soundtrack. Each student will be responsible for choosing her favorite chapter and selecting portions of five musical pieces to correspond to the introduction, rising action, climax, falling action and conclusion. To facilitate this task, time will be spent in small groups discussing what types of music could be used, and finding samples that would be appropriate for Chapter Three.

3. To get started, students will choose a chapter and fill out the plot development sheet. Give the students three or four days, including a weekend, to complete the musical portion of the assignment at home. Students may need to borrow tape recorders from the school.

Materials:
An audio tape for each student, a plot diagram for each student, cassette tape recorder, copies of *The Incredible Journey*, music to use as examples

Assessment / Reflection:
Students will share their completed tapes with the class. Each student will complete a self-evaluation of her work and receive feedback from peers in the form of "Three Pluses and a Wish," whereby peers share three things the presenter did well and one thing that needs improvement.

MI Extensions:

Interpersonal: Students will use conflict management skills to show another way to solve the problem in one of the chapters. This information will be shared with the class using either the plot diagram, role play, puppet show or flannel board story.

Intrapersonal: Each student will choose an event that happened in her personal life and apply it to the plot development structure, including the introduction, rising action, climax, falling action and conclusion. This event will be shared with the class using the student's choice of intelligence: musical, linguistic, spatial, logical-mathematical or bodily-kinesthetic.

Bodily-Kinesthetic: Students play charades in small groups. They choose a chapter that includes some action. All the components of plot development need to be evident in their actions.

Linguistic: Each student will create a poem about a chapter or about the entire story. Each of the major plot components should be included.

Logical-Mathematical: Students create a time line of major events in the story. They will also need to tell which events fall into the introduction, rising action, climax, falling action and conclusion of the entire story.

Spatial: Each student will create a mobile to show the five major plot components in his favorite chapter.

Activities to Support the Musical Intelligence

Interpersonal

- Design musical board games such as "Instrument Bingo" or "Composer Concentration"

- Turn a song into a finger game, story, puppet show or play

- Play circle games like "Miss Mary Mac," "Down, Down Baby," or "Sally Walker"

- Learn musical games from other countries

- Practice and invent jump rope rhymes

Intrapersonal

- Have music playing in the background during other activities

- Create a music montage

- Become a DJ for ten minutes and record selections to fit your mood

- Listen to music and think about how it affects you. What makes you move, lie still, smile, turn off the music?

- Compare yourself to a musical instrument or piece of music

Bodily-Kinesthetic

- Make up a dance with instrumental accompaniment

- Experiment with unconventional instruments and sound

- Interpret a rhythm through role-playing

- Lipsynch a song

- Use your body to make music

Linguistic

- Compose a song, rap, jingle or melody

- Say things to rhythm

- Spell to music by singing each letter to a beat

- Retell a story by rewriting the words to a familiar tune

- Find music to accompany parts of a story which demonstrate the mood

Logical-Mathematical

- Assign sounds to pattern elements and play the pattern

- Connect fractions with music, i.e., whole notes, half notes

- Compare and contrast musical styles from a historical perspective

- Sort instruments into the four basic groups — strings, brass, woodwind, percussion

- Sort and classify music by style, genre, or instrumentation

Spatial

- Paint a picture of musical instruments

- Make apple doll or puppet composers

- Listen to a musical work and draw the visual image you get or what you think the composer looks like

- Design a new musical instrument

- Create a symbol system to record music

A practical guide created by the faculty of The New City School ©1994

Identifying the Musical Intelligence in Your Students

Children function at many different levels within the intelligences. Through observation of everyday activities, one can create a profile showing the level of functioning within a particular intelligence and the intelligences in relation to each other. The levels described show increased engagement and proficiency. Use this record-keeping page to obtain a richer picture of a child.

Appreciates:

YES	NO	
		Consistently demonstrates interest and enjoyment; is able to differentiate qualities
		Enjoys music as a performing art
		Recognizes many tunes
		Distinguishes among musical styles or instruments
		Asks to listen to music
		Hears beat and rhythm in environmental sounds, i.e., copy machine, ticking clock
		Hums/mimics
		Moves body when music is playing

Performs:

YES	NO	
		Applies the intelligence to create an exhibit or demonstration, or problem-solve in a given situation
		Demonstrates skill (voice or instrument) in using pitch and rhythm
		Sings, plays an instrument, reads music
		Easily memorizes information presented musically
		Differentiates patterns and sounds
		Integrates musical activities into projects, centers, themes, i.e., writes raps, makes instruments
		Uses body to make musical sounds, i.e., tap on chest, cheek pops, knee slaps
		Uses sound to enhance language experience, i.e., poetry, math facts, spelling words
		Mimics intricate beats or rhythms

Creates:

YES	NO	
		Applies this intelligence to generate original work, to develop unique solutions to problems or create prototypes
		Designs and/or produces an original composition incorporating musical elements
		Designs/constructs a unique musical instrument
		Composes original music, i.e., writes songs or sound accompaniment to poetry
		Develops original notation related to the musical elements, i.e., rhythm, melody, harmony, form

Children's Resources

Books and Recordings:

Ackerman, Karen. *The Song and Dance Man.* Dragonfly Books, 1992. ★

Adams, Ron. *There Was an Old Lady Who Swallowed a Fly.* Child's Play Ltd., 1973. ★

Base, Graeme. *Animalia.* Scholastic Inc., 1986. ★

Bryan, Ashley. *All Night, All Day.* Atheneam, 1991. ★

Buffett, Jimmy and Susannah. *Jolly Mon.* Harcourt Brace Jovanovich, 1988. ★

Burnford, Sheila. *The Incredible Journey.* Little, Brown and Co., 1960.

Byrd, Baylor. *When Clay Sings.* Aladdin Books/MacMillan, 1972. ★

Cohlene, Terri. *Dancing Dream.* Rourke Corp, 1990. ★

Downing, Julie. *Mozart Tonight.* Bradbury Press, 1991. ★

Emberly, Rebecca. *City Sounds.* Little, Brown and Co., 1989. ★

Fillegard, Dee. *Brass.* Children's Press, 1988. ★

Fillegard, Dee. *Percussion.* Children's Press, 1987. ★

Fillegard, Dee. *Strings.* Children's Press, 1988. ★

Fillegard, Dee. *Woodwinds.* Children's Press, 1987. ★

Fleischman, Paul. *Rondo in C.* Harper and Row, 1988. ★

Gustafson, Scott, *Scott Gustafson's Animal Orchestra.* Contemporary Books, 1988. ★

Guthrie, Woody. *Pastures of Plenty - A Self-Portrait.* Harper Perennial, 1990.

Hard, Thacher. *Mama Don't Allow.* Harper and Row, 1985. ★

Haseley, Dennis. *The Old Banjo.* Aladdin Books/MacMillan, 1990. ★

Hayes, Ann. *Meet the Orchestra.* Harcourt Brace Jovanovich, 1991. ★

Holl, Adelaide. *Sylvester the Mouse With the Musical Ear.* Golden Press, 1963. ★

Husherr, Rosmarie. *What Instrument Is This?* Scholastic Inc., 1992. ★

Isadora, Rachel. *Ben's Trumpet.* Greenwillow Books, 1979. ★

Kampen, Vlasta Van and Eugen, Irene C. *Orchestranimal.* Scholastic Books, 1989.

Keats, Ezra Jack. *Apt. 3.* McMillian Child Group, 1986. ★

Komaiko, Leah. *I Like the Music.* Harper and Row, 1987. ★

Kraus, Robert. *Musical Max.* Simon and Schuster, 1990. ★

Kroll, Virginia. *Wood - Hoopoe Willie.* Cambridge,1992. ★

★ indicates a picture book

Kuslein, Karla. *The Philharmonic Gets Dressed.* Harper and Row, 1982. ★

Lionni, Leo. *Geraldine, The Music Mouse.* Pantheon, 1979. ★

Martin, Bill Jr. and Archambault, John. *Barn Dance.* Henry Holt and Co., 1986. ★

Martin, Bill Jr. *Brown Bear, Brown Bear, What Do You See?* Henry Holt and Co., 1992. ★

Martin, Bill. and Archambault, John. *Chicka Chicka Boom Boom.* Simon and Schuster Books for Young Readers, 1989. ★

Maxner, Joyce. *Nicholas Cricket.* Harper and Row, 1989.

Mitchell, Barbara. *Raggin': a Story About Scott Joplin.* Carolrhoda Books, 1987.

Peek, Merle. *Mary Wore a Red Dress and Henry Wore His Green Sneakers.* Clarion Books/Tichnor and Fields, 1985. ★

Pinkney, Brian. *Max Found Two Sticks.* Simon and Schuster, 1994. ★

Raschka, Christopher. *Charlie Parker Played Be Bop.* Orchard Books, 1992. ★

Rosen, Michael. *Little Rabbit Foo Foo.* Simon and Schuster Books for Young Readers, 1990. ★

Sage, James. *The Little Band.* M.K. McElderry Books, 1991. ★

Seeger, Pete. *Abiyoyo.* Macmillan, 1986. ★

Showers, Paul. *What Happens to Hamburger.* Harper Trophy, 1985. ★

Steinbeck, John. *The Pearl.* Barron's Educational Series, 1985.

Volkmer, Jane Anne. *Sing a Song of Chimimia: A Guatemalan Folktale.* Carolrhoda Books Inc., 1990. ★

Walter, Mildred. *Ty's One Man Band.* Four Winds Press, 1980. ★

Williams, Vera B. *Music for Everyone.* Mulberry Books, 1988. ★

Winter, Jeanette. *Follow the Drinking Gourd.* Dragonfly Books/ Alfred A. Knopf, 1992. ★

Yolen, Jane. *An Invitation to the Butterfly Ball - A Counting Rhyme.* Caroline House, 1976. ★

Zemach, Margot. *Hush Little Baby.* Dutton, 1976. ★

Games:

"Creating Word Pictures, The Five Sense Store." Aesthetic Education Program, CEMREL, Inc., Viking Press / Lincoln Center for the Performing Arts, 1981.

"Instrument Bingo." Jenson Pub., 1989.

"Music Maestro." Aristoplay Ltd., 1988.

"Music Mind Games." CPP, Belwin Inc., 1993.

"Musical Instrument Lotto." Nath, Jeux Nathan, S.A., 1987.

"Note Ability for Juniors." Tiger Electronics Inc., 1991.

"Rhythm Bingo." Jenson Pub., 1989.

"Simon." Milton Bradley, 1994.

"Songburst: The Complete Lyric Game." Hersh & Company, 1992.

Teachers' Resources

Beall, Pamela and Nipp, Hagen Susan. *Wee Sing and Play.*
   Price Stern Sloan Publishing, 1984.

Burton, Leon and Kurola, Kathy. *Arts Play.* Addison-Wesley, 1981.

Cassidy, John and Nancy. *Kids Song - One and Two.* Klutz Press, 1988.

Chapin, Harry and Sandy. "The Cat's in the Cradle," *Verities and Balderdash.*
   Story Songs Ltd., 1974.

Colin, Amy. *From Sea to Shining Sea.* Scholastic Inc., 1993.

De Regniers, Beatrice Schenk. *Sing a Song of Popcorn: Every Child's Book
   of Poems.* Scholastic Inc., 1988.

Ellington, Duke. "Bojangles." Recorded on Vi26644.

Guthrie, Woody. "My Dolly," *Woody's 20 Grow Big Songs.*
   HarperCollins, 1948.

Hart, Avery and Mantell. *Kids Make Music.* Williamson Publishing, 1993.

Haskins, James. *Black Music in America.* Harper Trophy, 1990.

Krull, Kathleen. *Gonna Sing My Head: American Folk Songs for Children.*
   Alfred A. Knopf, 1992.

Lomax, John and Alan. "Git Along Little Dogies," Folk Song.
   New American Library, 1947.

Mattox, Cheryl. "Lets Get the Rhythm of the Band," *Let's Get the Rhythm of
   the Band: A Child's Introduction to Music From African-American Culture.*
   JTG of Nashville, 1993.

Mattox, Cheryl. *Shake It to the One That You Love the Best.*
   Warren-Mattox Productions, 1991.

Palmer, Hap. *Homemade Band.* Crown Publishing Group, 1990.

Palmer, Hap. *Turn on the Music.* HiTops Video, 1988.

Price, Christine. *Dancing Masks of Africa.* Scribner, 1975.

Rubin, Roslyn, and Wathen, Judy. "Wheels on the Bus." *The All Year-Long
   Songbook.* Scholastic Inc., 1980.

Rubin, Roslyn. and Wathen, Judy. "Today Is Monday," *The All Year-Long
   Songbook.* Scholastic Inc., 1980.

Walther, Tom. *Make Mine Music.* Little, Brown and Co., 1981.

Warren, Jean. *Piggyback Songs.* Tatline Press, 1983.

Weisman, Julie. *Kids in Motion.* Alfred Publishing, 1993.

Wiseman, Ann. *Making Musical Things.* Charles Scribner's & Son, 1979.

Chapter 7:
The Spatial Intelligence

Contributors: Carol Beatty, Susie Chasnoff, Linda Churchwell, Joe Corbett, Eileen Griffiths, Jennifer Hartz Pass, Suzy Schweig, Monette Gooch-Smith, Denise A. Willis

"Art is the only way to run away without leaving home."
Twyla Tharp

Web of the Spatial Intelligence

Student quotes
Student quotes

List of characteristics

"I'm pretty strong in Spatial because I have a creative imagination and I can make it come to life when I am drawing."

"I like to draw a lot and I like to do hands-on activities. I draw on myself. I wear a lot of bright colors and designs. I wear colorful bows and ribbons in my hair."

"I'm spatial because I like to create original things. I like to bead necklaces, earrings and bracelets."

- Enjoys maps and charts
- Likes to draw, build, design, and create things
- Thinks in three-dimensional terms
- Loves videos and photos
- Enjoys color and design
- Enjoys pattern and geometry in math
- Likes to draw and doodle

Pablo Picasso is a famous twentieth century artist.

Maria Martinez, a Pueblo Indian, is synonymous with black pottery.

Faith Ringgold is a modern painter, quilter and writer.

I. M. Pei is an architect, famous for his work on the Louvre and his interpretation and integration of modern architecture and old buildings.

"We cannot create observers by saying 'observe,' but by giving them the power and the means for this observation, and these means are procured through education of the senses."

Maria Montessori

Famous people

Adult quote

A practical guide created by the faculty of The New City School ©1994

Spatial Intelligence: Through the Mind's Eye

by Monette Gooch-Smith

Torrey is sensitive to all environmental changes and personal changes in people, from a minor room rearrangement to a peer's new shoe laces. Chris can identify all of his peers by touch. Sarah can assemble puzzles upside down or sideways with as much speed and accuracy as her peers who are doing them the traditional way. Max has a remarkable ability to observe, to focus his attention and produce images through art; his work is extraordinary.

These kindergarten youngsters are often found closing their eyes to think, to concentrate and to problem solve. Visualizing images and seeing through their mind's eye is a way of life for them. They all possess an intuitive sense of spatial ability.

While these children are quite exceptional in their spatial aptitude, it is important to note that all students possess spatial ability in varying degrees. As educators we must work with youngsters at all levels. Spatial potential can be developed, nurtured and improved. Herein lies our challenge.

What Is Spatial Intelligence?

The realm of Spatial Intelligence involves an array of behaviors and abilities. This spatial domain involves the capability to see and to perceive stimuli accurately. It includes visual discrimination and recognition as a means to interpret and understand that which is seen. It involves the capacity to acknowledge change. The spatial domain involves the ability to conjure mental images and to think and see in "the mind's eye." This dominion is one of colors, shapes, patterns, designs, textures and pictures. It is one of discriminating relationships, including depth, dimension and movement. The spatial domain involves the ability to transfer internal and external images and to duplicate, manipulate, create and recreate them through concrete modalities.

This spatial domain involves the capability to see and to perceive stimuli accurately.

Involvement in the spatial arena is primarily, but not exclusively, out of the visual experience. Development of spatial intellect involves seeing the world, but seeing alone is not enough. One must perceive the world accurately by recognizing, interpreting and understanding what is seen. One need not have sight to possess spatial intellect. Blind youngsters can recognize shapes through tactile means. They can interpret tactile maps and navigate themselves to locations. They can make transformations internally and externally. And they can produce wonderful works of art through various artistic genre. Visually impaired individuals generally possess high degrees of spatial intellect.

Involvement in the spatial arena is primarily, but not exclusively, out of the visual experience. Development of spatial intellect involves seeing the world, but seeing alone is not enough.

People with a spatial orientation are likely to have some of the following characteristics. They often have the ability to:

- organize information visually
- think in three-dimensional terms
- navigate through space and have a "sense of direction"
- have active imaginations
- enjoy creating, inventing and building
- discern minute detail
- use visual information as a segue to other disciplines
- enjoy doodling, painting, sculpting, drawing and other art and craft activities
- decode maps, graphs, charts and diagrams
- become fascinated with machines, contraptions and things to take apart
- enjoy visuals like movies, slides, computers, videos, televisions and photographs
- manipulate images
- enjoy mazes, puzzles, hidden picture activities, chess
- get excited about color, shapes, patterns and designs
- understand perspective
- make figure-ground distinctions
- appreciate gestalt shifts and optical illusions
- remember scenes
- visually sequence events and form mental images
- dream

Developing the Spatial Intelligence in the Classroom

Integrating spatial activities throughout the curriculum is a way to develop, support and cultivate this intelligence. Children relish opportunities to engage their talents and minds by experimenting with a variety of art materials and strategies, no matter the subject area. These spatial experiences should also include occasions to develop visual perception and enhance visual processing, while facilitating an appreciation for art. This can be accomplished by providing some of the following activities:

- Set up spatial and visual art centers in the classroom. One of our kindergarten centers focuses on wet-messy projects like paints. The other concentrates on dry material like paper, markers, crayons, cloth, nature items and "found" junk.

- Invite local artists and spatially-talented guests to share their expertise and experiences. This is a wonderful way to help young children understand that there are many forms of art besides paint, and that there are many different kinds of artists.

During Math:

- Use Cuisenaire rods to teach fractions.
- Design and build with pattern blocks to reinforce shapes.
- Bake a batch of cookies to explain division.
- Use children as "live models" to demonstrate patterns.
- Sort buttons.
- Count, add and subtract actual students while taking attendance.

- Make predictions, guess-check, and estimating activities using real objects...a jar of M&M's, a jug of water, a bag of checkers.
- Provide opportunities to think, visualize and picture images and concepts.
- Compare and contrast art postcards featuring different artists and genre
- Construct math problems using first-hand and concrete materials.

During Language:
- Label art prints to reinforce vocabulary.
- Write poems, short stories and list all possible descriptors about art prints.
- Use story boards.
- Make puppets to retell a story.
- Draw, paint or sculpt the main character or a portion of the setting while listening to stories.
- Make a cartoon strip, flip book or board game to demonstrate understanding of concepts.
- Teach visual educational strategies like visual note taking and mind mapping skills.
- Create a dialogue from the artwork's perspective..."What could the people in this painting be discussing?"
- "If you were this sculpture who would you want to talk to?" "About what"?
- Perform a radio show or produce a real estate ad about buildings in the neighborhood. Learn historical information and use it in your visual aids.
- Debate the pros and cons for preserving the school building. If a new school was built, how might it look different?
- Provide opportunities for demonstration.
- Translate key concepts into poems, stories or songs.
- Make picture dictionaries or key word pictures.

During Social Studies:
Explore social studies through the art of different cultures. Children can appreciate art as it "speaks" to them—like music, like nature, like color. Art affects mood and feelings. Children can observe and enjoy art from a variety of artists and from diverse styles. Their reactions and interpretations are their own—personal and unique. Youngsters can make gross and, then, fine discriminations in art work. They are able to recognize styles and schools of art. They can offer evaluations as they form and share opinions.

Art affects mood and feelings.

People with strong spatial intellect can be found in all walks of life. Albert Einstein gathered his basic insights and inspirations from spatial models and imagery. Kevin Trudeau developed the Mega Memory system using images and picture association techniques.

Albert Einstein gathered his basic insights and inspirations from spatial models and imagery.

All students possess some degree of spatial talent. Spatial visualizers are often attracted to the arts when pursuing vocations and avocations. They become sculptors, designers, photographers, painters and architects. Others find outlets in the advertising, graphic design and drafting field. Navigators, chess masters, mechanics, coaches and inventors are talented in the visual-spatial realm, as are florists, carpenters, engineers and surgeons. Our challenge is to provide opportunities for youngsters to recognize their spatial talent and to provide experiences to facilitate its development.

Painting the O'Keeffe Way

Spatial
Preprimary
Art

MI Context: Students observe different artists' work throughout the year. In this lesson, students observe abstract paintings and other works of a particular artist.

Learner Outcomes: The students will interpret various paintings and then create a similar picture in the artist's style. The students will learn some facts about the artist.

Procedure:

1. Hang pictures and posters of Georgia O'Keeffe's paintings around the room and give students a chance to observe them.

2. Ask the students what they notice about the paintings. Write the responses on a chart.

3. Read the book *Georgia O'Keeffe* by Robyn Montana Turner. Be sure to highlight key points so students gain information about her life.

4. Refer to the list of observations and relate them to what the students are learning from the book. One of the observations may be "I see big flowers." The book mentions that O'Keeffe focused on big flowers.

5. Have each child choose one of O'Keeffe's paintings to duplicate. Students may work independently or with a partner. Have students closely observe the painting they have chosen. Be sure they pay attention to size, shape and colors.

6. Distribute white construction paper, watercolors, and black line markers. Have students draw their interpretation of the artist's work by first drawing with black marker and then painting with watercolors.

Materials:
Several pictures of O'Keeffe's paintings (reproductions of artist's work may be purchased relatively inexpensively at art museums in the form of postcards and posters), *Georgia O'Keeffe* by Robyn Montana Turner, 18" X 12" white construction paper, watercolors and brushes, medium point black markers

Assessment / Reflection:
Display the children's paintings. Have the students match each other's paintings to the O'Keeffe paintings. Are the children's similar enough to the original for them to be recognized?

MI Extensions:

Interpersonal: Using information learned from the story about O'Keeffe, make up a play about her life to perform for the class.

Intrapersonal: O'Keeffe lived half of the year in the desert and half of the year in the city. Where would you prefer to live and why?

Bodily-Kinesthetic: Using chalk outside on the sidewalk or playground, make large flowers in the style of O'Keeffe. The students could also use large paint brushes and water and draw the flowers on a wall.

Linguistic: Ask each student to write a sentence about themselves, the illustrator. Attach it to their picture. Laminate it and make a class art book.

Logical-Mathematical: Have students find ways to classify the pictures they painted.

Musical: O'Keeffe lived in New Mexico. While the students are painting, play music germane to that part of the country.

Map It!

MI Context: This lesson is used during a study of the USA or of mountains.

Learner Outcomes: Students will create a tactile map. Children will identify and use material to represent major mountain ranges in America. Later, students can follow the same format to investigate rivers.

Procedure:

1. Write the word *mountains* on the board. Let several children attempt to pronounce it.

2. In groups, let students share information they know about mountains.

3. Read *Sierra* by Diane Siebert. It is a poem about the mountain range.

4. As you read the poem, let students draw the mountains on butcher paper or tell them to close their eyes and try to picture the mountains in their "mind's eye" as you read.

5. Using a large floor map of the United States, locate several major mountain ranges. Use color-coded cubes to represent the different ranges, one color per mountain range. An outline map encourages children to focus on the task and not be distracted by colors used for states.

6. Have students re-create the mountain maps in small groups using outline maps and cubes.

7. Let students suggest material to represent mountains on outline individual maps, i.e., toothpicks broken and fashioned into triangles, playdough, plastic chips, glitter/glue, construction paper.

8. Make decisions about material and place mountains on individual mountain maps.

9. Share maps with the class.

10. Hang maps around the room or in hallway. They could be compiled into a mountain poem book.

Materials:
Board, markers, giant floor map of the USA, individual outline maps, wooden color coded cubes, butcher paper, toothpicks, Playdough, plastic chips, glitter, construction paper, *Sierra* by Diane Siebert

Assessment / Reflection:
Ask students, "What kind of feedback would you like about your project?"

Can students interpret maps while sharing with others?
How accurate are the maps?

MI Extensions:

Interpersonal: In groups, develop a way to translate the names of the mountain ranges into another made-up language or assign symbols for each range.

Intrapersonal: Let students reflect for a few minutes on how they are like mountains and how they are different from mountains. Share answers in small groups. Let students write in journals about being a mountain range.

Bodily-Kinesthetic: Draw a gigantic chalk outline of the USA on the playground. Children become the mountain ranges on the map.

Linguistic: Compose a visual word-picture poem about mountains.

Logical-Mathematical: Order mountain ranges from the smallest to the largest. Try to identify mountain ranges by touch only.

Musical: Teach "Mountain Ranges" song to the tune of "The Battle Hymn of the Republic":

Mountain Ranges
The Sierra-Nevada mountain range is west.
Wash-ing-ton state has the Cas-cades.
The Rockies are the largest. And the O-zarks are small.
Appalachian mountain range is east.

Refrain:
I know the moun-tain ranges,
I know the moun-tain ranges,
I know the moun-tain ranges,
in the USA.

Add other verses.

Spatial: Design a find-the-hidden-picture sheet.

A Parting of the Plant: Examining Plants

MI Context: This is part of a unit on fairy tales, specifically *Jack and the Beanstalk*. After reading several versions of this Jack tale, students plant a lima bean seed. This lesson is used when the students are observing the bean's growth.

Learner Outcomes: The child will draw a picture of his plant and recognize and name the leaf, stem and roots.

Procedure:
1. Students observe, touch and talk about their plants and make charts identifying the different parts. Explain the primary function of the stem, root and leaf as the students add them to their charts.

2. Each child draws a picture of his plant on white construction paper.

3. After laminating the pictures, children cut their pictures into four pieces, creating a puzzle. Pieces are stored in a re-closable plastic bag.

Materials:
Glue, markers, white construction paper, scissors, lima bean seeds, pots, soil, several versions of *Jack and the Beanstalk*

Assessment / Reflection:
Children put together each other's puzzle, naming the parts of the plant as they complete them.

MI Extensions:
Interpersonal: Working in pairs, students mix their eight puzzle pieces. Together, they must complete the two puzzles.

Intrapersonal: How are the students like a plant? What part are they most like?

Bodily-Kinesthetic: The children pretend to be seeds under the ground. Encourage them to remember what their seed looked like on the day it was planted. Re-enact the growth process.

Linguistic: Have a class discussion comparing at least two versions of the *Jack and the Beanstalk* story.

Logical-Mathematical: Gather leaves from outside, enough for each group of four students to have ten or twelve. Each group finds as many ways as possible to sort or graph the leaves.

Musical: Make lima bean music. Put several lima beans inside various containers to make shakers. Talk about the difference in sounds the shakers make. Some containers might be made of glass, plastic, cardboard and foam.

Beginning Poetry

Spatial
Primary
Language Arts

MI Content: This lesson is used to introduce a unit on poetry.

Learner Outcomes: By manipulating letter clues, students will discover they are beginning a unit on poetry.

Procedure:

1. Divide the class into several small groups and tell them they are about to begin a new unit. They must figure out what the unit is by the clues that you will give them.

2. Pass out envelopes which contain six index cards, each with a letter in the word "poetry." The groups try to figure out what the word is that the letters spell. When they have figured it out, they glue them on a piece of paper in the correct order.

3. When all the groups have finished, discuss what the word "poetry" means.

4. Children think of poems that they know and share them with the class.

Materials:
For each small group, an envelope with six index cards, each with a letter of the word "poetry," glue, construction paper

Assessment / Reflection:
What strategy did your group use to figure out how to make the word "poetry?" Was the task easy or difficult?

MI Extensions:
Interpersonal: Have children locate a copy of a favorite poem and put them in a designated spot all together. Each child writes the title of the poem he chose on an index card and puts it in a bag with everyone else's title. Draw a title out of the bag and read the poem indicated. By listening to the poem, children must decide whose favorite poem it is.

Intrapersonal: Students each find a poem that has special meaning for them, one they might like on a rainy day or on a cold winter day.

Bodily-Kinesthetic: Sew the title of the poem on cardboard or construct a poem banner to hang in the room.

Linguistic: Write an original poem or add a verse to an existing poem.

Logical-Mathematical: How many index cards were used during the exercise? How many vowels, consonants and syllables?

Musical: Choose a poem with a definite rhythm. Use symbols to represent the pattern. Use an instrument to keep the beat as the poem is recited.

The Four Directions

Spatial
Primary
Social Studies

MI Context: In order to better understand maps, countries and continents within the context of studying The Northeast Woodland Indians, children are first oriented to the four geographical directions.

Learner Outcomes: Children will be able to identify north, south, east and west in their immediate environment and on a map.

Procedure:

1. Identify the north, south, east and west walls of the classroom. Make labels to hang on the walls.

2. One at a time, the students follow the teacher's directions to move about the room, i.e., go three steps to the north, one step east, five steps north.

3. The members of the class give directional clues for the teacher to follow.

4. With a partner, students direct each other using directional clues.

5. On individual maps of the United States, each child labels north, south, east and west and makes a compass rose. As an orientation to the area where The Northeast Woodland Indians lived, have the students color the northeast portion of the United States.

Materials:
Cards labeled *north, south, east* and *west;* tape; markers; blackline map of the United States

Assessment :
Observe how well students follow oral directions, label and color map.

MI Extensions:
Intrapersonal: Look at a relief map of the United States and taking into account the physical characteristics of the land, each child decides where he would like to live. Children share their preference with others, looking for those with similar likes.

Interpersonal: Decide, with a partner, where to go on a camping trip, in the north, south, east or west. Decide what clothing and equipment will be needed. Be sure to take into consideration the climate.

Bodily-Kinesthetic and Musical: Sing and create movements to the song "Buttons and Bows."

Linguistic: Make a list of places and bodies of water. The students refer to a map and determine if the items on the list are located north, south, east or west of the northeast United States. The list might include the Atlantic Ocean, Canada, the Ohio River and the equator.

Logical-Mathematical: On a globe, use lines of longitude and latitude and the words north, south, east and west to find the location of the northeast United States. Students could also create a Venn diagram that shows the living conditions that students prefer (for example cold, warm, near ocean, by mountains), and have them place themselves in the appropriate areas.

A practical guide created by the faculty of The New City School ©1994

Dream On! Designing Your Ideal Room

Spatial
Primary
Art

MI Context: This lesson is used during a week-long introduction to the Seven Intelligences and the Brain.

Learner Outcomes: The students will challenge their Spatial Intelligence to transfer the pictures they see in their mind's eye onto paper.

Procedure:
1. Lead the children in a visualization activity to relax. Ask the children to find a comfortable place in the room to sit or lie down and relax. (This activity could also be done outside.)

2. Once they are comfortable say, "While you were away at Summer Camp (on a trip, at school, at your relatives), an amazing thing happened. When you returned home, you found that your bedroom had been redecorated. It was wonderful! You had been dreaming about your room while you were away, and now there it was! Just as you had imagined! You're at the open door looking inside your fantastic bedroom. Close your eyes and walk inside. You first look at the ceiling. Someone who knew you very well painted something there. You walk over to your bed and you notice the bed frame is not as it used to be. What is it now? Next to your bed are all the things you would like to have had that you thought were impossible. Picture in your mind what's on the walls, on the floor, what sounds you hear, what colors you see. Music is playing."

3. Continue with as many leading suggestions as the children seem to enjoy. Have them share their dream rooms with a partner or the whole class.

4. Give the students a large piece of construction paper to draw their dream room as it appeared in their mind's eye. It should be drawn as though it were a cross section of the house. Remind the students that they are using their Spatial Intelligence.

Materials:
Large construction paper, markers

Assessment / Reflection:
Display the dream rooms when they are completed. Have the children guess to whom each room belongs and discuss if it is possible to build. They must be able to explain their answers.

MI Extensions:

Interpersonal: One student draws someone else's dream room as they describe it. Together they discuss what is similar and what is different.

Intrapersonal: Students talk or write about how it felt to visualize, draw, and explain their dream rooms. Were they comfortable? Who would be allowed into the room? How is their room like their personality?

Bodily-Kinesthetic: What exercise equipment would be include in the dream room?

Linguistic: Create a fairy tale that takes place in the dream room.

Logical-Mathematical: Have the students draw their dream rooms to scale or compare their old rooms with their dream rooms in a Venn diagram. One circle is "old" and the other "new."

Musical: Students pick out the music that would be playing in their dream room.

Fashion Tee Reports

MI Context: This activity is a book report option for students.

Learner Outcomes: Students will design a tee shirt which illustrates their comprehension and interpretation of a book that they have read. They will concentrate on a character or a setting description and the importance either played in the book.

Procedure:
1. Tell students they will be designing a tee shirt for a book report and that these reports will have both linguistic and spatial elements.

2. Provide students with a preliminary check list to help them get started in thinking about the design. The tee shirt should be bold, colorful and eye-catching, easy to read, original, decorated and exhibit a good use of space. The design should be some sort of picture, logo or non-linguistic representation of the chosen character or setting.

3. Using fabric crayons, draw the tee shirt design on paper and iron it onto the T-shirt.

4. To accompany each shirt, the student writes a description of the book on an index card. These will be used as the narrative for the tee shirt fashion show that will follow. The information on the index card should include:

    • book title

    • the author's name

    • the book genre

    • a paragraph describing a character or a paragraph describing a setting

    • the character or setting's importance or role in the story

    • the student's own thoughts about the book

    The description should be at least ten sentences in length.

5. After all the tee shirts and paragraphs are finished, it is time for the fashion show. Wearing their shirts, students parade in front of the class while the narrator reads the description on the card.

Assessment / Reflection:
Were the students able to support the choices they had made in their description as far as character and setting?

Materials:
Plain tee shirts brought from home, fabric crayons, index cards

MI Extensions:

Interpersonal: Have students listen to the description and match the description to the tee shirt.

Intrapersonal: Using a scale of one to ten, go back to the criteria and rate how well it was followed in relation to the design and the paragraph.

Bodily-Kinesthetic: As the paragraph is being read, the author walks in front of the audience taking on the character about whom he wrote, or the main character in the story, if he wrote about the setting. How would that character have responded to the audience?

Logical-Mathematical: Brainstorm ways this activity could be graphed, i.e., character or setting, genre, words on tee shirt or no words, fiction or non-fiction. Choose one of the graphing ideas and create the graph.

Musical: Using the tune to "I'm a Little Teapot," make up a song called "I'm a Little Tee Shirt." Have the students learn it to teach to some younger children.

Radical Recess Room

MI Context: This lesson is used during a geometry unit to teach area and perimeter. The Spatial Intelligence is the primary intelligence being used; however, the Intrapersonal Intelligence is also used extensively as students plan what to include in their recess room.

Learner Outcomes: Each student will design his own radical recess room on grid paper. The room will need to include a space for each intelligence. The size of that space will correspond to the degree of strength the child feels in each intelligence. A child who feels he is very strong in the Musical Intelligence and weak in Bodily-Kinesthetic will have a large space for musical activities and a small space for bodily-kinesthetic activities. Each student will calculate the area and perimeter for each of the spaces as well as the total space of his recess room.

Procedure:
1. In small groups, students will brainstorm what would make the ideal recess room. They need to design a space for each intelligence, decide what equipment to include and how much space will be needed.

2. The class brainstorms ideas about what might be included in a radical recess room.

3. With the students, decide which room in the building would make a recess room of appropriate size. Measure that room. Using 11 x 17 grid paper, determine what the scale needs to be.

4. Students are shown on an overhead transparency of the same size grid paper how to determine area and perimeter. Then the teacher demonstrates how to calculate the space her exercise machines would need in the Bodily-Kinesthetic portion of the radical recess room.

5. Students then begin to work on individual floor plans. They must desig-nate the largest amount of space to the intelligences in which they feel the strongest. Space for all intelligences must be included, however.

6. Carefully label all the spaces and items within each space on the floor plan. The area and perimeter of each space must also be included.

Materials:
11x 17 grid paper, overhead projector, pens, transparency of grid paper

Assessment / Reflection:
Students trade floor plans and check the area and perimeter calculations for accuracy. Students share what they learned about each other by looking at the radical recess room floor plans.

MI Extensions:

Interpersonal: Students work in small groups to consolidate their individual plans into one plan. They must negotiate and compromise to complete the project so that consensus can be reached.

Intrapersonal: Look at the smallest area on your floor plan. What could be added to that part of the room to make it more appealing.

Bodily-Kinesthetic: Students construct a three-dimensional model of the room. Volume is introduced as students begin construction.

Linguistic: Students create word searches which include items that are in their radical recess rooms. Classmates exchange and complete someone else's word search to gain insights into that person.

Logical-Mathematical: Students call or visit local retailers to determine the cost of materials used in their room, such as paint, tile, carpet, wallpaper and equipment. They create a budget using this information.

Musical: Make the music space soundproof. What materials could be used to accomplish this task? Experiment and test the materials to see which ones are the most effective in insulating the sound.

A practical guide created by the faculty of The New City School ©1994

Native American Storyteller Dolls

Spatial
Intermediate
Social Studies

MI Context: This project will expose students to the clay medium while they learn about the origin of the Native American storyteller. This project takes place during a unit on folk art.

Learner Outcomes: Students will learn historical facts about the storyteller and storyteller dolls and their origins. Students will become familiar with the technical aspects of working with clay, including the shapes needed to create the dolls.

Procedure:
1. Begin by telling a Native American folktale, such as "Gluscabi and the Game Animals" found in the book *Keepers of the Earth*. Explain the importance of the storyteller in the culture. Include the following:

   • Through the storyteller, the children learned how to behave and how to live properly.

   • Traditions were passed on from generation to generation through stories.

   • Children learned social skills and how the members of the group were supposed to interact.

   • They did not read or have books, so the storyteller became very important to the Native American lifestyle.

3. Discuss Helen Cordera from the Cochiti Pueblo, the artist who began making storyteller dolls thirty years ago. (See the magazine *Faces*, Volume IX Number VIII, April 1993.)

4. Show pictures of storyteller dolls. Examples can be found in the book *Storytellers and Other Figurative Pottery* by Douglas Corigdon. Discuss the costumes, facial features and body structure. It is important to point out that the mouth is open because the doll is singing, the eyes are closed because it is thinking and that the dolls are seated. There are usually children attached to the doll.

5. Lead the students in a visualization: They are the storyteller dressed in traditional costume. Around them sits their family. What would they be wearing? How would they hold their head and hands? Would their eyes be open or closed?

6. Have the students draw their visualization in color. Encourage them to think about detail. Limit the colors to those used by the Native Americans or, more specifically, the Cochiti.

7. Demonstrate with modeling clay how to make a maquette, or model, of a doll. Discuss the shapes they will need to make to represent the body of the storyteller (for example, oval or round head, oval body, cylinder or coil shape for arms and legs). Discuss ways to show the facial features and hair. They may want to make these with clay or paint them on the head. This gives students an opportunity to put their ideas into three-dimensional form and practice before the final piece of art work.

8. Demonstrate techniques for working with the earthenware clay, including how to attach clay by scratching the areas to be joined and adding a little water. Be sure not to use too much water.

9. Allow the students to begin work on their own storyteller dolls. Their maquettes are their guides.

10. Let the clay figures dry and fire slowly.

11. Provide paints and small and medium size brushes. Remind the students to refer to their maquettes for details.

Materials:
Posters or any good pictures of storyteller dolls, drawing paper, pencils, markers, crayons, colored pencils, plasticine clay, earthware clay (low fire), slip (clay that has been wet down), clay tools, fetteling knife, needles, acrylic paint

Assessment / Reflection:
Display the storyteller dolls next to a card on which the students give information about the process they went through while making the dolls.

MI Extensions:
Interpersonal: Become a storyteller like the doll you have made. Your classmates are your family. What stories would they like to hear? What story do they need to hear?

Intrapersonal: Remember the role storytellers played, passing along history and special things that happened. What stories from your family should a storyteller tell to the next generation? What stories might your grandmother tell?

Bodily-Kinesthetic: Get in the same position as your storyteller doll. Is this a comfortable position? How long could you sit in that position to tell stories? How can you use your hands and body to help tell a story?

Linguistic: Find several different authors of Native American stories. Tell how their stories are similar and different. What do they tell you about the relationships among the tribes, their common heritage and their way of life within the different environments of this country?

Logical-Mathematical: Fold a large piece of rectangular butcher paper. On the fold side, cut a hole for the student's head. Using Native American designs and patterns create costumes that the students could wear while storytelling.

Musical: Use natural materials (for example, leaves, bark, grasses and sticks) to create music.

Activities to Support the Spatial Intelligence

Interpersonal
- Murals

- Collages

- Choreograph

- Blindfold activities

- Finger puppets

Intrapersonal
- Create an environment

- Make dioramas

- Design costumes

- Create architectual designs and construct
floor plans

- Be aware of one's body in space

Bodily-Kinesthetic
- Building with geometric solids, blocks or manipulatives

- Painting with different tools

- Quilting, clay, papier mâché and other crafts

- Orienteering

- Constructing models from plastic kits or making origami animals

Linguistic
- Story maps

- Flannel boards

- Comic strips

- Mind maps

- Posters and display boards

Logical-Mathematical
- Puzzles and mazes

- Pattern blocks and Cuisenaire rods

- Scale models

- Construction of maps and time lines

- Chess, checkers, and other strategy games

Musical
- Set up an orchestra using paper models of instruments

- Create a floor plan of the symphony

- Learn a dance

- Develop a musical notation system

- Make musical instruments

Identifying the Spatial Intelligence in Your Students

Children function at many different levels within the intelligences. Through observation of everyday activities, one can create a profile showing the level of functioning within a particular intelligence and the intelligences in relation to each other. The levels described show increased engagement and proficiency. Use this record-keeping page to obtain a richer picture of a child.

Appreciates:

YES	NO	
		Consistently demonstrates interest, respect and enjoyment within the intelligence and is able to differentiate qualities
		Enjoys building and taking things apart
		Shows interest in line, shape, color, pattern, texture
		Shows interest in concrete artistic expression of other cultures, i.e., clothing, jewelry, body ornamentation, crafts
		Shows interest in manipulatives, i.e., Legos, tangrams
		Enjoys working with art material, i.e., paint, markers, etc.
		Enjoys looking at pictures and talking about others' art work

Performs:

YES	NO	
		Applies the intelligence to recreate an exhibit or demonstration or problem solve within a given situation
		Demonstrates skill in use of line, shape, color, texture, pattern in projects
		Draws and reads maps
		Takes things apart and puts them back together easily, i.e., toys, appliances
		Draws a different perspective without seeing it
		Copies other artists' work with accuracy
		Draws mazes and intricate patterns
		Draws with varied lines and uses color with intention
		Uses texture to create depth in art work
		Has inner sense of where one is in space

Creates:

YES	NO	
		Applies this intelligence to generate original work, to develop unique solutions to problems or to create prototypes
		Produces an original work that conveys meaning visually
		Uses materials in a unique way
		Creates artwork with a recognizable style

Name: _____ Date: _____

Display Board Evaluation

On a scale of **1 - 10**, rate your **effort**.
(**1**= low, **10**= high)

1. Thinking of ideas   _____
2. Spacing the material   _____
3. Being neat   _____
4. Measuring for letters   _____
5. Using color   _____

Average effort: _____

This is what I learned about creating a display board:
_____
_____

If I were going to do it again I would _____
_____
_____

These are the ways I had to problem solve on the display: _____
_____
_____

Percent of parental help on this project:

[   ]

0%   50%   100%

A practical guide created by the faculty of The New City School ©1994

Children's Resources

Books and Recordings:

★ indicates a picture book

Baum, Arline and Baum, Joseph. *Opt: An Illusionary Tale.* Puffin Books, 1989. ★

Bjach, Christina. *Linnea in Monet's Garden.* Farrar, Straus and Giroux, 1987. ★

Bolton, Linda. *Hidden Pictures.* Dial Books, 1993. ★

Clouse, Nancy L. *Puzzle Maps U.S.A.* Henry Holt and Co., 1990.

Cummings, Pat. *Talking With Artists.* Bradbury Press, 1992.

dePaola, Tomie. *Art Lesson.* Putnam's Sons, 1989. ★

Everett, Gwen. *Li'l Sis and Uncle Willie.* National Museum of American Art, Smithsonian Institute, 1991. ★

Gardner, Beau. *The Turn About, Think About, Look About Book.* Lothrop, Lee and Shepard Books, 1980. ★

Garner, Alan. *Jack and the Beanstalk.* Doubleday, 1992. ★

Hoban, Tana. *Look, Look, Look.* Greenwillow Books, 1988. ★

Hoban, Tana. *Over, Under, and Through and other Spatial Concepts.* McMillan, 1973. ★

Jonas, Ann. *13th Clue.* Greenwillow Books, 1992. ★

Jonas, Ann. *Color Dance.* Greenwillow Books, 1989. ★

Jonas, Ann. *Round Trip.* Mulberry Books, 1990. ★

Kesselman, Wendy. *Emma.* Harper and Row, 1980. ★

Lawrence, Jacob. *Harriet and the Promised Land.* Simon and Schuster Books for Young Readers, 1993 ★ .

Lawrence, Jacob. *The Great Migration.* HarperCollins, 1993. ★

Lepscky, Ibi. *Pablo Picasso.* Barron's, 1984. ★

Lewis, Samella. *African American Art for Young People.* Hand Craft, 1991. ★

MacDonald, Suse. *Alphabatics.* MacMillan, 1986. ★

McPhail, David. *Something Special.* Little, Brown and Co., 1988. ★

Micklethwait, Judy. *A Child's Book of Art, Great Pictures, First Words.* Dorling Kindersley, 1993. ★

Newell, Peter. *Topsy and Turvys.* Dover Publications, 1964. ★

Peet, Bill. *Bill Peet, an Autobiography.* Houghton Mifflin, 1989.

Raboff, Ernest. *Van Gogh.* Harper and Row, 1988. ★

Rylant, Cynthia. *All I See.* Orchard Books, 1988. ★

Siebert, Diane. *Sierra.* HarperCollins Pub.,1991.

Sills, Leslie. *Inspirations: Stories about Women Artists.*
    Albert Whitman and Co., 1989. ★

Thomson, David. *Visual Magic.* Dial Books, 1991. ★

Turner, Robyn Montana. *Rosa Bonheur.* Little, Brown and Co., 1991. ★

Turner, Robyn Montana. *Georgia O'Keeffe.* Little, Brown and Co., 1991. ★

Venezia, Mike. *Getting to Know the World's Greatest Artists,
    Georgia O'Keeffe.* Children's Press, 1993. ★

Wolf, Aline D. *Mommy, It's a Renoir.* Parent Child Press, 1984.

Yenawine, Philip. *Colors.* Delacorte Press, 1991. ★

Yenawine, Philip. *Lines.* Delacorte Press, 1991. ★

Yenawine, Philip. *Shapes.* Delacorte Press, 1991. ★

Yenawine, Philip. *Stories.* Delacorte Press, 1991. ★

Games:

"Art Deck: The Game of Modern Masters." Artistioplay Ltd., 1985.

"Art Lotto: National Gallery of Art." Safari Ltd., 1990.

"Art Memo Game." Piatnik Vienna, 1989.

"Arts in Play." Intempo Toys, 1988.

"Brick by Brick." Binary Arts, 1992.

"Community Helper Lotto." Trend Enterprises, Inc., 1990.

"Good Old House: A Puzzle Game." Aristoplay, 1981.

"In the Picture: The Kid's Art Game." Intempo Toys, 1990.

"Jenga." Milton Bradley, 1986.

"Pictionary." Pictionary Inc., 1985.

"Set: The Family Game of Visual Perception." Marsha J. Falco, 1988.

Teachers' Resources

Block, Richard and Yuker, Harold. *Can You Believe Your Eyes?* Gardner Press, 1989.

Brookes, Mona. *Drawing with Children.* Jeremy P. Tarcher, Inc., 1986.

Brundin, Judith A. "Clay Storyteller Dolls." *Faces,* Volume IX, Number VIII, April 1993.

Caduto, Michael, and Bruchac, Joseph. *Keepers of the Earth.* Fulcrum Inc., 1988.

Congdon, Martin Douglas. *Storytellers and Other Figurative Pottery.* Schiffer Pub., 1990.

Evans, Livingston. "Buttons and Bows," "*Gene Autry's Greatest Hits.*" COL 1035.

Margulies, Nancy. *Mapping Inner Space.* Zephyr Press, 1991.

Pentagram. *Pentamagic.* Simon and Schuster, 1992.

Rubin, Roslyn and Wathen, Judy. "I'm a Little Teapot," *The All Year-Long Songbook.* Scholastic Inc., 1980.

Striker, Susan. *The Anti Coloring Book.* An Owl Book. Henry Holt Co., 1984.

Sullivan Charles. *Children of Promise.* Harry N. Abrams, 1991.

Vitlae, Barbara. *Unicorns are Real.* Jalmar Press, 1982.

Wycoff, Joyce. *Mindmapping.* Berkeley, 1991.

Part II.

Putting It All Together With the Multiple Intelligences

Chapter 8:
Diversity

by Barbara James Thomson

Diversity, tolerance, multiculturalism, anti-bias, gender bias: the words for differences swirl around us in and out of the education field. But we do not always take the step of connecting these words to issues related to how children learn. Yet the connection is there, and it is an important one.

The Multiple Intelligences theory recognizes seven discrete intelligences: Interpersonal, Intrapersonal, Musical, Bodily-Kinesthetic, Logical-Mathematical, Spatial and Linguistic. Educators who use this model support the development of children's skills and knowledge in all seven areas, rather than focusing primarily on the Logical-Mathematical and Linguistic talents usually associated with formal schooling.

Increasingly, the educators using the Multiple Intelligences framework are giving more attention to the Personal Intelligences: Intrapersonal, understanding one's self; and Interpersonal, being sensitive to and understanding others. No longer are classroom units called "Who Am I" or "Sharing and Caring" only the domain of early childhood educators. Instead, regular activities such as reflective journaling to focus on one's Intrapersonal Intelligence and small group discussions of how each student contributed to a cooperative learning project to focus on the Interpersonal Intelligence, are a part of classrooms from kindergarten to sixth grade and beyond.

MI and Multiculturalism
Self-understanding activities in schools using MI theory go beyond helping children appreciate their own interests, whether those interests are baseball cards, architecture, group sports, art or dance. In addition, the children learn about their own intelligences. A child who has strong gymnastics or soccer-playing abilities sees these as part of her bodily-kinesthetic strength. Knowing this about herself, she may use sports-related language activities to help motivate her work in other academic areas, such as reading and math. Of equal importance, students have regular opportunities to find out how they are seen by other children as their classmates give them feedback about their strengths and skills.

Students have regular opportunities to find out how they are seen by other children as their classmates give them feedback about their strengths and skills.

As educators have grown in their understanding of the need for multi-cultural education throughout the curriculum, attention has focused on the distortions and omissions in curriculum and textbooks. Among the other important aspects of appreciating diversity, understanding others as individuals and appreciating their talents are key points. When children or adults look at learning and learners through the broad lens of MI, they are much more likely to respect and appreciate the talents of a variety of peers. In a

Among the other important aspects of appreciating diversity, understanding others as individuals and appreciating their talents are key points.

Multiple Intelligence-based classroom, the "class clown" may be seen as someone with linguistic, interpersonal or bodily-kinesthetic talents, rather than as someone who simply doesn't conform to the class rules and regulations. Since book report options in this kind of a classroom are apt to include acting out the story or writing a play of it, the former "class clown's" talents are validated for both the child and her classmates. This does not mean that the "class clown's" behavior is suddenly acceptable or that she does not need to work to conform to the norms. It does mean that the "class clown," like all of the other students, is more likely to be understood and appreciated for the talents she possesses. This, in turn, is likely to lead to more success and, thus, a diminished need to play the role of the clown. In such a school setting, differences of ethnicity, socio-economic class or even gender loom less large because children know and appreciate the various strengths of other students. Focusing on a child's strengths, using them to help the child learn, becomes the norm.

Working Against Stereotypes

Understanding and appreciating individual strengths truly is a tool for combating stereotyping. Girls can be known and validated by themselves, by peers, and by adults, not only in the areas of language where they have traditionally been strong, but also for their bodily-kinesthetic or spatial talents. Boys, likewise, can be validated not only because of sports talents, but also as writers, and artists. Children fortunate enough to be in school settings with significant numbers of various ethnic and racial groups will also have regular opportunities to see the breadth of strengths and interests among children whom they otherwise might have seen primarily as different from themselves. The Multiple Intelligences theory offers another opportunity to work toward commonalties, focusing on what we share and value.

Children fortunate enough to be in school settings with significant numbers of various ethnic and racial groups will also have regular opportunities to see the breadth of strengths and interests among children whom they otherwise might have seen primarily as different from themselves.

Concerns have been raised about the possibility of using MI as a way of pigeon-holing students of color as strong in bodily-kinesthetic or musical. Unfortunately, this worry can certainly be understood because of the past educational experiences of African-Americans. Instead, the breadth of activities in an MI-driven classroom offers all students greater opportunities for self-understanding. Teachers, likewise, are apt to appreciate and use a greater variety of strategies for developing the child's strengths and using them to support learning in all areas. In addition, MI theory supports Jeff Howard's "Efficacy Theory" which puts the emphasis on effort, rather than innate ability, as the most important variable in learning situations.

Schools that support a diversity of intelligences truly build respect and connections among the children and families.

Classrooms using the MI model teach children about the various intelligences and then help them understand and develop their own particular combinations of talents. In doing so, they are also teaching children respect and appreciation for a wider range of talents possessed by others. Schools that support a diversity of intelligences truly build respect and connections among the children and families. In addition, they help all children see themselves as learners and problem solvers. Feeling good about themselves and appreciating their own talents and those of others, children taught within the Multiple Intelligences framework can appreciate the similarities and differences among learners, a crucial skill for the twenty-first century.

Chapter 9:
Science

by Susie Burge

As the science specialist at The New City School, I view the theory of Multiple Intelligences as a vehicle through which students learn. Students do not all learn in the same ways, and they use very different approaches as they structure meaning for themselves. I find that I am personally very Logical-Mathematical in my own approach to teaching and learning. I can have information beautifully organized in my own mind, logically present it to the students, step by step, crystal-clear...and yet some of them still won't get it! Those students need to utilize different intelligences to make the information meaningful to them.

Students do not all learn in the same ways, and they use very different approaches as they structure meaning for themselves.

Students Learn in Different Ways

One way I try to accommodate various learners is to present material in several different ways. Each topic is covered using methods from different intelligences.

Linguistic: written material, questions, fill in the blank, write a descriptive paragraph, explain to the class, research, write a report

Spatial: diagrams, charts, build models, create and work puzzles, draw examples of, graph, flow charts

Bodily-Kinesthetic: act out, take apart, experiment, dissect, demonstrate

Musical: listen to songs, background environmental tapes, write a song, mood music, chant to rhythm

Logical-Mathematical: light-up boards, matching cards, step-by-step descriptions and explanations, logic puzzles, reasoning games

Interpersonal: discuss with group, board games, flash cards, group projects

Intrapersonal: work alone, self-assessment

For example, when students learned about the digestive system, they had information to read and questions to answer for homework (Linguistic); they had to label diagrams of the digestive system (Spatial); they acted out food moving through the digestive system with each student playing a part (Bodily-Kinesthetic); they played a body-parts board game (Interpersonal); and they had to describe what happened to food from the time it entered the body until it left the body (Logical-Mathematical). Obviously, I cannot teach everything in seven ways, but I try as much as possible to teach everything in several different ways!

...they had to label diagrams of the digestive system (Spatial), and they acted out food moving through the digestive system with each student playing a part (Bodily-Kinesthetic).

Giving Students Choices

Some of my units are similar to independent study units. I give the students a list of the required things they must learn and a list of options. I have designed various activities around the intelligences, and students can choose how they want to learn the information. For example, they are required to learn the parts of a flower and how seeds are made. They may choose two or three activities from a list that includes dissecting, diagramming, reading, flow charts, puzzles and light-up boards. This is similar to learning centers, except a deliberate effort is made to incorporate activities that represent the various intelligences, and the activities all teach the same concept. This approach takes a lot of time to set up initially, but very little time in succeeding years.

Assessment in Science

Clearly, I want students to be able to construct meaning for themselves in the best way possible. However, they also need to be challenged to use the intelligences in which they are not as comfortable.

Ideally, I would also like students to choose how they will be assessed. They could choose how to demonstrate to me that they know the material: take a test, write a paper, tape record explanations, make a model and label it, act it out, write a song, or just tell me! Unfortunately, while this approach is the ideal, it becomes very time-consuming with a large number of students.

Often, I have a project at the end of a unit that requires students to incorporate the various things we have been learning. Students who are strong in a particular area can make their contributions to the project from their strengths.

Clearly, I want students to be able to construct meaning for themselves in the best way possible. However, they also need to be challenged to use the intelligences in which they are not as comfortable. I want to both let them learn in the ways that make the most sense to them, and help them improve in the ways that are difficult for them. If a child only works in areas of strength throughout the year, the child has not stretched and tried to improve an intelligence that is not perceived as a strength. Part of my job also includes making sure that all children work in all intelligences during the year.

Even with a "hands-on" approach to science education, provisions need to be made for students to construct meaning using various intelligences.

Even with a "hands-on" approach to science education, provisions need to be made for students to construct meaning using various intelligences. A deliberate effort made by the teacher to include a variety of methods representing the intelligences in classroom activities, learning centers, and projects will be rewarded by greater enthusiasm and understanding by the students.

Chapter 10:
Thematic Teaching

by Julie Stevens and
Suzy Schweig

Thematic teaching and the theory of Multiple Intelligences work together like "hand and glove" to create a new look in the elementary classrooms of the 1990's. Content is at the heart of thematic teaching and the seven intelligences serve as the arteries of learning for that content, suitable to each learner with her special needs and abilities.

How Does It Work?

In constructing our third-grade theme "Keepers of the Earth" and in keeping with our school's philosophy of diversity, we wanted the students not only to experience the native cultures of their own country but also to re-create as much as possible what the North American Indian suffered at the hands of our government during the westward expansion of the United States. The integration of the seven intelligences, through activities and choices within each component or unit of the theme, gave us that opportunity. First, we divided our theme into six components: Introduction to Native Americans; The Northeastern Woodland culture; The Southeastern Woodland culture; The Plains culture; The Pacific Northwest culture; and The Southwestern culture. Then we determined the actual content of each component, which we listed as key points or important facts to learn. Next, inquiries or activities were generated from the content and presented in the form of the seven intelligences. The students could choose the ones that would help them learn the content in the best way (see Figure A). Often, we found the students chose the same intelligence all the time, so we had to provide other opportunities in which they would experience all of the intelligences at one time or another. Because the seven intelligences often overlap one another, this was not hard to do. We use MI activities in several ways, either as a whole-group activity, as independent choices, for assessment or integrating skills into our theme.

We wanted the students not only to experience the native cultures of their own country but also to recreate as much as possible what the North American Indian suffered at the hands of our government during the westward expansion of the United States.

Whole-Group Activities

We know it is critical that the actual content of our theme should be both exciting and meaningful to our students. Therefore, we use the seven intelligences as a means to vary how we introduce the information we want them to learn. For demonstration purposes, we will use a portion from our component on the Plains culture which is generally familiar to all teachers, the Lewis and Clark expedition which opened the West to white settlers. First, we study the geography of the Lewis and Clark journey through published maps. Then the students design their own maps of the expedition and estimate the distances to and from the Pacific Ocean (Spatial and Logical-Mathematical). We read and discuss their journey through the eyes of Sacajawea, their Shoshoni Indian guide (Linguistic and Interpersonal).

We use the seven intelligences as a means to vary how we introduce the information we want them to learn.

As we read each chapter, the students pretend they are part of Lewis and Clark's crew. They are required to keep a personal journal with illustrations of their daily adventures (Linguistic, Spatial and Intrapersonal).

Independent Choices

These same types of activities are used throughout the theme for independent learning activities as well. The students have the opportunity to choose an MI activity which interests them. Some examples follow:

1. Write a letter to your parents describing your adventures with Lewis and Clark (Linguistic and Intrapersonal).

2. Research recorded statistics of supply numbers and distances traveled during the expedition to create and solve five mathematical problems (Linguistic and Logical-Mathematical).

3. Walk around a track for several miles to get a sense of how long it might have taken to carry a boat over land when the Missouri River ended at the mountains. (Bodily-Kinesthetic and Logical-Mathematical).

Assessment

Using various intelligences gives students a richer opportunity to learn and to show what they know.

Perhaps the most creative way to use Multiple Intelligences within the theme is through assessment. Using various intelligences gives students a richer opportunity to learn and to show what they know. Rather than take multiple-choice tests or write essays, students can use many of the intelligences to exhibit a "genuine understanding" of what has been taught. An example of this follows. The students design a talking travel brochure for one of the major places Lewis and Clark reached in their travels. They may use the Lewis and Clark journals, real travel brochures and other references to complete this project. The brochure should highlight geographical features of the location by showing maps and any recreational areas. It should include information on how Lewis and Clark had an impact upon the area by traveling there; what plants and animals are unique to that area; and, what discoveries and obstacles they encountered there. Upon completion, the students will present their brochures to the class. Peers will act as tourists and ask questions about the material presented while the teacher observes and assesses the activity. Almost all of the intelligences appear in this assessment: Intrapersonal, Linguistic, Logical-Mathematical, Interpersonal, and Spatial.

Integrating Skills Into the Theme Through MI

We have found that with a little imagination and practice, skills can be taught using multiple intelligences within a theme context.

Teaching skills within a theme has been an expressed concern for many educators. This has been a concern for us as well. However, we have found that with a little imagination and practice, skills can be taught using Multiple Intelligences within a theme context. Writing dialogue on a script and using end marks, commas and quotation marks in a narrative are all linguistic skills. We teach these skills within the context of the Lewis and Clark expedition. Examples of the MI activities we use follow.

1) Introduce dialogue-writing within a script by watching a five-minute segment of a television program. The students are introduced to the form a script follows. They are divided into groups and asked to brainstorm and write the next three minutes of dialogue for the television program using

the proper form. To the tune of a familiar song, they are then required to write a song which will teach these rules to the rest of the class (Spatial, Linguistic, Interpersonal and Musical).

2) The teacher chooses dialogue from a book about Sacajawea, removing all quotation marks and punctuation. The students edit the work (Linguistic and Intrapersonal).

3) Using Indian sign language, the students create dialogue with a partner to be presented to the class. The dialogue is later written to reinforce those skills (Bodily-Kinesthetic and Interpersonal).

Using Indian sign language, the students create dialogue with a partner to be presented to the class.

4) The students write dialogue between themselves and Lewis or Clark, using the rules they brainstormed in groups earlier (Linguistic and Intrapersonal).

Stretching the imagination to design ways to teach skills with a theme (instead of in isolation) and using the different intelligences is rewarding to both students and teachers.

In conclusion, integrating Multiple Intelligences into a thematic unit is no easy task, but it can be a reality. It takes patience, time, imagination, creativity and absolute dedication to the philosophy of making learning fun and meaningful for kids. Whether it is through whole-group instruction, independent choices, assessment or learning skills, as a teacher, you are providing opportunities that allow every child in your classroom to be challenged and become a success story. One of our success stories summed it all up last year by saying, "Every school should have MI!" We think yours should too!

FIGURE A

Key Point Activity	Intelligence	Bloom's Taxonomy	Subject
	Intrapersonal Interpersonal Body-Kinesthetic Musical Spatial Logical-Mathematical Linguistic	Knowledge Comprehension Application Analysis Evaluation Synthesis	Reading Writing Math Science Vocabulary Spelling Social Studies Art Music
	Intrapersonal Interpersonal Body-Kinesthetic Musical Spatial Logical-Mathematical Linguistic	Knowledge Comprehension Application Analysis Evaluation Synthesis	Reading Writing Math Science Vocabulary Spelling Social Studies Art Music
	Intrapersonal Interpersonal Body-Kinesthetic Musical Spatial Logical-Mathematical Linguistic	Knowledge Comprehension Application Analysis Evaluation Synthesis	Reading Writing Math Science Vocabulary Spelling Social Studies Art Music
	Intrapersonal Interpersonal Body-Kinesthetic Musical Spatial Logical-Mathematical Linguistic	Knowledge Comprehension Application Analysis Evaluation Synthesis	Reading Writing Math Science Vocabulary Spelling Social Studies Art Music

Chapter 11:
Sold On Simulations!

*by Carla Mash and
Denise A. Willis*

"You learn how to help other people and fight for your rights." "You might make new friends trying to stand up for people, and you have to work together." "It teaches you how to think for yourself." "Actions speak louder than words." "It's fun to feel like you are really traveling in a covered wagon." "It lets you trust someone you may not have trusted before, and it gives you empathy, not sympathy, for disabled people."

Simulations in our fourth-grade classrooms prompted these quotes from our students. Using simulations, we try to create an environment that allows children to participate in and experience situations that are close to real life. Our philosophy is that the children understand best when they can experience learning first-hand. This belief has strongly influenced us in designing a curriculum that both meets the objectives of our school's skills continuum and involves children in first-hand experiences.

Our philosophy is that the children understand best when they can experience learning first-hand.

Pioneers, Wheelchairs and Too Much Homework
We feel so strongly about simulations and their effectiveness that when the fifth-grade teachers came to us and said that our fourth graders needed to know more about government, we converted our two fourth-grade classrooms into city governments. Our students now sit in groups of four or five in wards and elect alderpersons to pass ordinances (classroom rules) and develop the judicial system (complete with a set of chairs set aside for problem solving and student mediators). Alderpersons have brought issues from their wards ranging from too much homework to finding strategies to deal with too much competition in physical education class. Through these experiences, students have gained more insight into concepts that are typically difficult for a nine- or ten-year old to understand and for teachers to teach.

We converted our two fourth-grade classrooms into city governments.

Actually traveling on the Oregon Trail is not a realistic possibility for our class, but our children still need to know about this time in our history. For the past five years, we have turned to a simulation entitled "Wagons West" by Interact (P.O. Box 997, Lakeside, CA 92040). This simulation requires a great deal of teamwork by the students and provides numerous opportunities to integrate linguistic and logical-mathematical skills. Each class is divided into two or three wagon trains, complete with wagon masters. The goal is to earn points through diary entries, trail decisions and projects while "traveling" from Fort Independence, Missouri to Hacker Valley, Oregon. In a survey we gave our classes, forty of forty-two students advised us to continue using this simulation with these comments: "It gives you a feeling of what real pioneers had to go through; there is lots of teamwork and problem solving involved"; "Kids learn more; it's more fun if you participate"; and

Each class is divided into two or three wagon trains, complete with wagon masters.

"You discover decision making." When we could not take a field trip back in time to Fort Independence in 1846, yet our students still needed to learn about this part of our past, it was Wagons Ho!

With our year-long theme entitled "Citizens Making a Difference," much of our emphasis in the fall centers around Missouri and its citizens, past and present, who have had significant influence on public life. We began in January, wanting to give our students the chance to make a difference themselves. Since diversity is a major thrust of our school's philosophy, we chose to look at issues of prejudice and discrimination relating to disabilities, race, gender and religion. With our belief that students need first-hand experiences, during this unit, each child spent six hours a day being blindfolded, wearing ear plugs, sitting in a wheelchair, or having limited use of arms and hands. This was done over a period of five days with partners. On a given day, one partner would simulate a disability while the other partner played the role of guide or helper. School was conducted as usual with students expected to problem solve situations that were made more difficult because of their disabilities. Individuals who have disabilities came as guest speakers. Their experiences, coupled with discussions and journals, played a large role in helping students understand the difference between empathy and sympathy. Numerous insights were gained through learning about each disability.

...each child spent six hours a day being blindfolded, wearing ear plugs, sitting in a wheelchair, or having limited use of arms and hands.

During the disabilities simulation, some students experienced discrimination because of other students' reactions to their disabilities and their limited access around our school. A simulation, "The Poverty Game," gave our students another experience with discrimination, this time based on socioeconomic status. The premise of this game was simple: students needed to complete a collage about themselves. At the beginning of the game, each child was given a bag containing a badge which determined his socioeconomic class and amount of supplies that would be appropriate for that economic class. The yellow triangles (top class, the wealthiest), received more than enough supplies and money, whereas the red circles (lowest class, the poorest) received a few or no supplies. It was through the parents who had joined us for the activity and who played predetermined roles such as shopkeeper, police officer, judge, and jail keeper, that blatant discrimination occurred. They treated children differently based on the badge they were wearing! The result of this simulation was to open the door to a powerful dialogue about issues of prejudice and discrimination. Additional issues that arose were the roles that police officers and judges played in the game and play in real life, as well as the amount of involvement the upper class did or did not take in the game. As you might imagine, we communicate a great deal with our students' parents. We want these experiences to feel as real as possible; parents should be informed about what has happened.

A simulation, "The Poverty Game," gave our students another experience with discrimination, this time based on socioeconomic status.

Does It Work?

The amount of positive feedback we've received from students about simulations over the years has been overwhelming. This year we asked our students, "Do you like to learn by participating in a simulation?" One hundred percent responded *yes*, and backed up their answer with examples, i.e., "I like to do something, not hear it or read it." "I like to experience things first hand." "It helps me to feel how others do or did." "I like to because it is an active way to learn." "I like to learn that way because I understand what it feels like to be disabled or poor or anything else."

Parent response has also been remarkably positive. For example, a parent who wrote curriculum for Teach 2000 included The Poverty Game. Another parent, an architect, observed our disabilities simulations in order to develop similar experiences for architects with the advent of the Americans with Disabilities Act. Besides adding more simulations to our curriculum each year, we facilitated The Poverty Game at a faculty inservice (Yes, it works with adults and was fascinating!), and our students have spoken about their simulations to our school's Board of Directors. One Board member stated that she felt good knowing that our future leaders have had these experiences.

Parent response has also been remarkably positive.

For some teachers, simulations will require an attitude shift. Cooperative learning is often a primary component. Student groups may encounter situations that we would not have planned for them, and this may require sitting back and watching students work around some very difficult obstacles. At times, this has proven to be a bit frustrating, as we have had to relinquish some of our control.

While simulations are a major component in our curriculum now, this hasn't always been the case. We began with one simulation and grew from there. An easy way to start would be to purchase a commercially-produced simulation, which would include all the information needed for beginning. We recommend sending for an Interact catalog.

We began with one simulation and grew from there.

The most powerful outcome of simulations that we've observed is "genuine understanding." Because students have made a difference in the roles they played, they have felt comfortable addressing issues that come up both in and out of school. When a group of students refused to let others join in playing tag, a town meeting was called and the conflict was resolved. We have had students call radio stations, send letters, sign petitions, and talk to teachers outside of school when faced with situations they wanted to change. Yes, this does work!

Simulations complement our philosophy. Our belief is that first-hand experience is essential in order to achieve "genuine understanding" (see Chapter 13). Based on years of positive feedback from students and parents, we feel confident that this is an effective way for children to learn and, despite the extra work that simulations sometimes require, they're well worth the effort. We're sold on simulations!

Our belief is that first-hand experience is essential in order to achieve "genuine understanding."

by Mary F. Daly

Chapter 12:

Learning Centers in the Preprimary Classroom

S everal years ago, our school began to study, and then to implement, Howard Gardner's Theory of Multiple Intelligences (MI). We had already recognized and valued the differences and similarities among our children. We recognized that children learn in many different ways, but we were still approaching education in many of the more traditional forms— Linguistic and Logical-Mathematical overload. We decided that if we really believed in the MI theory and valued this approach to educating our students, then MI should be reflected in our classrooms.

Children learning in a multitude of ways was not a new idea to educators. What was new was the concept that there are seven different intelligences and that educators need to address all these areas in classrooms at any level, giving emphasis and weight to each of the seven. Providing activities and lessons that incorporate the different intelligences and value different venues to demonstrate that knowledge was the challenge.

Children learning in a multitude of ways was not a new idea to educators. What was new was the concept that there are seven different intelligences and that educators need to address all these areas in classrooms at any level...

Our classroom went through a metamorphosis of sorts when we first began to look at Gardner's theory and how it related to our program.

Using Learning Centers to Address MI

One way to provide this exposure and variety of activities was through learning centers. Our classroom went through a metamorphosis of sorts when we first began to look at Gardner's theory and how it related to our program. We already used the learning center approach, but many questions poured out: What could we use that we already had? Would we need more centers, fewer centers? Were there intelligences we were not addressing enough, or at all? Should we rename our centers? Could we address more than one intelligence at a center? How often should we change the activities? How were we going to keep track of who is doing what and where?

We began by looking at our current structure. We had a four-teacher team with a teacher/pupil ratio of about fourteen to one. We had a "letter-of-the-week" emphasis in our learning centers (a different letter of the alphabet each week). We had twenty-five learning centers that we changed every two weeks.

Our room is a large square space with each of the four corners set up for small group work. We have "mirror image" centers set up on both sides, thus dividing the room in half for management purposes, and four centers that are shared in the middle of the room. The centers are coded by number, color or shape. The center signs have the name of the center, the color, number or shape and a "smiling face" tag to show children how many students can be there at a time. This allows the students to self-regulate the number of children working in any one place. We use a "Job Board" to assign center work to the students. To assign and monitor which students work at what centers, the children's names are listed down one side of the board and small tags (coded by color or number or shape) are placed next to each child's name with Velcro.

We knew we wanted to change the centers on a weekly basis but we also wanted less set-up time, so we combined some of the centers bringing the number down to twenty-one. We decided to have a monthly focus in the social studies and science centers. We also decided that the science center would reflect our year-long theme on the human body ("Busy Bodies"). We would continue with our letter-of-the-week focus. We also changed the name of several of the centers to incorporate some of the vocabulary of Howard Gardner's theory. This would reinforce for the children our beginning of the year study of the brain and the seven intelligences. The centers are now called: Logical-Mathematical, Games, Puzzles, Music, Science, Playhouse, Social Studies, Children's Desk, Library, Manipulatives, Visual Expression, Spatial Expression, Matching, Story/Words, Blocks, Workbench, Filling Station, Computer, Alphabet/Puppets, Listening and B/K (Bodily-Kinesthetic).

We decided to have a monthly focus in the social studies and science centers.

Designing Centers

Next, we looked at the centers themselves under the headings of the different intelligences, using the Personal Intelligences (Interpersonal and Intrapersonal) as an "umbrella" over the other five. Linguistic: Alphabet/Puppets, Listening, Computer, Story/Words, Social Studies and Library. Logical-Mathematical: Games, Logical-Mathematical, Puzzles, Science and Matching. Spatial: Manipulatives, Visual Expression and Spatial Expression. Musical: Playhouse, Music and Social Studies. Bodily-Kinesthetic: Blocks, Workbench, Filling Station and Children's Desk. We had nineteen centers that accommodated two or more students at a time, giving them a more interpersonal focus. It is important to keep in mind that, even when a child is working in an interpersonal situation, it does not mean they are interacting with others. They may be working completely on their own (and possibly the center becomes Intrapersonal for that child). We changed the Workbench, Library and the Children's Desk centers from two or three children to one, giving these centers an Intrapersonal focus.

We also decided to create two areas in our room that would address the Personal Intelligences exclusively. These would not be centers in the traditional sense of our room, but areas for children to relax or take a break from the busy atmosphere of "Choice Time," the time when the students are working in the learning centers. The "Social Tables," two tables in the middle of our room, became a place for children to meet and just enjoy each other. These tables accommodate about six or eight children at a time. We put a variety of materials (pencils, paper, crayons, markers) out for the children to use; they also can simply sit and talk. We also created a "Me Place"; one of our "turrets" became a place for one child to visit. (Our classroom has a castle motif.) There is a comfortable bean bag chair, and we hung a mirror on the wall. We occasionally put a book, a telephone, a doll or a stuffed animal in the space. Neither of these spaces are ever assigned, and children are free to visit them at their own discretion.

We also decided to create two areas in our room that would address the Personal Intelligences exclusively.

We have also learned that many of the learning centers lend themselves to multi-intelligence activities.

We have also learned that many of the learning centers lend themselves to multi-intelligence activities. The Social Studies, Science and Playhouse centers are particularly apt to become a multi-intelligence experience for children. Since we do not have an equal number of centers for each intelligence, we use many of the centers for cross over activities, i.e., the Listening center has a musical story (Linguistic and Musical), the Games center has a "one only" game in it (Intrapersonal and Logical-Mathematical), the Matching center has art prints to match and then copy (Spatial and Logical-Mathematical) and the Science center will have a variety of activities, a book about a body system (Linguistic) a body puzzle (Logical-Mathematical and Spatial), exercises to do (Bodily-Kinesthetic) and a song to learn about the particular system (Musical). A typical rotation of center activities for the letter "F" would be:

Linguistic:
Story/Words - Sort objects that begin with the letter F or add a page to the Person-of-the-Week book.

Alphabet/Puppets - Make a Friendly Frog puppet or make the letter "F" out of feathers.

Listening - Listen to "Frog Went A Courtin'" and put the pictures in order.

Computer - Play "Fun on the Farm" game.

Library - Look at "F" books with a friend.

Social Studies - Find St. Louis landmarks.

Logical-Mathematical:
Games - Play "Go Fish" or "Going Fishing."

Logical-Mathematical - Measure by the foot or use fraction stacks.

Puzzles - Assemble a flag or frog puzzle.

Science - Learn about feelings; draw a face that looks happy, sad, excited; or tell a teacher about a time you felt frustrated.

Matching - Match farm animals.

Spatial:
Manipulatives - Make a picture with the Fantacolors.

Visual Expression - Paint fancy feet or face painting.

Spatial Expression - Make the letter "F" out of clay or make a frog.

Musical:
Playhouse - Listen to "Fantasia" while you clean the playhouse.

Music - Listen to and sing in French, "Fais do do Colas," making rhythms with your feet.

Bodily-Kinesthetic:

B-K - Bounce a ball around a giant letter F; toss a football.

Blocks - Build a farm.

Workbench - Use a file to smooth a piece of wood.

Filling Station - Play with the funnels.

Children's Desk - Make a face book; draw a picture of a friend.

Our next task was to develop a method for keeping track of the jobs assigned as well as the choices children were making on their own during Choice Time. Structuring the learning centers to be as child-oriented and self-managing as possible frees the teacher to do more observations and have more one-on-one interactions with the students. It requires more planning and set-up, but Choice Time, with the students working in the centers, is spent observing and individualizing the program for each student. A simple checklist with the students' names down one side and the names of the centers across the top, with corresponding boxes in the middle, gives the teacher a one-sheet record of where the students were assigned and where they chose to be during Choice Time. Spaces can also be added to keep track of whether they were working alone, with a partner or in a group, and whether they finished assigned jobs. These sheets can be changed on a weekly basis and a simple tally sheet kept for long-term findings (by semesters, quarterly or yearly).

Structuring the learning centers to be as child-oriented and self-managing as possible frees the teacher to do more observations and have more one-on-one interactions with the students.

Incorporating the seven intelligences into the learning centers was a challenge for our team. We began to view children in a different way and to plan activities that stretched everyone to use all of their intelligences. It has kept our energy level high. We are constantly changing and reassessing what we do, it has never been the same two years in a row. MI has changed the way we teach; it has changed the way we use Learning Centers. It has enriched our program and the kinds of things we can do through the centers. This, in turn, addresses the strengths in every child we teach.

by Tom Hoerr

Chapter 13:
Genuine Understanding

Assessment is the engine that drives curriculum and instruction. Whether or not we like it, what is measured and how it is measured determines what is taught and how it is taught.

But too often when we assess, we merely focus on acquisition of information and mastery of skills. Students learn enough to parrot the answer or pass the test but do not truly understand what is taught. If you doubt this, ask a teenager or adult to divide fractions, 3/4 divided by 5/6 for example. While many won't know how to do this, a "mathematically proficient" teenager will know enough to invert and multiply; the computation is now 3/4 times 6/5, and can be solved. But then ask why that process works, what was taking place when the numerator and denominator were inverted. Very few individuals can respond correctly. Similarly, ask an adult why it is warmer in the summer than the winter; chances are you'll hear that it's because the Earth is closer to the sun, (rather than the correct answer, that the angle at which the sun's rays hit the Earth has changed). What these examples share is that the respondents no longer know — because they didn't truly learn — the concepts that they were taught in school, concepts that they and their teachers thought they understood.

Although the case can be made that successful teenagers and adults do not need to know this specific information, this lack of comprehension prevents other learning from taking place. Because assessment drives curriculum and instruction, the extensive use of multiple-choice tests and paper/pencil exams has limited what happens in the classroom to working toward mastery of information, not comprehension of concepts.

A New Way to Look at Understanding

In contrast to this approach, Gardner and his colleagues at Harvard Project Zero have developed a model for assessment called "Genuine Understanding" (sometimes referred to as "Teaching For Understanding"). While Genuine Understanding, or GU, should be the goal whether or not MI is being used, pursuing GU works particularly well with the multiple entry points approach to learning that is the basis of MI. The two approaches, MI and GU, complement one another.

In his book *The Unschooled Mind* (1991), Gardner says, "Such performances [of Genuine Understanding] occur when students are able to take information and skills that they have learned in school or other settings and apply them flexibly and appropriately in a new or at least somewhat unanticipated setting." David Perkins and Tina Blythe, in the February 1994 issue of *Educational Leadership*, offer examples of GU: "...being able to do

Because assessment drives curriculum and instruction, the extensive use of multiple-choice tests and paper/pencil exams has limited what happens in the classroom to working toward mastery of information, not comprehension of concepts.

a variety of thought-demanding things with a topic — like explaining, finding evidence and examples, generalizing, applying, analogizing, and representing the topic in a new way." At New City, our shorthand way of defining GU is "using skills or information in new and novel settings."

Rather than asking for the "right" answer, GU requires the student to synthesize her understanding and produce a conceptually complex response. Lower-order skills such as mastering math facts or dividing words into syllables, while important to a child's development, do not lend themselves to GU. Seeking GU in assessment, then, enriches the curriculum by ensuring that what is taught goes beyond the basics.

Rather than asking for the "right" answer, GU requires the student to synthesize her understanding and produce a conceptually complex response.

A Performance Perspective to Assessment

It is perhaps easiest and most appropriate for a student to demonstrate that she has GU through a project, exhibition, or presentation (PEP). By definition, GU is a synthesis of skills and/or knowledge, not a specific skill or a particular piece of knowledge, so a PEP approach, a performance perspective, readily lends itself to this kind of evaluation.

GU is not limited to a PEP approach, however. GU can also be assessed through having students respond either orally or in writing to complex questions. The question, for example, "How might the infrastructure and economy of the United States be different today if the initial settlements had taken place in San Diego, not Plymouth?" requires specific knowledge and GU about migration patterns, economic development, the effect of geography on migration and settlement, and even race relations. Although children's developmental levels vary and a third grader's response to this question would be less sophisticated than that of a sixth grader, in any case it is important for the teacher to go beyond the simple "The U.S. Capital would be in California" answer and elicit a deeper level of analysis and understanding.

Another example of a GU problem that could elicit a written or oral response would be to ask students to determine, beginning with $3,000 in the bank, whether it is a better economic decision to lease or buy a car; then ask how that answer might change if one started with only $500 in the bank. As in the settlement example, the leasing question requires an understanding of many variables and how they interact. To respond correctly, the student will need to do more than simply compute the principal and interest payments of purchasing and compare them to leasing. At a minimum, she will also need to consider the effect of lost (or gained) potential earnings from the savings in her bank, the cost of auto taxes and upkeep, the different effect of these payments on her income taxes, and the merits of leasing versus purchasing at the end of the lease. (Chapter 14 in this book, "Student-Created Museums," offers an example of how GU can be approached with primary-aged children. The museum example, too, could be done, at a more sophisticated level, with older students.)

While demonstrating GU for the settlement and leasing questions could indeed be done orally or in writing, it would be better (and would be more likely to incorporate MI) if shown through a PEP approach. Answering the settlement question in narrative form requires strong linguistic skills; allowing the student to present her response through a project, exhibition, or presentation capitalizes on her MI strengths. Similarly, although formulas could be used to demonstrate GU of the leasing question, allowing the student to share her knowledge through a performance enables her to use her various abilities in MI. The PEP Approach is also more "intelligence-fair" (Krechevsky, Gardner, and Hoerr, 1994), allowing students to use the relevant intelligence(s) to demonstrate understanding.

...allowing the student to share her knowledge through a performance enables her to use her various abilities in MI.

An Integral Part of Curriculum

Although the settlement and leasing examples are specific questions which address GU, it is far preferable to incorporate GU on an on-going basis throughout the curriculum (as described in the chapter "Student Created Museums") as part of a overall theme or generative issue. If a unit on transportation, for example, begins on Labor Day and continues to Thanksgiving, in addition to planning for the final PEP in which students would demonstrate their understanding of the entire unit, the teacher should be asking what could be done along the way, each day, to ensure that kids were gaining GU. What are the smaller clusters of concepts, covered throughout the unit, for which GU can be shown? In her daily and unit planning, a teacher should ask herself how the curriculum could be designed differently to lead to GU; she should not be satisfied with her students' development ending with acquisition of knowledge or mastery of skills. Assessment of GU should be viewed as an integral, on-going part of curriculum and instruction.

In her daily and unit planning, a teacher should ask herself how the curriculum could be designed differently to lead to GU; she should not be satisfied with her students' development ending with acquisition of knowledge or mastery of skills.

Generative Topics

For this kind of curriculum planning and instruction, GU is best seen as part of generative topics, overall themes. Generative topics are central to what is being taught, lend themselves to a GU approach and are amenable to students making connections among various subject matter areas. They are rich with possibilities and interesting to both students and teachers. A generative topic for primary grade students might be "How has technology helped and harmed us?" For intermediate grade students, asking "How does geography shape culture?" is ripe with possibilities. Creating semester- or year-long themes and topics, and finding ways to integrate skills and content into these overall themes and topics, makes learning more meaningful, integrated and interesting. It also reflects the real world, in which disciplines meld together and are not separated artificially by the signal of a bell ringing or textbooks being put away. After generative issues are in place, specific goals for understanding ("students will understand...") can be developed.

Rather than simply responding to the teacher's request for the right answer or filling in the appropriate small circles, when moving toward GU, students must define the problem, choose the appropriate routes to its solution and demonstrate their understanding.

GU places responsibility on the teacher to design and evaluate her curriculum in order to determine generative issues and learner outcomes. Once that is done, the onus of responsibility shifts to the student. Rather than simply responding to the teacher's request for the right answer or filling in the appropriate small circles, when moving toward GU, students must define the problem, choose the appropriate routes to its solution and demonstrate their understanding. This process of teaching for understanding is not always easy for teachers or students, but it is always beneficial. If we want our students to learn, we must teach to and assess their genuine understanding. To do less does them a disservice.

by Christine Wallach

Chapter 14:
Student-Created Museums

If you walked into The New City School during the last week of school, you would find the first graders enthusiastically involved in their biggest project of the year, a plant museum. You would have no sense that the school year is almost over. Instead you would see children fully engaged and for whom the end of the year is a big disappointment.

Planning and Establishing Criteria

It all started when my three teaching colleagues and I began to explore "genuine understanding" and how a first grader would demonstrate it. We defined "genuine understanding" as using something learned in a new or novel way. Because it was our last unit of the year, we decided that plants would be the context for this exploration. We set several objectives: we needed to involve all fifty-two students in a meaningful way; we wanted them to create a project; we wanted them to interact with the community through the project; and we wanted them to have many opportunities to evaluate and reflect.

We decided that the creation of a museum would meet these criteria and so introduced the idea of a plant museum to the students. Their questions led us immediately into an inquiry of what makes a good museum. While we served as recorders, they brainstormed and listed all the museums in the St. Louis area. Next they selected one museum and listed on paper what they liked about that particular museum. In groups of four, the children shared their ideas, recorded them on chart paper and taped them to the walls. At this point, they visited the other first-grade classrooms and read the other charts. They were each given two orange stickers and were instructed to place them next to the two ideas with which they agreed. In this way the children developed their criteria for what makes a good museum. This initial step was extremely important to us. It laid the foundation for reflection and future evaluation of their efforts and made it possible for their museum to be more than just a place to display projects that they had already made.

We decided that the creation of a museum would meet these criteria and so introduced the idea of a plant museum to the students. Their questions led us immediately into an inquiry of what makes a good museum.

Using Their Criteria

The next step was to see how the local museums measured up. The children were divided into three groups. Armed with clipboards and the rating sheets we created from their charts, they set off for the Art Museum, the Science Center or the Zoo's Living World. Each museum received an overall rating in three areas, how they looked, the kinds of interactions they provided, and their performance level (for example, explanatory videos or docent talks). The rating sheet contained a Likert scale with a smiling face at one end and a frowning face at the other end. Later that day, during math class, the students collected the data and created graphs showing how each museum measured up. What they learned was that the museums that received the highest ratings were those that allowed the visitor to become a participant.

We began to create our museum by challenging the children to find ways that they could share what they had learned about plants. They were asked to recall their museum criteria because, of course, they wanted visitors to enjoy their museum. They knew that the museum would have to be interactive. The idea that visitors might also learn while attending the museum led to a discussion of Multiple Intelligences. Students knew the names of the seven intelligences and could repeat the names, but they had never been asked to use this information in a new way, to create a learning environment based on the intelligences. The children themselves decided that, in order to be interesting to all the people, the exhibits would need to address all seven intelligences.

Shivers ran up our spines as one idea led to another, and we realized that they were already taking ownership of this museum.

As the children generated ideas, the teachers again became their recorders. Shivers ran up our spines as one idea led to another and we realized that they were already taking ownership of this museum. My teammates and I took their list and discussed ways we could help them make their exhibits a reality. Because this was the first time they had been asked to work with a strict deadline, we created time lines for them. The museum was to open the last week of school, and there was no way we could delay that.

Creating the Museum

The children consciously used all of their intelligences in designing and preparing exhibits that would, in turn, address the many intelligences of the museum-goer.

We became facilitators while the students made decisions. The children consciously used all of their intelligences in designing and preparing exhibits that would, in turn, address the many intelligences of the museum-goer. For example, a visitor could walk down a maze while learning facts about a desert (Bodily-Kinesthetic). Another exhibit invited the participant to create a page for a book entitled, "If I were a plant I would be ..." (Linguistic and Intrapersonal). Giant puzzles were on the floor depicting farming in different parts of the world, pattern blocks lured the children into creating and recording their own plants (Logical-Mathematical), and flower model foldouts illustrated how a flower creates a seed (Spatial). Dioramas and songs about plants as habitats were on display and videos of the children teaching others about experiments they had conducted were running (Interpersonal). The students had also video-taped dances and musical numbers created to depict plants in their habitats (Musical). For those who were mathematical, there were estimation problems (How Many Seeds Are in the Bag?) and story problems that used plants as subjects.

Of course, one of their favorite exhibits was not an exhibit at all—the gift shop! One day Tim brought in stationery he had made on his home computer. He asked if they could create a gift shop for their museum. After generating ideas for a shop, we introduced the students to the notion of market research. This time they set out with a list of products on their clipboards. They visited other classrooms and asked the students and teachers which items they might be interested in purchasing and how much they would be willing to pay. After collecting the data, the students knew what to make and how much to charge. The gift shop earned fifty dollars which the students donated to the fund to build our new playground.

Opening Day

On the day the museum opened, the children pinned on name tag badges and took their places. They had applied for jobs and were put into work crews of ten, each with a shift in the museum. As visitors approached the museum, housed in the lobby of the school theater, they were handed a gallery guide by the greeter seated at the information desk. The students served as curators, docents, gift shop clerks, and, of course, security guards. One day Sam approached me as I was helping some students solve a problem. He was serving as curator and noticed that the gift shop was about to run out of plants. I told him I could not help him just then. He left the room. Several minutes later I walked into the room next door and found him quietly gathering milk cartons, filling them with soil, and planting cuttings for the museum. He knew what to do, how to solve the problem, and took the initiative to see that it was done. Their ownership of the museum gave them a sense of responsibility for it.

As visitors approached the museum, housed in the lobby of the school theater, they were handed a gallery guide by the greeter seated at the information desk. The students served as curators, docents, gift shop clerks and, of course, security guards.

Reflection

On-going evaluation became an important part of this study. The children used a variety of rating sheets and questionnaires to help them reflect on what they had done well and what they could improve. This involved both the intrapersonal level, examining what they knew about themselves, and the interpersonal level, determining how they had worked with other people. They also asked others to fill out rating sheets. One day one of the students, Susan, told the class, "When we have something important to do that we all want to work on, we don't waste time by arguing. We get along and get it done."

On-going evaluation became an important part of this study. The children used a variety of rating sheets and questionnaires to help them reflect on what they had done well and what they could improve.

Joan, another student, said it best, "Our plant museum was the best because we made it for the kids." In this way she succinctly stated what every visitor to the plant museum knew. She and her classmates had demonstrated a "genuine understanding" of Multiple Intelligences and how to create an interactive museum.

by Sally Boggeman

Chapter 15:
Assessment and Portfolios

There has been much talk of alternative assessment in schools in the last few years. Performance assessment, authentic assessment, portfolios and exhibitions are all gaining credibility in schools across the nation. It is becoming clear that there need to be ways, other than paper and pencil tests, to assess the multiple intelligences. We also know that one must assess the *process* as well as the *product of* a child's learning and understanding. This assessment can take place through observations, dialogue, student reflection, written work, exhibitions and projects. Regardless of how it is done, however, assessment must be ongoing and frequent, and the student must be provided with feedback about the performance.

Approaches at New City

At New City, we use several different forms of assessment. Teachers make notes of their observations of children and keep anecdotal records as students work and interact. When students are given choices of activities involving the intelligences, we keep track of what they choose and look for patterns in these choices. Such observations are not focused on proficiency, but rather on student interest. The video camera is playing an ever more important role in assessment. Not only can the camera capture projects and presentations that cannot be recorded on paper, it also offers an avenue for self-reflection, developing Intrapersonal Intelligence, as students watch their performance and alter their behavior as a result of what they have learned.

In assessing a unit of study to determine how well the students have mastered the objectives and understood the content, a project is often used as the culminating activity upon which students are assessed. The final assessment outcomes are clearly stated for the students at the onset, often in the form of a rubric. The rubric delineates what must happen or be demonstrated to result in the *best,* in a *mediocre* or in an *unacceptable* project. Part of the students' learning is understanding the standards against which they are being measured. Through teacher observations, conversations and presentations made by the students, the teacher is able to evaluate the learning and understanding that has taken place.

Rather than just doing a research paper on a tribe of their choice, each child in the third grade does a research paper and then applies the resulting knowledge to a diorama and presentation on a Native American tribe. Students in the fifth grade study the stock market. They do more than follow a few stocks in the paper for a few days. They are assigned an adult in the building for a couple of weeks and they function as brokers and work up a stock portfolio for the adult. The adult has a certain amount of money to spend

When students are given choices of activities involving the intelligences, we keep track of what they choose and look for patterns in these choices.

Part of the students' learning is understanding the standards against which they are being measured.

and chooses ten stocks. The student follows the rise and fall of the stock and advises his client when to buy and sell. The adult is presented with a complete stock portfolio at the completion of the project. After studying "people who made a difference," fourth graders research a person of their choice, dress as that person and become part of a Living Museum in the library. Other classes come to the Living Museum, push a button on the box on which the person stands like a statue, and suddenly the statue begins to tell the listener about his life, information he has gleaned from research. To share with others what they learned about ancient Egypt, first graders dress in the costumes, including make-up, of ancient Egyptians, construct a papier mâché mummy, write hieroglyphs on the cardboard tomb wall, do Egyptian dances, make amulets and posters about Egyptian gods. This performance assessment incorporates all seven of the intelligences.

After studying "people who made a difference," fourth graders research a person of their choice, dress as that person and become part of a Hall of Fame in the "living" library.

The Personal Intelligences

New City puts a great deal of emphasis on the Personal Intelligences. Students do much self-reflection during many phases of the learning process, on both their academic and social performance. Depending on the grade level, one might find math journals, cooperative learning reflections, reading and writing surveys, research evaluations, field trip reflections, reflections on how well the student felt he worked with a substitute and a response to a report card. Samples of most of these forms can be found in this book.

Students do much self-reflection during many phases of the learning process, on both their academic and social performance.

Feeling that the Personal Intelligences are the most important, rather than something that can be described in a small box on the last page of the report card in which the teacher mentions "effort" and "gets along with others," the entire first page of our progress report is devoted to the Inter- and Intrapersonal Intelligences (see page 244). Children are assessed on such attributes as motivation, responsibility, confidence, problem solving, appreciation of diversity and teamwork, by means of a checklist and teacher narrative. Many teachers have the children assess themselves in these areas and use that information as part of the report. To support teachers in assessing these intelligences and completing this page, the faculty created a booklet of activities and behaviors to be observed.

A new aspect of assessment at New City is the MI Profile. It relates to parents where the classroom teacher sees the student functioning in each of the intelligences. The MI Profile is a grid on which the classroom teachers report (annually) the level at which they see the child's proficiency in each of the intelligences in their classrooms or at outside play. Specialist teachers already report how they see the child in their classes (art, performing arts, physical education, library and science), but we feel it is important to capture a child's proficiency and evolution in all settings. Children are assessed on a continuum (appreciates, performs, creates) described elsewhere in this book. It is important to note that by reporting the child's level of functioning, we are NOT implying that every child should be at "the top" (creates) in each or any area. Rather, our goal is simply to help each child develop to his potential in every intelligence; the MI Profile captures how the child is seen by the classroom teacher.

The MI Profile is a grid on which the classroom teachers report the level at which they see the child's proficiency in each of the intelligences in their classrooms or at outside play.

Another major assessment tool at New City is portfolios. A portfolio is a purposeful collection of student work that shows growth, strengths and turning points and may utilize a variety of media. Each child has a portfolio that is passed on with the child as he moves through the grades. Typically, portfolios are used primarily to monitor a child's writing, reading and math. But because we at New City believe that students have strengths in several areas, the portfolios reflect all seven intelligences. They are not just a container full of stuff like "Friday spelling tests" and unit tests and papers marked 100%. They are not portfolios of Best Work only. Instead, inside the large redboard portfolios are published stories, as well as rough drafts, pieces of art work, self-assessment sheets, material with sewing, physical fitness awards and students' musical compositions. Much of what happens in the classroom, and much of what needs to be assessed, cannot be confined to paper and fit conveniently into a portfolio. Each student has a video tape, audio tape and photographs capturing anything from role-plays, large projects, costumes they created, finishing the mile run, dance and interviews.

...because we at New City believe that students have strengths in several areas, the portfolios reflect all seven intelligences.

With each and every portfolio inclusion is a Reflection Sheet on which the child tells about the process he went through and why the piece should be in the portfolio. This dated reflection is critical for charting growth. Because student reflection is an essential part of the learning experience, the pieces included in the portfolio are generally chosen by the students (rather than the teacher). The teacher does have the option of including something, but it must be indicated on the reflection sheet that the child did not choose it. If a teacher is aware that a student has not included a piece from one of the intelligences, she may do so. Our goal is to have at least one item from each intelligence placed into the portfolio each year.

To more easily see growth over time, there are some things that are required of all students in their portfolios. In addition to a video tape, there is an audio tape on which the student reads a book (or portion thereof) of his choice, or in the case of preprimary children, talks, in September and again in May. The student reflects on the differences he notices. An annual self-portrait is also required, as well as an autobiography. Portfolios are stored where students have easy access to them. A couple of times a year the students are given an opportunity to look through them.

Taking Charge of Assessment

The message from schools, however, is often that test scores are what is important.

Children present the content of their portfolios to the parents so they can see first-hand the growth that their child has made during the year and over the years.

Teachers have been known to complain that students' parents are overly concerned about standardized test scores. The message from schools, however, is often that test scores *are* what is important. If we only report to parents about standardized test results, what are they to think is important? At New City, standardized test scores are sent home, but we also have a Portfolio Night in the spring when parents are invited to come and view the portfolio with their child, listen to tapes and view videos. Children present the content of their portfolios to the parents so they can see first-hand the growth that their child has made during the year and over the years. Their child is seen as someone who has talent and interest in seven different intelligences, not just someone who scores XYZ on a standardized test.

It is true that such alternative forms of assessment are time-consuming and more difficult, less reliable and more subjective than paper-pencil forms of assessment. However, regardless of how we define intelligence, portfolios are invaluable as one looks at the whole child. If a teacher believes in the MI model, understanding that students have strengths and weaknesses in at least seven different areas, then the kinds of alternative assessment that I have described are essential.

A practical guide created by the faculty of The New City School ©1994

New City School • 5209 Waterman Avenue • St. Louis, MO 63108
Progress Report

Name_____ Date_____

Attendance: Absent_____ Tardy_____

Teachers:

Key: ED = Exceeding Developmental Expectations

DA = Developing Appropriately

AC = Area of Concern

= Needs Added Attention

Intrapersonal Development
Can self-assess; understands and shares own feelings

Reporting period:	1	2	3

I. Confidence
- Is comfortable taking a position different from the peer group
- Engages in appropriate risk-taking behaviors
- Is comfortable in both leader and follower roles
- Copes with frustration and failures
- Demonstrates a positive and accurate self-concept

II. Motivation
- Demonstrates internal motivation
- Is actively involved in the learning process
- Shows curiosity
- Shows tenacity
- Exhibits creativity

III. Problem Solving
- Shows good judgment
- Asks for help when needed
- Can generate possible hypotheses and solutions
- Shows perseverance in solving problems
- Accepts and learns from feedback

IV. Responsibility
- Accepts responsibility for own actions
- Accepts responsibility for materials and belongings
- Handles transitions and changes well
- Accepts limits in work and play situations.
- Uses an appropriate sense of humor

V. Effort and Work Habits
- Participates in activities and discussions. . . . .
- Works through assignments and activities carefully and thoroughly . . . .
- Keeps notebook, desk, and locker/cubby organized . . . .
- Has age-appropriate attention span . . . .
- Works independently. . . . .
- Follows written and oral directions. . . . .
- Listens attentively . . . .
- Uses time effectively . . . .

Interpersonal Development
Can successfully interact with others

I. Appreciation For Diversity
- Makes decisions based on appropriate information, rather than stereotypes
- Understands the perspectives of others, including those of other races and cultures
- Shows concern and empathy for others
- Respects the individuality of others

II. Teamwork
- Cooperates with peers and adults
- Works at conflict resolution
- Behaves responsibly in groups
- Demonstrates an ability to compromise
- Expresses feelings and gives feedback constructively and appropriately

MI Profile

This grid indicates the levels at which your child functioned this year, *in the classroom*, in each of the Multiple Intelligences. We hope that it, along with the remainder of the Progress Report and the Specialist teachers' reports, will give you a full picture of your child's development. The definitions of the terms are listed below the grid. "Limited interest observed at this time" simply means that in the classroom, your child has not displayed much interest in this area.

Our goal is to help each child reach his/her potential in all seven of the intelligences. Our expectation is not that each child will function at the "creates" level in each of the intelligences.

	Appreciates	Performs	Creates	Limited interest observed at this time
Bodily-Kinesthetic				
Interpersonal				
Intrapersonal				
Linguistic				
Logical-Mathematical				
Musical				
Spatial				

Appreciates . Consistently demonstrates interest and enjoyment; is able to differentiate qualities

Performs . . . . Is able to apply a given intelligence to recreate an exhibit or demonstration, or problem-solve a given situation

Creates . . . . . Is able to apply a given intelligence to generate original works

MI Choices

When given choices, your child typically chooses activities in the following intelligences:

Spatial
Musical
Bodily Kinesthetic
Linguistic
Logical-Mathematical

Your child prefers to work: **Alone** **With others**

A practical guide created by the faculty of The New City School ©1994

New City School Portfolio Reflection Sheet

Title of Work_____   Name_____

(Or Description)   Date_____

                                                                              Teacher_____

This work exhibits the following of my multiple intelligences:

☐ Logical/Mathematical   ☐ Linguistic   ☐ Spatial/Artistic

☐ Musical   ☐ Bodily-Kinesthetic   ☐ Interpersonal

☐ Intrapersonal

Reflection
What I like about this piece is_____

_____

_____

_____

If I could change or have done one thing differently with this piece I_____

_____

_____

_____

Product
I worked on this project:

☐ alone   ☐ with the help of a teacher and/or friend

☐ in a group   ☐ other_____

I have chosen to include this piece in my portfolio because:

☐ it is work that I am proud of   ☐ it shows my learning process

☐ I have done my personal best   ☐ I feel that it is creative and/or original

☐ I was asked to put this piece in by_____

Comments_____

_____

_____

This work shows that I know about_____

_____

_____

Rate Yourself in the Intelligences

Name_____ Date_____

Rate yourself with the scale below for the following statements.

Rarely   **Sometimes**   **Always**
1————|2 ———— |3 ———— |4 |————5

3	I like to hum or sing to myself.
3	I learn best when working with others.
3	I like arranging things in space (i.e., pattern blocks, maps).
1	I like logical-mathematical choices.
1	Expressing my ideas in writing is easy.
2	It helps me to touch something to understand it.
3	I can use music to learn new information (i.e., number fact raps, jingles, hand claps).
2	I prefer the company of others during recess.
3	I need to see something to understand it.
1	I like number puzzles, logic boxes, and/or mathematical riddles.
5	Reading is enjoyable.
4	I draw, doodle, move my feet, tap, and/or change my positions even when I'm listening.
4	Group activities are my favorite.
2	I like having music on in the classroom.
2	I like to/wish I could exercise in class.
3	It makes me anxious when we have to do art activities in class.
4	It helps me to learn when I write things down.
5	I'm sensitive to the needs and feelings of others.
5	I like to have musical choices.
3	It's hard for me to evaluate myself.
	I like having B-K choices.
1	I like opportunities to draw.
3	I like to learn new words.
4	I understand other people's points of view.
3	I like to reflect about myself.
4	I feel comfortable working alone.
3	I can read people and change my behavior if needed.
3	I like spatial choices.
5	I'm easily frustrated when working with logical-mathematical activities.
1	I like linguistic choices.
5	I understand my strengths and weaknesses.
3	At recess I enjoy hanging out by myself.
3	I like arranging things on paper (i.e., posters, collages, tables, charts).

II.)   Rank the seven intelligences in order from one to seven (1 is your strongest intelligence — 7 is your weakest intelligence).

_____	**Intrapersonal**	_____	**Bodily-Kinesthetic**
_____	**Logical-Mathematical**	_____	**Linguistic**
_____	**Spatial**	_____	**Musical**
_____	**Interpersonal**		

A practical guide created by the faculty of The New City School ©1994

Part III.
Multiple Intelligences, Parents and Teachers

by Betsy Giles Blankenship

Chapter 16:
Communication:
A Key To Success

For the theory of Multiple Intelligences (MI) to be fully implemented, everyone involved in the school needs to understand the model. This means that from the youngest students, to the busiest parents, to the wisest board member, everyone must have some knowledge of MI. Therefore, how to share this information with all members of a school's community becomes a key consideration.

Bringing Everyone on Board

For communication to be effective, it must be multi-faceted; schools need to take every opportunity to instruct the students' families and make MI come alive for them. We don't want parents to just read about it, we want them to see it, to hear it, and to touch it. We want them to experience MI as they learn about it—just like their children!

Using the Walls to Educate

Walk in the door of The New City School and MI will welcome you. First, a large bulletin board proclaims "New City School — Where We Are Smart in Many Different Ways." The bulletin board tells about each of the intelligences with a brief description. There are also pictures of staff members and an intelligence they exhibit. As you stand there reading the bulletin board, you hear music wafting down the hall, and another sign informs you of the day's musical selection. As you look around, you can't help but notice the art work adorning the walls. You might notice drawings by the children in which they mind-mapped pictures of themselves. The explanation accompanying the pictures tells you that the children used their Intrapersonal and Spatial Intelligences to tell about their likes, dislikes and special talents. MI is all around you.

Communicating With Parents

Continue your walk to a classroom and outside you will find a parent bulletin board. Often these boards also share the MI message. Collages created by the youngest children indicate that even a four year old can find a picture of someone using her Bodily-Kinesthetic Intelligence or his Musical talent. Teachers in our preschool and Kindergarten classes send a letter home explaining how various centers and choices in their classrooms relate to the intelligences. Block building is certainly Spatial, Bodily-Kinesthetic, and often Logical-Mathematical; dramatic play uses Linguistic, Interpersonal, and Intrapersonal; and the water table can help develop Bodily-Kinesthetic, Interpersonal and Logical-Mathematical Intelligences. It helps parents see the value in the play, and understand how MI relates to their child's daily activities.

We don't want parents to just read about it, we want them to see it, to hear it and to touch it. We want them to experience MI as they learn about it—just like their children.

The explanation accompanying the pictures tells you that the children used their Intrapersonal and Spatial Intelligences to tell about their likes, dislikes and special talents.

The preprimary teachers aren't the only ones to use their linguistic abilities to spread the word on Multiple Intelligences. Reading just about any piece of print material generated at our school will give additional information on MI. Classrooms send home weekly newsletters and teachers make a conscious effort to include descriptions of classroom activities related to the intelligences. Students do much of the writing and illustrating of these weekly notes, sharing their linguistic and spatial abilities.

School-Wide Communication

Weekly letters from the School's director often highlight special events that relate to the incorporation of MI into the classrooms. These might include information on the first grade's Plant Museum, the fourth grade World's Fair exhibit, or the third grade's Native American Day. His letters might share an informative quote from a recent article on the subject, or a recommendation of a notable book to read. It's always exciting when a parent has read something on MI and wants to share it!

It's always exciting when a parent has read something on MI and wants to share it.

Our bi-annual newsletter also has made MI a focus. The first newsletter, published after New City began implementing MI, focused almost exclusively on explaining MI and described the process we were using to implement it. The highlight of the newsletter was the two-page center section featuring drawings by students depicting each of the intelligences. All subsequent newsletters have shared information on the progress we have made thus far in our implementation.

Print material used for recruiting purposes also shares the MI message. A trifold brochure focuses on MI and serves as an introduction to the model for prospective parents and other visitors to the building. It again uses students' drawings and simple definitions for each intelligence to summarize the theory. We have even prepared a separate piece on MI to give to the many educators who visit New City.

Student Assessment and MI

Student assessment takes several forms at The New City School, each aimed at knowing and reporting on the child's development in all the intelligences. One tool is the use of Parent-Teacher Conferences for sharing information. Conferences held in March and May allow for typical reporting to parents about the students' growth. However, our first conference of the year takes a different approach. Planned for late September, our Intake Conference allows parents the opportunity to tell us about their children. Their strengths, weaknesses, afternoon activities, hobbies, special needs and special talents are all shared from the parents' perspective. Teachers have the opportunity to ask if there are any intelligences the children might be involved in at home that we haven't seen exhibited at school. The Intake Conference serves as a valuable tool to understanding and knowing each child more fully and, at the same time, building communication with the parents.

Progress Reports (Report Cards) are another linguistic tool for sharing information about MI. We are continuing in the process of revising the present reports so they more effectively represent our commitment to MI. The first page of the reports, which used to be titled "Social-Emotional Growth, " has been renamed "Interpersonal and Intrapersonal Development." That change, along with rethinking many of the items listed under those headings, has strengthened our commitment to the Personal Intelligences. We believe that the Personal Intelligences are extremely important, so we choose to begin our Progress Report with them. In addition, teachers use written comments to share information about the other intelligences. It is not uncommon to read comments like: "John is spatially talented. His mural depicting the senses from *Charlie and the Chocolate Factory* was delightful." Another example might be "Susan is very bodily-kinesthetic; she loves to role-play stories and is remarkably adept on the climber." Such examples share valuable information with the parents and show how the Multiple Intelligences theory can help their child learn more easily and effectively.

Open Houses (Plural) and MI

Another key component of our parent education program is our schedule of Open Houses. Each section (Preprimary, Primary and Intermediate) has an Open House within the first three weeks of the school year. These Open Houses are at least an hour and one-half in length. This time frame allows the teachers to not only explain their program fully, but also allows time for the parents to actually become involved in several experiential MI activities. Parents might be asked to work in a cooperative group creating an art project with limited materials, or another class might have the parents visiting centers and taking part in choice time, much as their children do during the day. Another grade level might share a short story and then ask the parents to choose one of the suggested activities to show what they learned. The parents come away with a first-hand experience of what it means to learn using the MI model.

Parents might be asked to work in a cooperative group creating an art project with limited materials, or another class might have the parents visiting centers and taking part in choice time, much as their children do during the day.

However, classroom Open Houses are not our only hands-on experience for parents. Specialist teachers also host an Open House in which parents rotate from class to class experiencing what each of those classes (Performing Arts, Art, Physical Education, Science, and Library) offer. This is important because, although the classroom teachers give children numerous opportunities to use their various intelligences to help themselves learn, the specialist classes give children the opportunity to focus on a particular area of intelligence. The specialist teachers have particular expertise and can focus on a specific interest or talent a child might have. They are able to give the child an opportunity to explore an intelligence in a more in-depth manner. It is helpful for the parents to see the similarities and the differences in how the various intelligences are addressed in the classrooms and the specialists' rooms. By being given the chance to actually perform with the performing arts teacher, use their bodily-kinesthetic abilities with the PE teacher, or create with the art teacher, the parents, like their children, can have a real life experience with MI. As you can see, at New City there is not *one* Open House event, there are *four*.

It is helpful for the parents to see the similarities and the differences in how the various intelligences are addressed in the classrooms and the specialists' rooms.

Portfolio Night

Another worthwhile experience for parents and children is our Portfolio Night. Held during the last month of the school year, children share their portfolios with their parents while teachers play a facilitator role. The schedule is designed to allow three to five families to come during the same thirty-minute period. The teacher is available to answer questions. The evening is a huge success. Feedback from parents indicates that they not only enjoy sharing the papers, photos and projects with their children, but that they also gain a better understanding of their child. Many parents comment that they have never had such an in-depth conversation with their child!

In the future, we plan to also distribute our MI Profile as part of Portfolio Night. The MI Profile is a document created as a result of on-going assessment and revision of the Progress Report. It is designed to serve as a tool to share information with parents. It indicates at what level their child is performing in each intelligence. Are they at the "Appreciates" level, enjoying activities, observing or possibly being an involved spectator? Does the child function at the "Performs" level, recreating performances, projects or activities? The next level is the "Creates" level, where the child creates new projects and activities, or sees things in a different way and acts upon those differences. In addition, the Profile also tells which intelligence a child prefers to use when given options. This may be very different from how a child performs within the intelligences at home or with the specialist teachers.

Involving parents in the process of MI can only strengthen the program in a school.

Involving parents in the process of MI can only strengthen the program in a school. The more parents, board members and friends of the school understand the theory, the more supportive they can be. It is our responsibility to look for and use as many communication keys as possible to open the doors of knowledge for parents.

Chapter 17:
Getting Started in the Classroom With MI

by Christine Wallach

"The state and the district have a curriculum and guidelines that I am required to follow, and I have over twenty-five children in my class-room. Some of them are discipline problems. How am I supposed to address all the intelligences, meet my district and state mandates and manage students in that kind of setting?" These are questions that are often asked at the end of any presentation on Multiple Intelligences, and it seems only logical that some readers might be asking these questions right now. However, it is possible to organize instruction to address the intelligences, follow state and district guidelines and manage the logistics of students making choices.

Begin With What You Already Do
The easiest way to begin is to look carefully at your existing program to see what you are already doing that reflects the Multiple Intelligences. Language arts, the linguistic intelligence, is a part of every elementary school curriculum. Perhaps you already ask children to write in a journal as part of their language arts instruction. By asking students to reflect on topics and how they relate to those topics while writing in their journals, you are beginning to address the Intrapersonal Intelligence. By increasing the specificity of the writing prompt, the students will develop the ability to focus their reflection. For example, helping a student become aware of her thinking by asking her to write about the thoughts she had during each step of a project is very different from asking her how she liked the assignment.

Next, examine the way you present information to the students and how they share what they have learned with you and each other. For example, how often do students work with manipulatives or other hands-on activities? This is the Bodily-Kinesthetic Intelligence. Do you have students do projects? Many of these incorporate one or more of the intelligences. Are there spatial components? Do you ask your students to make presentations to the class? These involve the Interpersonal Intelligence if the students are reading the audience and responding to feedback. Do the students listen to music during the day or learn songs? Both activities are starting points for the Musical Intelligence.

Organizing Reading Instruction
Most basal reading programs ask the students to extend their reading through enrichment projects. If, on the other hand, your school has adopted a whole language philosophy, your students are probably sharing literature through book projects. Look carefully. Many of these extensions within your reading program already address one or more of the intelligences. For example, if you ask your students to make a poster about a book they have

Examine the way you present information to the students and how they share what they have learned with you and each other.

Do you ask your students to make presentations to the class? These involve the Interpersonal Intelligence if the students are reading the audience and responding to feedback.

just read, they are using their Spatial Intelligence. If they act out the story, the Bodily-Kinesthetic Intelligence is being activated.

Especially in the area of character analysis, projects related to the intelligences are easy to create and facilitate. Some book or reading assignments are given to the whole class; others are given as choices. To facilitate choice centers in a limited space, put the instructions for the center on a piece of construction paper, laminated for future use. Then place all the supplies in a plastic tub. For example, if the center uses the spatial intelligence, the tub might contain water-color sets, brushes, paper, towels, some empty cups for water and a gallon jug filled with water. When introducing the choice, show the students the tub and place it in a handy location in the room. Students can get supplies from the tub and return to their desk or work in the area where the tub is placed, depending on the physical layout of the classroom.

To facilitate choice centers in a limited space, put the instructions for the center on a piece of construction paper, laminated for future use. Then place all the supplies in a plastic tub.

Any number of books can be used in this way. *Meet Addy* by Connie Porter is one of the books in the American Girls series. The richness of these books makes them a must in both the reading and social studies program. This book can serve as an example of how a teacher can create activities that support character study and comprehension skills using MI. The main character, Addy, experiences the horror of life as a slave and the uncertainties of the escape to freedom. Students use the Intrapersonal Intelligence by comparing themselves to her. How would they feel if they were in her situation? One particularly good discussion starter is Addy's father's statement, "We're free on the inside." To address the Musical Intelligence the students can learn the song, "Follow the Drinking Gourd." During this study last year, the students who were adept at the piano used the sheet music to play the notes. Other students, fascinated by this musical ability, asked for their assistance to learn to play part of the song. The players became teachers in a quick lesson on how to read music. Their apprentices struggled happily. Still other students practiced singing the song with the accompaniment of the keyboard players. For that teamwork to be successful, the students drew on their Interpersonal skills. For the student who might choose to work in the Logical-Mathematical Intelligence, give students the option of drawing a map of the route Addy took to freedom. Our requirements were to look at a real map of the area as a reference and to include a key, compass rose, and scale of miles on the map they drew. To address the Bodily-Kinesthetic and the Spatial Intelligences, the students build a model of one of the forms of transportation that was used on the underground railroad. Finally, those who want to work within the Interpersonal Intelligence are instructed to work with a partner to conduct an interview. One student plays the part of Addy; the other student the part of the interviewer. In this way, the students gain the opportunity to work within their strengths to share what they learn from the book. Other students use the opportunity to reinforce other intelligences through the choices they made.

For the student who might choose to work in the Logical-Mathematical Intelligence, give students the option of drawing a map of the route Addy took to freedom.

Mathematics and MI

A wonderful way to begin bringing other intelligences into the mathematics curriculum is through literature. There are many books available that can help the teacher get started. The book *Ten Little Rabbits* by Virginia Grossman and Sylvia Long can be used with any grade level. The illustrations contain beautiful Native American blankets with intricate patterns.

Students can be challenged to create their own patterns and blankets. Drawing these patterns on paper makes the lesson spatial. By allowing the students to actually sew the blanket, the fine motor aspect of the Bodily-Kinesthetic Intelligence is added. The book is a counting book and so lends itself to consecutive number problems. After reading the book, intermediate level students can be challenged to determine how many rabbits are pictured in the book and then to write an equation for the problem.

Math programs like "Box It and Bag It" or "Mathematics Their Way" for the primary grades already address many of the intelligences. When the students make sound patterns, the Musical Intelligence is being stimulated. Often the students are asked to act out story problems, thus using the Bodily-Kinesthetic Intelligence. Strategy games require the Interpersonal Intelligence and manipulatives like pattern blocks, base ten blocks and Cuisenaire rods allow children to use their Spatial Intelligence to understand concepts like fractional numbers, number operations and place value.

Organizing Social Studies Instruction

The intelligences can easily be incorporated into an existing social studies curriculum. When studying other countries, add a traditional dance or games component to address the Bodily-Kinesthetic Intelligence. Listen to music as a starting point for the Musical Intelligence. Folk tales add a linguistic component while currency and population numbers are an introduction to the Logical-Mathematical Intelligence. After you establish a comfort level and a foundation, begin to extend the unit using the intelligences. During a recent unit on Africa, the first grade used MI to extend thinking skills. Instead of being a traditional unit on Africa, the focus was changed so it would be concept-based, "cultures are diverse yet share the human condition." The goal was to allow students to refine their knowledge by comparing and contrasting the Asante culture of Ghana to their own. After developing a definition of *culture,* the students embarked on a research project. Within each intelligence, the students gathered pictures and samples of the Asante culture and the culture of the United States. Clothing, music, art, food, games, dance, holidays, religion, architecture, and jewelry were explored. The students made collages, constructed replicas of houses, danced, and made head wraps to name a few of the projects. In the end, the students put all this work together to create a village where visitors had an opportunity to explore the intelligences by dressing up, learning a dance, listening to storytellers and making Akua-ba dolls.

Instead of being a traditional unit on Africa, the focus was changed so it would be concept based, "cultures are diverse yet share the human condition."

Organizing Science Instruction

Your science curriculum probably already addresses many of the intelligences. Much of the scientific process utilizes the Logical-Mathematical Intelligence. When students are involved in experimentation, they must think logically and use their mathematical skills to collect and organize data. Linguistic skills are used when students read texts to collect information and when communicating findings. In addition, most classes require students to work in groups during hands-on experiences because of a shortage of supplies. By asking students to analyze and respond to the way they work as a team, the Interpersonal Intelligence is developed.

When students are involved in experimentation, they must think logically and use their mathematical skills to collect and organize data.

Part IV.
And Finally

Bibliography

Armstrong, Thomas. *In Their Own Way.* St. Martin's Press., 1987.

Armstrong, Thomas. *Multiple Intelligences in the Classroom.* ASCD, 1994.

Armstrong, Thomas. *Seven Kinds of Smart.* Plume, 1993.

Bruer, John. *Schools for Thought.* The MIT Press, 1993.

Campbell, Bruce, Campbell, Linda and Dickinson, Dee.
   Teaching and Learning Through Multiple Intelligences.
   New Horizons for Learning, 1992.

Csikszentmihalyi, Mihaly. *Flow.* Harper and Row, 1990.

Csikszentmihalyi, Mihaly. *The Evolving Self.* Harper and Row, 1993.

Fallows, James. *More Like Us.* Houghton Mifflin, 1990.

Gardner, Howard. *Creating Minds.* Basic Books, 1993.

Gardner, Howard. *Frames of Mind.* Basic Books, 1983.

Gardner, Howard. *Multiple Intelligences: The Theory In Practice.*
   Basic Books, 1993.

Gardner, Howard. *The Unschooled Mind.* Basic Books, 1991.

Howard, Jeff. "Getting Smart: The Social Construction of Intelligence."
   "Efficacy." The Efficacy Institute, 1991.

Kovalik, Susan. *ITI: The Model – Integrated Thematic Instruction.*
   Books for Educators, 1993.

Krechevsky, M., Gardner, H., & Hoerr, T. "Complimentary Energies:
   Implementing MI Theory From the Lab and From the Field." A paper
   prepared for J. Oakes and K. H. Quartz (Eds.), Creating New Educational
   Communities: Schools and Classrooms Where All Children Are Smart.
   National Society for the Study of Education Handbook, 1994.

Lazear, David. *Seven Ways of Knowing.* Skylight, 1991.

Lazear, David. *Seven Ways of Teaching.* Skylight, 1991.

Margulies, Nancy. *Mapping Inner Space, Learning and Teaching Mind
   Mapping.* Zephyr Press, 1990.

Margulies, Nancy. *Yes, You Can Draw!* Zephyr Press, 1991.

Marzano, Robert. *Dimensions of Learning.* Association of Supervision
   and Curriculum Development, 1992.

Perkins, D. & Blythe, T. "Understanding Up Front."
  Educational Leadership, February 1994.

Perkins, David. *Smart Schools.* The Free Press, 1992.

Routman, Regie. *Invitations: Changing as Teacher and Learners K-12.*
  Heinemann Educational Books, Inc., 1991.

Thomson, Barbara. *Words Can Hurt You.* Addison-Wesley, 1993.

About the Authors
Art work by The New City School students

Betsy Giles Blankenship:
Betsy earned a BS in Education from the University of Missouri-Columbia and a MA in Early Childhood from Southern Illinois University in Edwardsville. She has been in education for twenty-four years, eighteen years at The New City School.

Susie Burge:
"MI has made me realize that by teaching in only one way, I will miss some of the kids who are stronger in other intelligences. My logical approach doesn't get through to everyone." Susie has a BA in Biology from the University of Missouri-St. Louis. She has taught for five years, four of which have been at New City.

Carol Beatty:
"MI has helped me to focus on the strengths of my students while helping them to develop other interests many people may consider as weaknesses. I find watching a child engaged in his interests is what learning is all about." Carol has taught for eight years, completing her first with New City. She holds a BA in Special Education from Fontbonne College.

Sally Boggeman:
"Working with the Personal Intelligences and bringing more B/K and music into the classroom has made it a place where all children can grow and learn by focusing on and developing their own talents. I don't have to have strengths in the intelligences to have them available for my students." Sally has a BA in Elementary Education from Hiram College. She has taught for twenty years, ten of which have been at New City.

Susie Chasnoff:
Susie has always believed in addressing the needs of the whole child. "MI has provided me with the intellectual underpinnings to explain why I teach as I do and has helped me specifically identify and strengthen areas of my curriculum." Susie has taught for twelve years, four at New City. She earned her BS in Elementary Education from Case Western Reserve University.

Joe Corbett:
"Because of MI, I have a new awareness, reaching students in a number of areas. It has not changed my teaching as I'm too new to have changed." Joe has taught for three years at New City. He earned a BA in History and a MAT from Webster University.

Carla Carroll:
"Being conscious of MI has helped the curriculum and activities in the classroom be richer and broader since I make sure that the intelligences are reached during themes taught." Carla has her BA in Elementary Education from Webster University. She has been at New City for one year and teaching for six.

Linda Churchwell:
"Knowledge of MI has first affected me personally, leading me to reassess my own educational experiences. I am learning to better address the variety of personalities and learning styles, and wish that I'd had a similar educational experience as a child." Linda has taught for five years, two with New City. She earned a BA in History from Spelman and an MAT from Wayne State.

Diane Davenport:
"MI has not changed my teaching. The theory has validated my mission in seeing an arts integrated curriculum." Diane has been in education for twenty nine years, seven with New City. She earned her Bachelor of Music Education from Millikin University and her Masters in Aesthetic Education from Webster University.

Bonnie L. Frank:
"MI has challenged me to look at various ways of approaching the same topic of study." Bonnie has taught for seven years, six at The New City School. She attended Miami of Ohio where she earned a BS In Elementary Education.

Mary F. Daly:
"MI has allowed me to view my students differently. It has given me seven different ways to plan my lessons." Mary has spent all her seven years as a teacher with New City. She holds a BA in Early Childhood Education from Fontbonne College.

Danielle Egeling:
"MI validated what we've always felt, that all kids have talents and gifts." Danielle has taught for seventeen years. Eight of them have been at New City. She earned her BS from the University of Missouri-Columbia in Elementary Education and her MA in Education from Washington University.

Joycelyn L. Gray:
Joyce has been teaching for four years, three at The New City School. She earned her BS degree in Early Childhood Education from the University of Missouri-St. Louis.

Jean Blockhus Grover:
"Because of MI, I've provided more opportunities for my students to have choices on how to show their understanding." Jean has been in education for eight years, five at New City. She earned her BA in Elementary Education from the University of Northern Iowa and an MA from Maryville University.

Monette Gooch-Smith:
"As a result of MI, I have created centers that reflect the Intra-personal Intelligence. There are spaces in the room where a child can be by herself and know that it is OK, even encouraged." Monette received her AAS from Forest Park Community College in Child Care, her BA from Fontbonne College in Early Childhood/Special Education and her MS in Early Childhood/Special Education from Southern Illinois University in Edwardsville. She has taught for thirteen years, twelve of them at New City.

Eileen Griffiths:
Eileen earned her BA in Education with a major in English from Wilmington College and a MAT from Webster University. She has been in education for thirteen years, eight with New City.

Elizabeth King:
After earning her BS in psychology from Spring Hill College and her MAT in Elementary Education from Webster University, Betsy completed her first teaching assignment with New City.

Susan Matthews:
Susan received her BA in History from Indiana University and her MA in Education from Maryville University. She has taught for six years, all at New City.

Tom Hoerr:
"MI has been a wonderful tool to use collaboratively with our faculty. It has helped us look at kids in different ways, increasing their opportunity for success." As well as being the Director of The New City School, Tom also directs the Non-Profit Management Program at Washington University. He received his BA in Education from Harris Teachers College, his M. Ed. in Administration from the University of Missouri-St. Louis, and his PhD in Policy Making and Development from Washington University. Tom has been in education for twenty-five years and the Director of New City for sixteen.

Carla Mash:
"MI has led me to have the children do much more of their own assessing, setting goals and talking about their strengths and weaknesses." Carla has taught for nineteen years, nine at New City. She holds a BS in Education from Eastern Illinois University.

Lauren M. McKenna:
"MI has pushed me to a different level." Lauren has been in education for thirteen years, five at New City. She earned a BA in Education from the University of Missouri-St. Louis with a major in Physical Education.

Suzy Schweig:
Suzy has spent five years in the field of education, all as a New City teacher. She earned a BA in Psychology from the University of Kansas and an MA in Elementary Education from Southern Illinois University in Edwardsville.

Nancy J. McIlvain:
"MI has brought a new sense of excitement to New City. It has helped us all grow—personally and professionally." Nancy has worked in the field of education for twenty-two years, seven years with New City. She holds a BS in Secondary Education from Southeast Missouri State University. She earned her elementary certification from the University of Missouri-St. Louis and an MAT from Webster College with an emphasis in Math.

Jennifer Hartz Pass:
"MI has changed my awareness of the students' needs and how each individual may respond better with a different intelligence. It has helped me, even as an art teacher to present my lessons in a much more creative way." Jennifer earned a BS in Education with a major in Art from the University of Missouri. She has taught for eight years, four with New City.

Nancy Solodar:
"MI has broadened my vision of what a school can be and how teachers and students can learn. Try it! Don't be afraid to fail sometimes!" Nancy has taught for a total of sixteen years, thirteen of which have been at New City. She received her BA from Mt. Holyoke in Russian Language and Literature, and her MAT from Yale University in Teaching Russian.

Stephanie Young:
"MI has made me more aware of activities that I can do to bring out all children's strengths." Stephanie has a BA in Speech Communication from the University of Maryland and a Master of Science in Early Childhood and Elementary Education from Bank Street College of Education. She has taught for four years, completing one year at New City.

Joan Moldafsky Siwak:
"I've always felt a good early-childhood program should have many different centers to reach all kids. Now I feel good knowing the whole school reflects this and supports the centers approach." Joan earned her BA in Early Childhood Education form Maryville University. She has been in education for twenty years, six at New City.

Denise A. Willis:
After earning a BS in Elementary Education from Shenandoah University, Denise has spent nine years in education. She has just completed her fifth year with New City.

Susie Tenzer:
Susie has taught at New City for five of the thirteen years she has spent in the field of education. She has a BS in Elementary Education from the University of Missouri-St. Louis.

Christine Wallach:
"MI has added another dimension to the way I design instruction. Now I look for ways to help students refine knowledge leading to understanding and meaningful use of what they have learned. Chris has taught for nineteen years, two at New City. She earned a BS in Education from Southeast Missouri State University with a major in French and an MA in Elementary Education from Southern Illinois University Edwardsville.

Barbara James Thomson:
"Multiple Intelligences Theory puts the emphasis on creating curriculum to match children's strengths rather than trying to mold children to fit curriculum." Barbara earned a BA in History from Cornell University and an MAT from Webster University in Early Childhood Education. She has been in education for twenty years, eight with New City.

Julie Stevens:
"I used to be a very traditional teacher. MI has given me the context in which to creatively design a curriculum which addresses the learning styles of each child." Julie has been in education for twenty seven years, six at New City. She holds a BA in English Literature from the College of New Rochelle and an MA in Educational Administration from Illinois State University.

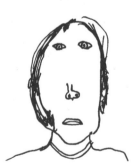

Stephanie Cunningham Wiles:
Stephanie earned her BS in Elementary Education and BS in Early Elementary Education from The University of Missouri. She has been at New City for five years.

About The
New City School

It is appropriate to share a bit about The New City School, to give the reader a context for our work. As noted, New City is a unique educational setting. Formed in 1969 by neighbors who were concerned about declining property values, New City is an independent school located in the Central West End of the City of St. Louis. Our neighborhood is socioeconomically diverse, as is our student body. The School is housed in a large two-story building that was built as a girls' high school in 1901.

New City is an independent elementary and preschool, with its own board of directors. We say that New City offers a unique combination of academics, ambience and diversity. Since its founding, the school has always maintained a commitment to racial and socioeconomic diversity. In the 1993-94 school year, for example, 26% of our 355 students (beginning at three years of age and going through the sixth grade) were minorities, almost all African-American; and 22% of our students, minorities and non-minorities, received need-based financial aid. Our students come to us from forty-seven different zip codes.

We believe that learning should be fun. New City features experiential, constructivist and developmental approaches to learning and high academic achievement. The majority of our students average two to three years above grade level on standardized achievement tests. Our pupil-teacher ratio ranges from 10:1 with three-year-old students to 20:1 in grades four through six. We have always had a commitment to aesthetic education and, prior to learning about MI, had full-time teaching specialists in art, performing arts, and physical education, a librarian and a half-time remedial reading teacher.

During the 1988-89 school year, our director, Tom Hoerr, read *Frames of Mind* by Howard Gardner. He felt that MI fit well with the values of New City and that it could be a powerful tool for identifying and nurturing our students' various abilities. He shared his excitement about MI and asked our teachers if they were interested in learning about MI and pursuing how it might be used at New City. One-third of the staff decided to meet regularly to learn more about MI. The Talent Committee met after school and during the summer, beginning by reading *Frames of Mind*.

We wanted to carry our school's commitment to experiential learning to our investigation of MI. Committee members, working in teams, took responsibility for presenting portions of the book to the group by using each of the intelligences in learning and teaching about them. When presenting the concepts from the bodily-kinesthetic chapter, for example, the teachers who presented had the committee members engaged in activities in which they used both their small- and large-motor skills. The committee learned about the spatial chapter by completing puzzles and working through a maze.

In fall 1989, more teachers joined the Talent Committee. The group also visited the Key School in Indianapolis, the first school to implement MI. The faculty began to see the MI model as a useful tool, a way to help them to identify and build upon the strengths of their students.

Our MI implementation has been exciting, but it has not been without its difficulties. While our students' parents are wonderfully supportive, as you might imagine, they have asked good, hard questions about MI and where we were heading. Fortunately, we have always had good answers, even if the answer was, "We don't know, this is new ground for us! But we will work on it and get back with you."

And there have been some wonderfully rich discussions (INTENSE!) at faculty and committee meetings, talking, for example, about the use of the MI Profile and what exactly it means when a child is at the "creates" level (see Chapter 15). But that's as it should be. Education is an art not a science, and fine teachers are wonderful artists who continue to grow. Having a building full of wonderful artists working collegially, discussing issues with thought and passion, is not always easy. But it is always fun. And most important, our kids benefit form the questioning, the dialogue and the innovation.

For us, MI is more than a theory of intelligences. It has become a way for us to look at how kids can learn, how teachers can teach, and how schools should operate. It has been a fun and exciting journey, and we look forward to learning even more!

Index

A practical guide created by the faculty of The New City School ©1994

Order Form

To: The New City School
5209 Waterman Avenue
St. Louis, MO 63108

BOOK TITLE	# of COPIES	COST	TOTAL
Succeeding With Multiple Intelligences: *Teaching Through the Personal Intelligences*		@ $34.00 each.	
Celebrating Multiple Intelligences: *Teaching for Success*		@ $29.95 each.	
Individual grade level assessments: Linguistic and Logical-Mathematical rubrics and Progress Reports Check: preschool: (3/4s, 4/5s, & KG) ☐ grades: 1 ☐, 2 ☐, 3 ☐, 4 ☐, 5 ☐, 6 ☐		@ $20.00 each	
Entire set of grade level assessments: Linguistic and Logical-Mathematical rubrics and Progress Reports, preschool through grade 6 ☐		@ $125.00 each	
		Add Shipping and Handling 7% ($2.50 minimum)	
		TOTAL	

I have enclosed a check for _____

Credit Card purchases can be made by telephone or fax.
Telephone: (314) 361-6411
Fax: (314) 361-1499

If you are paying by credit card please complete the
following:

☐ MasterCard   ☐ VisaCard

Card Number

Expiration Date

_____
Cardholder's Signature

If paying by credit card, please complete the following if different from the "Ship to" information.

Name _____

Address (No P.O. Box Number) _____

_____

City _____ State _____ Zip _____

Ship to:

Name _____

School (if applicable) _____

Address (No P.O. Box Number) _____

_____

City _____ State _____ Zip _____

Daytime Telephone (___) _____
             Area Code

If you are missing the following page with the MI Survey
Sheet and would like a copy, please contact us at:

The New City School
5209 Waterman Avenue
St. Louis, MO 63108
Telephone: (314) 361-6411
Fax: (314) 361-1499

It Can Be Lonely Out There

We believe that the best way to implement MI is by learning with and from others, growing in a supportive manner. With this in mind, we are thinking of creating an MI network, a list of people who are working with MI. If you would like to be part of this group, please complete and return this form to us. Feel free to make copies for others too. Thanks!

Return this form to:
Tom Hoerr
New City School
5209 Waterman Avenue
St. Louis, MO 63108

MI Interest Survey
(please print)

Name _____

Work position/title _____

☐ Home or ☐ work address _____

City, state, zip _____

e-mail address _____

We are in the very early stages of thinking about doing a book that would contain articles and lesson plans from around the country, not just from New City. If you would like to know more about this possibility or be a part of it, please check here:

Questions or comments: _____

_____

If you are missing the Order Form on the preceding page for our MI books and rubrics, please contact us for a copy at:

The New City School
5209 Waterman Avenue
St. Louis, MO 63108
Telephone: (314) 361-6411
Fax: (314) 361-1499